THEY CALLED THEM SOLDIER BOYS

A Texas Infantry Regiment in World War I

Gregory W. Ball

Number 11 in the War and the Southwest Series

University of North Texas Press
Denton, Texas

10 9 8 7 6 5 4 3 2 1

Permissions:
University of North Texas Press
1155 Union Circle #311336
Denton, TX 76203-5017

The paper used in this book meets the minimum requirements of the American National Standard for Permanence of Paper for Printed Library Materials, z39.48.1984. Binding materials have been chosen for durability.

Library of Congress Cataloging-in-Publication Data

Ball, Gregory W., 1969-
They called them soldier boys : a Texas infantry regiment in World War I / Gregory W. Ball. -- 1st ed.
p. cm. -- (Number 11 in the War and the Southwest series)
Includes bibliographical references and index.
ISBN 978-1-57441-500-1 (cloth : alk. paper) -- ISBN 978-1-57441-511-7 (ebook)
1. Texas. National Guard. Infantry Regiment, 7th--History. 2. United States. Army. Infantry Regiment, 142nd--History. 3. World War, 1914-1918--Regimental histories--United States. 4. World War, 1914-1918--Campaigns--France. I. Title. II. Series: War and the Southwest series ; no. 11.
UA4747th .B35 2013
940.4'1273--dc23

2012045566

They Called Them Soldier Boys: A Texas Infantry Regiment in World War I is Number 11 in the War and the Southwest Series

Book design by Jimmy Ball.

To
Mom and Dad

CONTENTS

ILLUSTRATIONS
(*BETWEEN PAGES 124 AND 125*)

MAPS

TABLES

ACKNOWLEDGMENTS

I would like to thank the Donley County Historical Society and the Burton Memorial Library, Clarendon, Texas; the Southwest Collection at Texas Tech University, Lubbock; the Texas State Library and Archives, Austin, Texas; The Abilene Public Library, Abilene, Texas; the Foard County Library, Crowell, Texas; the University of Texas at Arlington Libraries Special Collections Branch; Pat and Woodene Simpson; the Texas Military Forces Museum, Austin, Texas. Thanks also to Ron Chrisman and Karen DeVinney at UNT Press. I would also like to specifically thank Dr. Randolph B. Campbell, my major professor at the University of North Texas, for his advice and friendship over the past five years, as well as Dr. Richard B. McCaslin and Dr. Alfred Hurley. From the USAF history and museums program I would like to thank Dr. Charles J. Gross, Mr. David Anderson, Dr. Sue Rosenfeld, and Mr. George W. "Skip" Bradley. I would like to thank my parents for all they have done for me over the years, my brother, Jimmy, for designing the book and the maps, his wife Oanh and my nephew Ethan. Finally, I want to thank Sarah. I'm so glad you're here for this.

INTRODUCTION

In a small Texas town, thousands of miles and nearly a century removed from the battlefields of France, the influence of World War I on the Lone Star State can still be observed. Two worn statues stand on each side of a World War I-era German artillery piece in the courthouse square of Crowell, the county seat of Foard County, Texas, in the northwestern part of the state. The statues are copies of E. M. Viquesney's famous *Spirit of the American Doughboy* and *Spirit of the American Navy*. Both statues rest on pedestals and strike similar poses. The doughboy holds a grenade in his raised right arm but the left arm is missing below the elbow. The sailor's arm is also aloft although the hand is missing. The artillery piece is spotted with rust. These three pieces form a monument to World War I soldiers from Foard County. The stories of the soldiers who came from Crowell and who brought back to Texas a German artillery piece deserve to be told, as do the stories of the many others who came from this region and fought in Europe.[1]

Texas has a long military tradition, dating from the Texas Revolution and carried on through the War with Mexico, the Civil War, and World War II, although perhaps it is felt less in the present because military organizations are no longer established on a regional basis. Nevertheless, the military experiences of Texans generally have been amply documented, although less so for those who fought in World War I. For instance, the collection of essays edited by Joseph G. Dawson, *The Texas Military Experience: From the Texas Revolution through World War II* largely overlooks the Texas military experience during World War I. However, the oversight is corrected in part with the recent publication of *To the Line of Fire! Mexican-Texans in World War I* by Jose Ramirez, and *Texas and Texans in the Great War* by Ralph Wooster.[2]

Prior to the publication of those works, Lonnie J. White was the only historian to write extensively on the World War I Texas military experience. He examined the organization, training, and combat of the two Texas-Oklahoma divisions organized by the War Department in 1917 in Fort Worth and San Antonio, both of which saw combat in France. White's *The 90th Division in World War I: The Texas-Oklahoma Draft Division in the Great War* focused on the division comprised predominantly of Texas and Oklahoma draftees. That division, known later as the "Tough 'Ombres," was organized in San Antonio's Camp Travis and saw extensive service in France. In 1984, White published *Panthers to Arrowheads: The 36th (Texas-Oklahoma) Division in World War I.* This work remains the only full study of the 36th Division in World War I, a unit that initially consisted mainly of Texas and Oklahoma National Guardsmen. While White's works provide an excellent starting point for a study of the Texas military experience in World War I, he wrote in the preface to *Panthers to*

Arrowheads, "This study is not envisioned as the final word on the subject. Rather, it is hoped that it will open the way for more in-depth investigations of units, events, activities, battles, and individuals." In essence, White perceived what he called "a notable gap in the military history of Texas and Oklahoma." Unfortunately, White's expectation that other scholars would study in greater detail the division's units and personalities has been met with silence for the past twenty-five years. This study of one of the division's regiments is in response to White's call.[3]

This work tells the story of the 7th Texas Infantry Regiment, one of the Texas National Guard regiments that formed the 36th Division. Over a period of two years, the soldiers of that regiment, predominantly from North and Northwest Texas, joined the Texas National Guard, were mustered into federal service, trained at Fort Worth's Camp Bowie, travelled to France, experienced combat, and returned home in the summer of 1919. Although their experiences in the Army and in combat were not necessarily unique among soldiers in World War I, their stories serve to broaden understanding of how World War I affected Texans. What those soldiers experienced, what they felt, and how they expressed themselves to their loved ones back home is important to the history of World War I and of Texas, as their experiences form an important, albeit neglected, part of the Texas military experience.

Concepts of the Texas military experience are rooted in the Revolution and the Alamo, the Texas Republic, and the Civil War. During that period, residents of the state developed the idea that Texas soldiers were particularly courageous and adept in combat, although such stories and beliefs about Texas soldiers' prowess in battle might be based more on myth than on fact, and it is difficult, if not impossible, to determine how much of the Texas military experience is based on fact or legend. What is clear is that the Texas military experience has been developed for over a century and includes elements of regional and ethnic cultures: southern, western and frontier on one hand, and a blend of Spanish, Mexican, Anglo, and African-American cultures on the others. This coalesced into a perception that Texans experience war uniquely. While other states such as Virginia, New York, and Oklahoma have claimed distinct military experiences, it has been suggested that the Texas military experience more closely resembles other nations rather than other states in the Union. While the idea of a unique Texas military experience is debatable, a more important question is: How did the military experience of Texans in World War I clarify or sharpen that perception of a unique Texas military experience? This can be answered in two ways. First, by the way the Texas soldiers and Texas residents viewed their combat experiences. Second, the question might be answered in a broader military context by comparing this regiment with other units to determine how those Texas soldiers were similar or different regarding their training, their equipment, and their overall combat effectiveness.[4]

More than 1,900 men formed the 7th Texas Infantry, yet it was only one National Guard regiment out of more than a dozen infantry, cavalry, and artillery units organized by the state of Texas for possible service in the war, and the 7th Texas did not quite represent 1 percent of the nearly 200,000 Texans who eventually served in the United States military during the Great War, and it cannot be proven that the men of the 7th were "typical" of World War I soldiers in general. However, a demographic and economic profile of those who served in the 7th offers a worthwhile characterization of one unit and establishes a basis for comparison with soldiers from other parts of Texas, soldiers from other states, as well as African-American and foreign-born soldiers.

It is difficult to understand any group of soldiers without being aware of the society from which they came. During the first two decades of the twentieth century, many Texans remained tied to their state's nineteenth-century southern, agricultural, and rural past. The legacies of the Texas Revolution and the Civil War remained strong in the minds of many Texans, tempered only by the experiences of post-Civil War Reconstruction. Within this context many Texans perceived and understood loyalty, courage, and cowardice, and used their understanding of those concepts to connect with their historic past and military tradition. While many looked to the past, important changes occurred within the state during the early twentieth century.[5]

Texas underwent a population boom during the first two decades of the twentieth century. The state's population, which numbered slightly more than 3.8 million in 1910, grew to 4.6 million by 1920. The economic situation of the state, however, did not change as much. The vast majority of Texans lived in a rural environment, and many considered cotton the state's "money crop," although ranching was also a powerful economic pursuit.[6]

Socially, the southern outlook of the state fostered a culture of segregation as the African-American and Hispanic populations were marginalized as second-class citizens. Texas, in common with the South, had enacted a wide range of "Jim Crow" segregation laws aimed at keeping the African-American population subordinate to white society. There was little chance of minorities participating in local or state government or improving themselves socially and economically. The social characteristics of Texas mirrored other southern states, and this southern culture also influenced Texas politics well beyond minimizing the participation of African-Americans and Hispanics.

In Texas, single party politics were the norm, and the Democratic Party dominated the political culture of the state. The Republican Party, while it existed in Texas at the time, had not played a significant role in the state's politics for decades. However, this single party system of the Democrats did not mean that political conflict was lacking. On the contrary, political conflict within this system generally revolved around a struggle between Texas conservatives and those who sought reform, whether it was economic, political, or social.[7]

The region and the counties in which the 7th Texas was recruited mirrored the social, economic, and political characteristics of the state as a whole. The regiment included companies from across a wide swath of North, Northwest, and West Texas rather than just a narrow region of the state. In North Texas, companies were established in Cooke, Denton, Wise, Tarrant, and Johnson counties. To the northwest, companies were raised in Wichita, Wilbarger, Hardeman, Foard, and Childress counties. In the Panhandle and West Texas, officers organized companies in Donley, Potter, Lubbock, and Taylor counties. Those fourteen counties consisted of an overwhelming percentage of white residents with few African Americans and even fewer foreign-born residents. In total, those fourteen counties counted 329,539 residents, approximately 8 percent of the state's 1910 population. All of those counties, with the exception of Tarrant and Johnson counties, were predominantly rural, and agriculture based on cotton dominated in most while ranching led in the Panhandle counties of Lubbock and Potter, and in eleven of the fourteen counties (78 percent), more people lived in rural conditions than urban centers. The three counties with urban populations greater than their rural population included Tarrant (Fort Worth), Wichita (Wichita Falls), and Potter (Amarillo) Counties. The larger percentage of rural population also matched the state as whole. All of those counties supported the southern and conservative way of life that dominated the state. Perhaps most important, this conservative, rural, and agricultural way of life was what the soldiers of the 7th Texas knew; this was the land and the culture that affected how they perceived the war and shaped their understanding of service and duty.[8]

Finally, while this study focuses on one group of soldiers, the 7th Texas technically ceased to exist as a military organization in the fall of 1917 after President Woodrow Wilson federalized the National Guard and the Army reorganized it according to War Department rules. At that point, many of the soldiers who made up that Texas National Guard regiment, including the commanding officer, were combined with the 1st Oklahoma Infantry to become the 142d Infantry Regiment. Still, in spite of those organizational changes, it is possible to track many of the soldiers of the 7th Texas throughout their service. While there were many acts of heroism and valor among soldiers of the 142d Infantry, and the regiment included many hundreds of Oklahoma soldiers as well as draftees and soldiers from other parts of the country, the focus on members of the old 7th Texas Infantry is not meant to slight the actions of other members of the regiment or the other regiments in the brigade and division. In fact, an important part of the story of this particular regiment and its World War I services lies in its innovative use of members of the Choctaw Nation to transmit messages in combat, the first known instance of using Native American language to disguise communications in modern combat. This in itself is ample reason to study this particular regiment. And while those Oklahoma National Guardsmen who spoke their native language were members of the old 1st Oklahoma rather than the old 7th Texas, they nevertheless were part of the same regiment and went through the same experiences as the Texans.

Additionally, this study of the 7th Texas analyzes common characteristics of World War I Texas soldiers, such as their ages, occupations, and marital status and therefore provides a better understanding of how the "Great War" affected the lives of many thousands of the state's citizens. No full study of a Texas regiment that served in World War I has yet been written, and yet such a study can help answer two important questions: who were those Texans who volunteered to leave their families and homes, become soldiers, and go to France to fight and perhaps die in the service of their country? More importantly, how did they experience World War I?

THEY CALLED THEM
SOLDIER BOYS

1

RECRUITING THE 7TH TEXAS INFANTRY

On April 2, 1917, President Woodrow Wilson addressed a joint session of the United States Congress where he responded to a number of events, including the resumption of unrestricted submarine warfare by Germany and the disclosure of the infamous Zimmerman Telegram. He then asked Congress for a declaration of war. Congress debated the president's request for several days, and approved a declaration of war in the Senate on April 4, 1917, and two days later in the House.[1]

Although there was debate across the nation as well as within Texas regarding the president's request for a declaration of war, most Texans supported the president. Once war was declared, a different topic became the center of debate in the nation and in Texas: How would the United States raise and field an army large enough to make a difference on European battlefields? The answer to that question affected millions of young men across the nation and thousands in Northwest Texas. The debate hinged on whether or not the United States should raise an army by relying on volunteers or through a mandatory system of service. Such a debate was not new to the nation, and as late as February 1917, the government had expected to rely primarily on voluntary enlistments to increase the army's size. By April, however, the debate became more urgent and crystallized around which system would allow an army to be raised more quickly.[2]

Texans debated the implications of volunteerism as opposed to conscription, but in the end many residents supported selective service and expected their congressmen to as well. On April 28, 1917, Congress passed the Selective Service Act, and President Wilson signed it into law three weeks later. Drafted men would form the "National Army," and along with the Regular Army and a federalized

National Guard, those three sources of manpower would represent the Army of the United States on the Western Front. Once the president signed the Selective Service Act, the administration of the draft proceeded quickly, primarily because the registration of all men between the ages of twenty-one and thirty would take place on June 5, 1917. The focus then shifted from the national to the local level, where the process of registering, selecting, examining, and sending men off to training camps took place.[3]

While the men of the 7th Texas were not drafted, the passage of the Selective Service Act and its implementation at the county level spurred increased recruiting efforts by the Army, Navy, and Marine Corps, and figured in the decision making calculus of the men who eventually joined the 7th Texas. It is not difficult to imagine the pressure on millions of young men who were uncertain about how the draft would actually work and who were surrounded by patriotic displays and recruiting officers urging them to enlist. While patriotic rallies, drill sessions, and rhetoric did not require a commitment, the enlistment of a soldier could be construed as a much deeper, and in some cases final, commitment to the war effort. The rhetoric of speeches and newspaper articles was one thing; it was something else for a young man to offer himself to his country. Across North and Northwest Texas, communities tested the patriotism of young men with the increased recruiting tempo spurred by the declaration of war. More than participating in military drills or talking about joining, when the recruiting sergeants visited their communities many young men were pressured to enlist, although the pace of enlistment never appeared to match the patriotic fervor of communities in North and Northwest Texas. Furthermore, the Army, Navy, and Marine Corps had to compete for recruits with another organization: the Texas National Guard, which during the summer of 1917 started its own campaign to fill up its ranks.[4]

In those first few weeks after the declaration of war, the counties across North and Northwest Texas were swept up in the worldwide conflict. Thousands displayed their sense of patriotism through a variety of means, including parades, speeches, and rallies. The men often joined together and engaged in military drill, while women frequently joined Red Cross organizations and participated in numerous events to show their own patriotism. Likewise, African-American and foreign-born citizens showed their commitment to the war. African-Americans formed their own drill companies, while occasionally foreign-born citizens displayed an inflated sense of patriotism in order to downplay their foreign heritage and to protect themselves from citizens who would not or could not believe that they had severed ties to their nation of origin. Furthermore, a paranoid fear of German spies roaming across the state tainted the atmosphere in the months after the declaration of war. Rumors of German spies committing sabotage swept across Northwest Texas while many foreign-born citizens were watched closely and often faced the threat of violence. That paranoia exploded into public view when the leaders of the Farmers and Laborers Protective Association (FLPA) were arrested and tried in Abilene during the summer and fall of 1917 for alleged opposition to the draft.[5]

Within this atmosphere of patriotism and paranoia, the Texas National Guard sought to recruit its ranks to full strength. By the end of the summer of 1917, nearly two thousand men would make their choice to serve in the Texas National Guard's 7th Infantry. They made their choice under difficult circumstances, perhaps unsure if they should enlist in a particular service or wait to be drafted, although with the draft there was no certainty about where they might end up and who they might serve with. Within such a climate, officers of the Texas National Guard arrived in counties across North and Northwest Texas in June of 1917, where they spent the summer recruiting, organizing, and training fifteen new companies of soldiers.

On June 28, 1917, barely three weeks after the national draft registration, the *Wichita Daily Times* printed an announcement sponsored by the Wichita Falls Chamber of Commerce. The announcement read: "Attention! You who have registered for [the] Army draft, the Texas National Guard will take 300 men from Wichita, Clay, Archer, and Knox Counties. This opportunity to enlist with National Guard expires Sat. June 30, 1917." The notice enumerated the many advantages of joining the National Guard rather than being drafted as part of the "National Army." For example, the advertisement hinted that a recruit would be able to "select your own associates" and "know your own officers." The prospective Guardsman would receive "efficient training, beginning at once," and might have an opportunity to become an officer in other Texas Guard units. Furthermore, the recruiting advertisement claimed it would be easier for a Guardsman to prove his identity "in case of injury or on application for pension." The final two reasons, however, might have been the Guard's strongest selling points: a Texas Guardsman would "receive the attention, love and respect of the people at home, who are able to give your companies special attention; boxes from home, etc." Finally, he would receive the same pay as a soldier in the Regular Army. The announcement concluded by pointing out that a mass meeting for recruiting draft-registered men for the Texas National Guard would soon be held in the city. Local business leaders who attended the rally were asked to "state that they will hold open all positions now held by men who desire to enlist, and will give back these positions, or better ones, to them when they return." The announcement finished with a phrase popular at the time: "Be a 'went' instead of a 'sent'—if you must go sooner or later, why not go with the boys from home?"[6]

Although the National Guard recruited across the United States during the war, that organization faced competition for recruits from the Army and Navy. In

Texas, senior National Guard officers planned to use every advantage available to secure enough men. Indeed, by the summer of 1917 the nation had been at war for two months, the decision had been made to hold a selective draft, and nearly ten million men had already filled out the Selective Service registration paperwork, including nearly one million in Texas alone. The business of creating the army that would go to Europe to fight alongside Great Britain, France, and other nations became the focus of thousands of military officers and civilians nationwide, and National Guard leaders expected their organization to play a significant role in the conflict. However, as late as April and May of 1917, the government had not yet decided to increase the size of the National Guard, and when official word finally came to recruit men for new units, there was little time to waste.

While the militia tradition was older than the nation itself, efforts to professionalize the National Guard and put it on a more equal footing with the Regular Army did not take hold until the early twentieth century. The Dick Act of 1903 re-organized the militia and formally titled it the National Guard, and although legislation authorized the Guard a strength of 180,000 in early 1917, it was nowhere near that mark. While President Wilson mobilized the National Guard in 1916, and 112,000 served on the Mexican border that year, by early 1917 most of those National Guard units had demobilized and were returning home. Several Texas National Guard units served on the border, including the 2d, 3rd, and 4th Infantry Regiments, the 1st Cavalry Squadron, and various engineer, artillery, and hospital units. At the end of 1916, the state's military officials designated the Texas National Guard troops on the border as the 6th Separate Brigade, commanded by the adjutant general of Texas, Brig. Gen. Henry Hutchings, a veteran of the Spanish-American War. Hutchings' command numbered approximately 4,755 men, and was in the process of demobilizing when the Wilson administration released the Zimmerman Telegram on March 1. The Zimmerman Telegram highlighted Germany's attempts to draw Mexico into the war and infuriated many American citizens. That, as well as deteriorating relations with Germany, prompted the president to suspend the National Guard's demobilization in March of 1917. New orders arrived on March 21, 1917, and the 2d, 3rd, and 4th Infantry regiments of the Texas National Guard remained on active duty.[7]

Soon, however, the federal government finally authorized a number of states, including Texas, to raise additional National Guard units to be brought into federal service by August of that year. In turn, the states had less than four months to organize and recruit these new Guard units. In Texas, Gov. James Ferguson and General Hutchings determined that the Texas National Guard should expand by about 12,000 men and be organized into two infantry brigades of three regiments each, one separate infantry regiment, one cavalry regiment, two regiments of artillery, one battalion of field engineers, one field signal battalion, as well as supply train, military police, and ambulance companies. The units with border service—the 2d, 3rd, and 4th Infantry—were organized as the first brigade under the command of Brig. Gen. John A. Hulen, a Texas National Guard officer and like Hutchings a veteran of the Spanish-American War as well as the Philippines Insurrection. The second brigade consisted of the newly recruited 1st, 5th, and 6th Texas Infantry under the command of General Hutchings, while the 7th Texas would be recruited as a "separate" regiment, not assigned to one of the two infantry brigades. To build the officer corps of those new units, Governor Ferguson and General Hutchings approved the commissions of 417 individuals in the expanded Texas Guard. Those officers then fanned out to particular areas across the state with the authority to raise companies and regiments of National Guardsmen. The officers were assigned geographical regions of the state in which they could recruit. As it turned out, officers of the 1st and 2d regiments recruited in the southwestern portion of the state; the officers of the 3rd and 5th regiments recruited in the southeastern area; and the 4th and 6th regiments sent officers to North and Northeast Texas. The "separate" regiment, the 7th, recruited men across North and Northwest Texas. The governor selected Austin attorney and veteran Texas Guardsman Col. Alfred Wainwright Bloor as that regiment's commanding officer.[8]

Bloor was not a native Texan, having been born in Pennsylvania in 1876, although by 1880 Bloor's father had moved his family to Austin. Bloor graduated from the Agricultural and Mechanical College of Texas (now Texas A&M University) in 1895, and shortly thereafter joined the 1st Texas Militia Regiment and then served as a sergeant with the Texas Volunteers in the Spanish-American War. His father died in 1899 during Bloor's stint in the Army, and his mother returned to Pennsylvania where she listed Bloor as a resident of that state on the 1900 Federal Census. However, after his service in the Spanish-American war, Bloor returned to Texas, married, and worked as a general practice attorney. In 1910, Bloor was thirty-two years old and had served continuously in the Texas National Guard. By 1914 he held the rank of major and served as the third-ranking officer of the 2d Texas Infantry, a position he had held since 1903. From 1914 to 1917, he served as lieutenant colonel of the 2d Texas and deployed to the Mexican border. After receiving his commission as colonel of the 7th Texas, he set about building the regiment that he might one day lead overseas. Other members of his staff included his deputy, Lt. Col. John Jennings, and battalion commanders Majors Davis E. Decker, Alvin M. Owsley, and William Culberson, a relative of United States Senator Charles Culberson. These men oversaw the regimental recruiting effort and set up headquarters in Wichita Falls, a central location for their Northwest Texas recruiting area. Culberson, a former high school administrator from Hillsboro, and

Owsley, eldest son of a prominent Denton County resident, would later broaden their experience by serving as commandant and executive officer of two officer training camps held at Fort Worth's Camp Bowie in January and May 1918.[9]

While General Hutchings continued his duties as the state's adjutant general, General Hulen took responsibility for recruiting the Texas National Guard with the "authority to call into the state service such officers and enlisted men as he may deem necessary." Shortly thereafter, he issued a statewide announcement that the National Guard would recruit seventy-three units to fill up the four new regiments authorized by Governor Ferguson. This equated to 12,000 men from across the state. Of this number, the 7th Texas would account for about one-sixth. With this announcement, and with the new officers of the regiment having received their commissions, the "prospective commanders" fanned out across the state and set about recruiting their companies.[10]

Recruiting the 7th Texas.

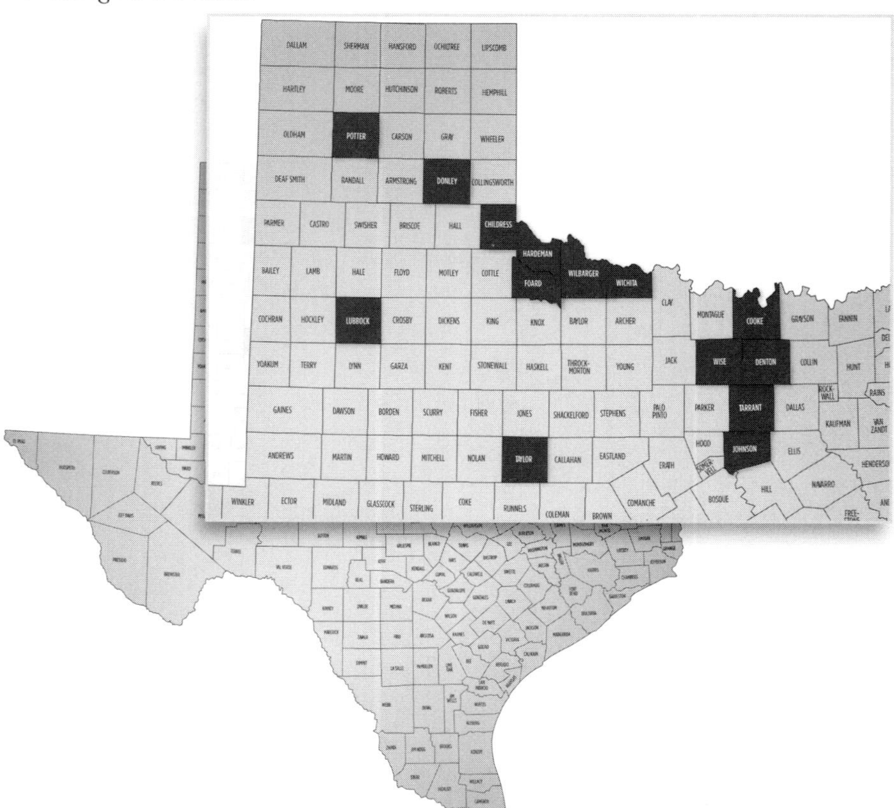

Companies for the 7th Texas Infantry, Texas National Guard were formed in these fourteen counties in the summer of 1917.

Most of those "prospective commanders" received their authority to recruit their companies in June of 1917, and immediately began organizing their units. Each officer faced time pressure because once the draft began the National Guard could no longer recruit draft-eligible men. As mentioned, they also faced competition for recruits from Army and Navy recruiters. However, many of the newly minted officers of the 7th Texas were from North and Northwest Texas, and nearly all of them received extra support from local communities. The officers received basic recruiting instructions, which, besides their own skills at convincing men to join their units, were their only guidelines to build their companies from the ground up. While they were often on their own, the regiment's senior officers travelled around the region and assisted where they could.[11]

The men charged with raising the companies of the 7th Texas varied in their backgrounds and experience. In Cooke County, Capt. William Tyler returned from Houston to begin recruiting his company. Tyler, a Gainesville resident whose father and grandfather had both been soldiers, served for a number of years in the Texas National Guard as a lieutenant and captain, although that unit had been mustered out of service two years earlier.[12]

In Amarillo, Capt. Thomas D. Barton returned to the town where he had earned a living in the newspaper and drugstore business to begin recruiting in the Panhandle. He was in his early forties and became the oldest of the regiment's company commanders. His military career had started in 1892 when he served as a private in the 6th Texas Infantry. Later, he gained experience in the Philippines. In Taylor County, Lt. Alan J. McDavid, originally from near Tyler in East Texas, became the first Texas National Guard officer to start recruiting in Abilene. McDavid opened a recruiting office in the Abilene Gas and Electric Company in the Sayles Building. The company commander, Capt. Robert M. Wagstaff, was in Brownsville at the time but locals expected his return by early July. He would not actually make it to Abilene until July 20, after his company had been mustered into service. Wagstaff was a well-known resident of the town, and the son of Judge J. M. Wagstaff, a prominent local citizen. Captain Steve Lillard, a Decatur resident for twenty-three years and a graduate of the Agricultural and Mechanical College (now Texas A&M), where he played football, had not yet reached thirty years of age when he returned home to Decatur to recruit in Wise County in North Texas. In Vernon, Capt. H. A. Baker, a former Wichita Falls science teacher, received an appointment to raise the National Guard Company in Wilbarger County.[13]

In Denton, Maj. Davis E. Decker visited the city to gauge the feel for recruiting a company there and came away less than favorably impressed. He had offered commissions to several local men, all of whom turned them down except for James B. Stiff, who accepted a commission as second lieutenant. Decker's unfavorable report reached General Hulen, who shortly thereafter dispatched another National Guard officer, Capt. Noah Roark of Dallas, an attorney who had previously lived in Denton, to take another look at the situation to determine "what grounds, if any, there are for giving up the plan of raising a National Guard unit in Denton and Denton County." Once in Denton, Roark concluded that a company could, in fact, be raised there. General Hulen then appointed him as the company commander and charged him with raising the company.[14]

In Wichita Falls, two weeks after the declaration of war, the local paper reported that if an individual wanted to join the Texas National Guard, he should look elsewhere as there was "apparently no opportunity for a Guard organization here at present." Shortly thereafter, General Hulen sent a telegram to local resident Sneed Brewster Staniforth that a National Guard company would be raised in Wichita Falls. In fact, Hulen pointed out that in all probability Wichita County would be authorized to raise two companies. Staniforth, a short and stocky man, had previously served with the Texas National Guard in Gainesville, rising from private to captain and eventually serving as company commander. In Wichita Falls, he worked as an assistant general manager of a brick and tile company. Local residents described him as a "young man of soldierly qualities." Throughout April and May, Staniforth's "company" remained an informal organization, with men showing up for drill practice but holding to no legal commitment until receipt of official word in June of the expansion of the Texas National Guard. This message also formally announced that two companies would be recruited in Wichita Falls as expected. Capt. Duncan M. Perkins received responsibility for the second Wichita Falls company. Like Staniforth, Perkins was well-known in the Wichita Falls area and a veteran of the military, having served in Cuba during the Spanish-American War. He also had eight years experience as an officer in a state militia company. Perkins apparently took over the recruiting for both companies while Staniforth attended the officers training course at Leon Springs, Texas. Staniforth, however, secured an early release from the course through General Hulen's intervention. Still, in his short time at the camp, Staniforth earned a reputation as "one of the brightest young officers in the camp." He arrived back in Wichita Falls at the end of June to assist Perkins, who had been slow in recruiting, evidently spending much of his time "getting his affairs into order for his military service." The two officers were friends, however, and worked together to recruit the three hundred men needed for the two companies rather than competing against each other for recruits.[15]

Clyde Graham arrived in Foard County to begin his recruiting efforts, telling locals that Foard County earned the chance to raise a company because soldiers of the area had reputations for being "champion" marksmen. To the east, Capt. Eugene T. Underwood arrived in Johnson County to raise his company. Underwood, a "high-toned gentleman," hailed from East Texas rather than Johnson County, although the local paper reported that he "comes highly recommended." James E. Wiley completed the officers training camp at Leon Springs and at the camp's conclusion wired the city of Quanah that he would be arriving to raise a company in Hardeman County. In Clarendon, Capt. Ethan Simpson, a local lawyer, lost fifty pounds by running and dieting on "buttermilk and tomatoes" so he could attend the officers training camp. Upon graduation, he returned to Donley County and with a local ranch foreman named Star Johnson began recruiting in the area. Likewise, Harold T. McGrath assumed responsibility for Fort Worth and Tarrant County, while Homer Troy Merrill began the work of raising a company in Lubbock. Merrill had attended the New Mexico Military Institute and served as a member of the Philippine Constabulary from 1912 until 1916, when he unsuccessfully sought a commission in the Marine Corps. Still, while he was in the Philippines, senior officers recognized his "good moral character" and his "energy and willingness to do his duty," and he received a commendation for "excellent work in the capture of some outlaws."[16]

By mid-June, as those officers were starting their recruiting campaigns, many of them carried out their work with the expectation that they could only recruit for their units until the draft occurred, at the time scheduled for the first week of July, although it actually occurred on July 20, 1917. The Texas National Guard also recruited men with the understanding that each recruit who signed up would count against that particular county's draft quota until the end of June. For example, prior to the draft, if a county received a quota to provide 200 men for the draft but 50 men joined the National Guard or the Regular Army or Navy, then the county needed to provide 150 men. The Texas National Guard, at General Hulen's insistence, also discouraged the use of the word "conscript" as a demeaning term for "persons who shall be selected for service under the selective draft system." According to General Orders No. 2, no Texas Guardsman was to "make use of such terms, or similar expressions" to demean the draft system. The order, however, pointed out that it was "proper to direct attention to any special advantage that may be claimed for any particular unit or arm of the service." Finally, Hulen's order urged that "all public utterances should be directed to stimulating recruiting … and the heartiest cooperation should be practiced" between the Army, Navy, and National Guard.[17]

The Texas National Guard recruited men for six-year enlistments, three years "in the service with the organization," and three years "on furlough attached to the National Guard." Each company also needed a certain number of recruits of different ranks, and in the summer of 1917 the standard company included 150 men. The men received pay ranging anywhere from $53 per month for the company first sergeant, to $40 for cooks, and $30 per month for each of the 87 privates. While 150 men equated to full strength, because medical exams and other things subjected some Guardsmen to disqualification, most officers tried to over-recruit. Married and single men between the ages of eighteen and forty-five were eligible to enlist.[18]

As their instructions pointed out, the officers' first priority was to take "immediate steps to provide, at your own expense, an office or place in which to carry on organization work." In order to do this, the recruiting instructions stressed local cooperation, pointing out that officers should contact local newspapers and "procure the cooperation of the leading businessmen." In many cases, this extended to local government officials as well. Finally, officers were given the latitude to use their imaginations as their instructions told them to "take all other steps which may occur to you which are proper towards securing recruits." Because most of the officers hailed from the communities in which they recruited, local residents eagerly assisted them and did so in a number of ways. For some, this assistance came early in the form of office space. In Gainesville, Captain Tyler received space in the Chamber of Commerce and Clyde Graham opened an office in Crowell on the ground floor of the Bell Building. Likewise, Captain Wiley in Quanah opened a recruiting office in Jones' Tailor Shop, and Captain Barton in Amarillo opened a recruiting station in the Nunn Building, where he expected to raise his company within a week, telling a reporter that "we will go and return as an Amarillo Company ... say to my friends to come at once and let's all get together." Capt. Eugene Underwood in Cleburne pitched a tent on the courthouse lawn and received the "hearty cooperation of the best men in this city and vicinity." All of the officers of the 7th Texas, upon arrival, managed to find office space near their respective courthouse squares.[19]

As soon as the offices opened, the recruiting began, although some were not sure what the government would use them for. Captain Tyler held out hope that the men he recruited would stay together through their entire term of service, although he, and many others, believed the Guardsmen stood a good chance of spending it on the Mexican border rather than overseas. Just one day after opening his doors, he secured four recruits but also turned away several men for medical reasons. Perhaps Captain Tyler had an edge in recruiting men because General Hulen, who oversaw recruiting for the state, had started his own National Guard career in Gainesville, and Tyler used that as a recruiting point. Taking an approach common among Texas recruiters, Lt. Alan J. McDavid equated military service with past tradition and urged men to come to his recruiting office and "offer himself, as did his forefathers and fathers." Indeed, within a week after Lieutenant McDavid's arrival, the *Abilene Reporter* mentioned that seventeen men had enlisted and that the "National Guard company being formed here continues to grow each day."[20]

In Foard County, Captain Graham posted a statement in the *Foard County News* urging men to join the "Crowell Company of National Guards" but to do it before the draft started. If they did so, he assured them, they would not only be helping the National Guard but themselves as well. He reported that thirty-five men had signed up, but he wanted seventy-five as quickly as possible. In Quanah, Captain Wiley signed up sixteen men rapidly and placed an ad in the *Quanah Tribune Chief* stressing the need for more volunteers.[21]

Recruiting in Denton started slowly although the pace picked up. By the end of June, Captain Roark had thirty-three men. A week later, however, his company increased to seventy men. But it was not until the city held a recruiting rally, and Roark and Lieutenant Stiff travelled throughout the county speaking at places such as Krum, Bolivar, and Sanger, that Roark had enough men to establish the unit. Many of these communities in North and Northwest Texas were plastered by recruiting posters, most of which echoed standard recruiting themes. One in Wichita Falls read: "Don't be drafted, VOLUNTEER in the National Guard of Texas ... don't be a slacker. Your friends around you are all going. What are you going to do? Get into line and answer the bugle call!" A second poster appealed: "In after years, don't let your children be embarrassed when they are asked 'where was your father in 1917?'"[22]

Perhaps the toughest recruiting challenge for the 7th Texas came in Fort Worth, where the 7th Texas competed with the 4th Texas Infantry, National Guard artillery units, Army and Navy recruiters, and National Guard units in nearby Dallas County. By June 21, Capt. Harry McGrath had signed up just four men, one of whom was Fancher D. Reagan, the first man to sign up for service with McGrath's company, who would later be killed in France. Because of the slow pace of recruiting in the city, McGrath and the other recruiters pinned their hopes on a "big rally" to be held in early July. A headline in the *Fort Worth Record* morosely opined: "Although [the] selective draft goes into effect soon, recruiting drags; National Guard still needs many men." Indeed, Captain McGrath opened a second recruiting station and took advantage of a display window offered by a local store to advertise the Texas National Guard. This may have helped because in a burst of recruiting on the final Saturday before the end of the June Captain McGrath signed up five additional men, the highest total in the city that day among all recruiters.[23]

Not only did many communities assist the officers of the 7th Texas by providing them areas in which to conduct their recruiting and printing numerous newspaper articles, local communities also held recruiting rallies that often featured speeches from prominent citizens supporting the Texas National Guard. Although some of those rallies included Army and Navy recruiters, the evidence suggests that the Texas National Guard received much more community interest than the other services, although residents did not disparage any man who joined another branch.

At these events, leaders often referred to the Texas military experience and frequently followed the lead of a widely published appeal from General Hulen, which read in part: "From a military standpoint the achievements of the Lone Star State stand foremost of the states of the union. The heroic and unselfish deeds of her sons have been written indelibly upon the pages of history." According to Hulen's appeal, the time had come for Texans of 1917 to make their mark upon history: "The dark 'pall' of despotism is 'stalking' through Europe. Texas' young men are needed. The need is as great as when that hero of the Mexican war said, 'who will follow old Ben Milam to San Antonio.' " Hulen believed that the "young men of the state must answer again as did their forefathers" by joining the Texas National Guard. In Quanah, the *Tribune Chief* echoed that theme: "Blood will tell! Most of the boys who are enlisting now of their own free will had fighting ancestors," while "Men who skulked and sneaked during times that tried men's souls are recognizing the same characteristics in their sons." The Texas National Guard relied heavily on such ideas to entice men into its ranks, although it is unclear to what extent those connections were effective in convincing men to join.[24]

In Gainesville, citizens held a patriotic rally for the purpose of "arousing a spirit of enlistment in the National Guard service among young men of Gainesville and Cooke County" and Captain Tyler sent letters to men who had registered for the draft, urging them to enlist in the Texas National Guard and avoid being drafted. In Amarillo, residents marked Texas National Guard recruiting week with a large parade. In Cleburne, Democratic National Committeeman William Poindexter made a special call to recruit men from Johnson County for the Texas National Guard and helped organize a patriotic rally, which "secured 24 additional enlistments in the Johnson County Company." In Vernon, residents held a "mass meeting in the interest of the Texas National Guard" with prominent Wichita Falls resident Frank Kell speaking on Captain Baker's behalf.[25]

Likewise, the citizens of Wise County held recruiting rallies three days in a row in an effort to complete the recruitment of the local company. Capt. Steve Lillard attended each day's rally and kept his office in the City National Bank open until midnight to enlist men before the recruiting deadline arrived. Decatur residents also received an introduction to Maj. Davis Decker, whose battalion included the Wise County company. Decker was one of several of the regiment's senior officers who travelled throughout Northwest Texas supporting recruiting efforts for all of the companies. Speaking to the Decatur residents, Major Decker asked them why "the hardy young manhood of this town and county was not answering the call for volunteers?" Decker announced that Lillard's company needed just a few more men, and advised anyone who desired "to escape the draft" to "cast their fortune with Captain Lillard's company."[26]

In Fort Worth, residents held what they considered a successful recruiting rally, although Fort Worth's enlistments did not improve enough to prevent an officer from Texas National Guard recruiting headquarters in Houston from writing to Fort Worth Mayor W. D. Davis asking him to hold a second rally. Davis was reluctant to do so, however, writing back: "We have just finished with a big patriotic meeting and recruiting rally, plenty of speakers and lots of music. What more can we do?" Instead of another rally, the mayor drew on the support of local groups such as the Young Men's Business League, the Chamber of Commerce, and the Lions and Rotary Clubs to push for recruits during the final days of June.[27]

As the companies began to take shape and fill out through early July, the state filled the remaining company officer positions. In Gainesville, Captain Tyler gained the assistance of 1st Lt. Horace Clark Jennings and 2nd Lt. Thomas D. Mitchell, both of whom hailed from Gainesville and recently graduated from the officers training camp at Leon Springs. Jennings was considered one of Gainesville's "leading young businessmen" and had served in the former Gainesville unit of the Texas National Guard. Mitchell was attending the University of Texas when President Wilson mobilized the National Guard in 1916 for service on the Mexican border. He enlisted and progressed through the ranks, becoming one of twenty-five sergeants in his regiment selected to attend the officers training camp in 1917. The local paper also observed that the two officers would be permanently assigned to the company if they succeeded in recruiting it to full strength. Several weeks later, 2nd Lt. Bert H. Davis completed the complement of officers for the Gainesville Company, also having graduated from the officers course at Leon Springs.[28]

In Johnson County, Captain Underwood welcomed Lieutenants E. J. Litteer and William R. Lockett. In Wise County, Tully V. Terrell, son of prominent Decatur resident and Texas State Senator Charles Vernon Terrell, received an appointment as a lieutenant in Captain Lillard's company. Bertram Bloor, the regimental commander's younger brother, served as the second lieutenant in the company, and Lt. Thomas W. Newsome filled out the staff. As late as July 15, however, the lieutenants of the two Wichita Falls companies had not been named, and residents speculated about who would be appointed. Finally, Daniel S. Blue and Gordon R. Porter received commissions as lieutenants in Captain Staniforth's Company F on August 2, 1917. Shortly thereafter, Captain Perkin's Company G welcomed the arrival of 1st Lt. Joe A. Kell, son of prominent resident Frank Kell, and 2nd Lt. Alfred H. Carrigan Jr., also from a well-known Wichita Falls family.[29]

Other junior officers appointed to the regiment included Lt. Robert W. Armstrong of Lubbock, and Lieutenants Wilson, Tyson, and Ogden of the medical detachment, commanded by Maj. Everett Jones. Lieutenants William H. Brownell and George O. Thompson assisted Capt. Thomas Barton in Amarillo, while in Clarendon, Lieutenants Nat S. Perrine and John K. Bonnan reported to Captain Simpson. In Childress, Lieutenants Vivian Brady and George H. Klutts assisted Capt. Alonzo Drake, while in Quanah, Lieutenants William M. Murphy and Stayton M. Hankins served with Captain Wiley. In nearby Vernon, Captain Baker welcomed lieutenants Jim Bomar and Lester T. Burns. Lieutenant Bomar managed the Herring-Johnson Ranch and also worked with Captain Graham in nearby Foard County. In Taylor County, Lt. Alan J. McDavid organized the company in Captain Wagstaff's absence, and welcomed Lt. Edwin B. Sayles, a young man with prior military experience hailing from a well-known local family. Finally, Captain McGrath's other officers were Lieutenants Thompson Henry and Young B. Yates, while in Denton, Captain Roark's junior officers were Lieutenants James B. Stiff and Clark Owsley, the younger brother of battalion commander Maj. Alvin Owsley. That completed the complement of 7th Texas officers, and those men would eventually lead the regiment to Camp Bowie near Fort Worth.[30]

While the National Guard pressed its officers to recruit men prior to the implementation of the draft, the delay in implementing the draft until July 20, 1917, allowed the Texas National Guard more time to fill its ranks. Because the Texas Guard had not yet met its goal, Governor Ferguson designated the week of July 4–11, 1917, as National Guard Recruiting Week. The governor urged citizens to "devote his time to urging recruits to join the ranks." Again recalling the Texas military experience, the governor hoped the "spirit" of the recruiting week would be carried out by "men interested in Texas maintaining the traditions of the past." However, the need for a "recruiting week" illustrated a deeper problem that officers at the county level were already dealing with: less than a month before the Texas National Guard was to be federalized it had failed to recruit all of its units to full strength. Despite the flag waving and patriotic speeches, the young men of Texas had not rushed to join the Texas National Guard as expected. In part, this might have been a reflection of individuals waiting to see how the draft would turn out. Regardless of the reason, however, the state had not met its goal and National Guard officers tried to do something about it. As the *Gainesville Daily Register* reported, "Unless Texas 'gets busy' immediately Texas will disappoint the government and fail in the task assigned her." In Wichita Falls, only twenty men had signed up by mid-June, and locals realized that "filling two infantry companies is a large order for a town like Wichita Falls."[31]

In a second telegram widely published statewide, General Hulen pleaded once more with Texans to do their part: "Texas needs 12,000 men. She must have them ... young men of Texas must maintain the honor of the commonwealth for which their forefathers died." Another Texas National Guardsman, Col. Oscar Guessaz, wrote that it was an "affront to the state and nation" for a man not to fight when called. In his view, "men of Texas should hide their faces in shame, if they permit the call of the National Guard of Texas to go unanswered." Guessaz also appealed to their masculinity: "Let every young man in Texas think for just a moment of those near and dear to them. Let them read the history of the grand women who gave birth to their fathers ... Do you not think we ought to take good care that these good women may not meet the fate of the thousands of women in Belgium and France? Men of Texas awaken, before it is TOO LATE!"[32]

National Guard Recruiting Week appeared to work well for Captain McGrath in Fort Worth. Perhaps the rhetoric of Colonel Guessaz had worked. He also received assistance from Lieutenant Colonel Jennings and benefited from another recruiting rally sponsored by the Chamber of Commerce. As the *Fort Worth Record* reported, the Chamber of Commerce "grimly decided to bring to life the dormant young panthers who have been allowing a glorious opportunity to go to seed. In short, the local companies of the National Guard are going to be recruited to war strength in less than a week." Their efforts met with success as just over two weeks later the muster roll of Captain McGrath's company included 137 men.[33]

In Gainesville, Captain Tyler was "anxious" to raise his company to its full complement. According to Tyler, while full strength equated to 150 men, the company could be organized with 74 men, approximately half the total and termed "war strength." Nevertheless, Tyler made a strong push to secure more recruits as he moved into the final recruiting days. In Amarillo, Captain Barton urged the men of Texas to join a unit that had "state insignia." He claimed that by joining the National Guard they would stay together in the "passage across the waters" and "when the Germans pour their shells into their trenches, and if necessary die together, or to return home together." By July 14, Barton had enlisted eighty-six men in his company, and the next day had reached ninety-five and successfully secured its establishment. In Denton, Captain Roark recruited more than ninety men before announcing the organization of his company was a "foregone conclusion."[34]

Cleburne faced a similar situation, where by the end of the first week of July Captain Underwood had recruited eighty-eight men although just a few days later his company exceeded the 150 men for full strength. Many of the other companies, however, had not reached that point so early in the month. Underwood, like other officers, tried to over-recruit to offset the inevitable failure of some men to pass their physical exams. He also received a telegram from Colonel Bloor telling him to continue his efforts, but to make sure he publicly announced that once an individual had been drafted, they could no longer enlist in the National Guard. Recruiting in Wilbarger County met with considerable success as well, with Captain Baker enlisting 122 men by the middle of July. Additionally, citizens of Wilbarger County could boast that 325 of its residents had joined the Army, Navy, or National Guard, which was more than three times that county's draft quota.[35]

In Abilene, by the end of June, Lieutenant McDavid recruited 92 men and expected that in the next twenty-four hour period the company could grow beyond the 150 mark. McDavid passed that information along to Captain Wagstaff, who replied from Brownsville that "We have good prospect of having one of the best companies in the Guard and I shall be greatly disappointed if the Abilene country doesn't furnish the entire amount by enlistment." Wagstaff had little to fear, however, as two days later McDavid reported that the company stood at 141 men.[36]

In Wichita Falls, recruiting efforts finally met with success, with the two companies enrolling 310 recruits by July 1, 1917. A number of the men who joined in Wichita County came from the oilfields of nearby Burkburnett, including fifty-four men who joined as a group. Those men made eight dollars per day in the oilfields, or close to $160 per month. Compared to the $30 per-month salary of a private, they were taking quite a pay cut to enlist in the Texas National Guard. In fact, recruiting turned out so well in Wichita County and the surrounding area that General Hulen sent local officials a congratulatory telegram, and others followed from around the state seeking National Guard recruiters from Wichita Falls to help other communities. Lieutenant Colonel Jennings called Wichita Falls an "inspiration to the rest of the state," a statement that no doubt pleased the city fathers.[37]

Initially, National Guard officers referred to each company in the 7th Texas by the name of the county seat where its recruiting headquarters resided. Once each company recruited enough men that its establishment was assured, the process of mustering each company into state service began, including giving each company its state designation. For example, in Gainesville, Captain Tyler received word from General Hulen that his company had been designated as the regimental "Machine Gun Company." Tyler and his lieutenants were "enthusiastic," and Tyler claimed that "machine gun work is one of the best branches of the service." In Amarillo, the Texas National Guard originally designated Captain Barton's soldiers as the Supply Company. A short time later, however, state officers changed it to an infantry company and designated it Company A, while Captain Merrill's Lubbock Company became the regimental Supply Company. The following table provides an overview of the 7th Texas Infantry upon its arrival at Camp Bowie in September 1917:[38]

Table 1. Composition.

Composition of the Seventh Texas Infantry Regiment on arrival at Camp Bowie, September 1917			
Commanding Officer	Recruiting County	Seventh Texas Designation	Number of Persons
Captain Thomas Barton	Potter County	Company A	160
Captain Ethan Simpson	Donley County	Company B	128
Captain Alonzo Drake	Childress County	Company C	112
Captain James Wiley	Hardeman County	Company D	106
Captain Harry Baker	Wilbarger County	Company E	106
Captain Duncan Perkins	Wichita County	Company F	107
Captain Sneed Staniforth	Wichita County	Company G	119
Captain Steve Lillard	Wise County	Company H	139
Captain Robert Wagstaff	Taylor County	Company I	142
Captain Harold McGrath	Tarrant County	Company K	122
Captain Eugene Underwood	Johnson County	Company L	159
Captain Noah Roark	Denton County	Company M	126
Captain William Tyler	Cooke County	Machine Gun Company	75
Captain Homer Merrill	Lubbock County	Supply Company	92
Captain Clyde Graham	Foard County	Headquarters Company	78
		Total:	1771

Note: Total does note include regimental officers, medical detachment, or band section.

C.H. Barnes, *History of the 142nd Infantry Regiment of the Thirty-Sixth Division*, October 15, 1917 to June 17, 1919 (Blackwell Job Printing Company, 1922), 218-243

In late July, the companies prepared to be mustered into federal service, after which they would be drafted by President Wilson on August 5, 1917, and begin their training. Until they were mustered into federal service, the companies existed only on paper and the men were not required to report to any sort of a camp, but instead remained at home ready to report when called. However, some companies, such as Abilene's Company I, held military drills twice a week. While not mandatory, Lieutenant McDavid made it clear that "the member who attends will be that much ahead when the company finally goes into training."[39]

Waiting to be mustered into service became a burden for some soldiers because they received no pay until mustering in and the state provided each man just thirty cents subsistence allowance per day. This caused many recruits to struggle because they had already left their jobs to enlist. In response, many Northwest Texas communities shifted their emphasis from helping recruit soldiers to raising funds or finding jobs for the local National Guard companies. In Wilbarger County, Vernon businessmen defrayed the expenses of Captain Baker's recruits, covering the cost of room, board, and "necessary expenses" of each man. Baker's men were eventually put up in an "armory," and had their laundry done. In Wichita Falls, community leaders funded the living expenses of recruits believing that the lack of pay until mustering in caused men to refuse to join. In Johnson County, Captain Underwood's men asked city officials to give them work until they were mustered in.[40]

Because of the lack of adequate funds to take care of the soldiers prior to mustering in, local citizens felt obligated to assist in some way whether they wanted to or not. In Gainesville, Captain Tyler personally solicited local businessmen in an effort to raise $1,000 as a mess fund for his company, while in Abilene, members of Company I took it upon themselves to raise funds for purchasing books and musical instruments "in order that the men may pass their leisure hours more pleasantly." The *Abilene Reporter* commented that the soldiers' fund should be "heartily supported" as the city had no plans, at least in early July, to fund their mobilization camp. Nevertheless, the Abilene company raised more than $400 by the first week of August. Conditions were similar in Donley County, where Captain Ethan Simpson appealed to the local townspeople "to raise money necessary to keep the local militia company until they are officially mustered into Federal Service." Even the Clarendon girls' honor guard pitched in by collecting knives, forks, spoons, towels, and soap for Simpson's soldiers. A similar situation existed in Hardeman County, where residents held a meeting to raise money for Captain Wiley's company, and the local paper wrote that it was "up to the Quanah Folks to see that they do not lack for grub." Organizers eventually raised more than $200 for the local Guardsmen. Many residents in those communities also believed that a fund to support local soldiers would not be needed once the company exchange, or store, was established, but those would not be established until after the men were mustered in.[41]

In Cleburne, citizens of Johnson County stepped forward and took care of the men in their local company after rumors arose that the men went hungry and did not have places to sleep. To dispel such rumors, the *Cleburne Daily Enterprise* explained that a committee of four prominent Cleburne residents, including the county attorney, had been placed in charge of a fund to which citizens could contribute and which the soldiers would use to purchase supplies. The paper also described the care the men received: beds had been placed in the upper story of the courthouse, and an "arrangement" had been made with a local café to feed the men "as good meals as they received at home." The men also secured permission from the county judge to sleep on the courthouse lawn if they found the courthouse too warm at night. Leading residents urged locals to contribute one dollar each to a fund so the Guardsmen could buy "such delicacies as they cannot secure in the army."[42]

Prior to the companies being ordered into federal service, they underwent physical examinations. Military doctors traveled throughout Northwest Texas performing those physicals, which occurred in mid to late July. Lieutenant Arthur Stuart Brown examined several companies of the 7th Texas, including Abilene's Company I, in which 141 out of 161 men passed their physicals, and Captain Merrill's Supply Company, although it is not known how many men failed their physicals in that unit. In Cleburne, Captain Underwood's 185-man Company L lost almost thirty men due to the stringent physicals. While the *Wichita Daily Times* crowed that 310 men signed up in early July, only a few days prior to the federal mustering in Company F reported just 92 men, while Company G reported 93 on its roll, which represented a serious loss of men, although it is not clear if physical exams accounted for the drop. In nearby Electra, doctors rejected 75 percent of the men examined for service. Because of those disqualifications, the Texas National Guard in Wichita Falls needed to recruit about 100 more men in order to meet federal requirements for mustering in. However, by the time a Regular Army officer inspected the two Wichita County units, Company F had 136 men on its muster sheet, while Company G boasted 132 men. Lieutenant Colonel Jennings mustered the companies into state service and several days later they were inspected by a regular officer and recommended for federal service. What caused the sudden rush to service in Wichita Falls? While it is unclear if there was any specific reason, both officers most likely pushed the idea of joining a local company rather than facing the uncertainty of the draft. As the time for the draft approached, men might have been more susceptible to the rhetoric of serving in the National Guard, and perhaps even succumbed to the desire to live up to the experiences of Texas soldiers in previous wars.[43]

Once the physical exams were complete, the companies mustered into service in late July. In Foard County, Captain Graham published General Order No. 1, requiring all men to report to Crowell in preparation for the mustering in but wrote that each man had to pay his own way to get to Crowell. In Gainesville, Captain Tyler prepared for the July 18 mustering in ceremony, while in Abilene, Lieutenants McDavid and Sayles stayed "busy … making out the muster rolls, getting everything in shape …," while they waited for the battalion commander, Maj. Alvin Owsley, to arrive and conduct the ceremony, something he also did for Company L in Cleburne.[44]

The inspection of Capt. Robert Wagstaff's Company I in Taylor County was typical. The officers lined up the men and marched them to the courthouse square where the "company was inspected as a whole." After that, the "detail work of the inspection" took place on the third floor of the armory. Additionally, all of the soldiers of the company took an oath of "allegiance and loyalty." According to the *Abilene Reporter*, the "men made a splendid showing," and were neat and alert. Finally, they were pronounced to be a "husky bunch" that could "stack up" better than other units. In Cleburne, officers told Captain Underwood's soldiers that they "they were the most uniform in size of the men of any company." They also believed they would be in France by October, a rumor that proved off the mark. Indeed, most of the companies at this time still had not received their uniforms and continued to wear civilian clothes.[45]

Not surprisingly, those communities that hosted National Guard companies frequently took it for granted that their company was the best in the state. For example, after officers inspected Captain Simpson's Donley County company, the local paper claimed their "fitness was so apparent there was no hesitation on the part of the regular army officers in accepting them." As the paper attested, Captain Simpson and Lieutenants Perrine and Donnan had "a fine bunch of men in the home company and we are sure they will develop into first rate fighting men," something the reporter believed would reflect greatly on "Old Donley, who mothered them." According to the *Gainesville Daily Register*, Captain Tyler's machine gun company consisted of "as fine a looking bunch of young men as ever enlisted under the flag. They are our boys and we are proud of them." In Wichita Falls, the local paper described the soldiers of Companies F and G as a "particularly husky bunch," and had "as good raw material in these companies as can be found anywhere." In Crowell, Major Culberson and Captain Baker of Vernon visited Captain Graham's company and the local paper reported that the two officers "had some very flattering remarks" to make about the company, including "their uniformity." The two officers also reported that the Crowell company was "a fine bunch of boys in every particular."[46]

Not only did communities take pride in their local companies, but state officers expressed similar views that the Texas Guardsmen displayed those masculine qualities that many assumed would translate into good soldiers. For example, the Texas Guard's chief medical officer, Maj. John O'Reilly, stated that the Texas Guard "will provide Uncle Sam with as fine a body of men as ever donned uniform." O'Reilly based that assessment on his travels throughout the state, participating in the physical examinations of thousands of Guardsmen. Overstating the facts slightly, O'Reilly claimed that Texas was known "for her big men, strong and sturdy and of wonderful vitality and endurance," and these soldiers represented the "best men of Texas, both physically and mentally," who would stand the test of war better than men from any other state. After the war, the regimental chaplain, an Oklahoman, described the 7th Texas as "the kind of men who would help make any organization famous, when it came to the test." Indeed, according to that officer, the

7th Texas' soldiers were "big hearted because they had a big state with a big history back of them; ready to lay down life, for their forefathers had sacrificed when Texas was a Republic within itself." Even those outside the regiment and the state drew connections between those Texas guardsmen and the state's past, and some noted that the soldiers had not even suffered childhood diseases such as the measles and mumps. Nevertheless, such rhetoric indicated to many observers at the time that those Texas soldiers would perform better than others for the sole reason that they were from Texas, whether that had any basis in reality or not.[47]

While numerous observers described the superior physical characteristics of the Texas National Guardsmen, other states did not fare as well. For example, physicians discovered that nearly 60 percent of Alabama National Guardsmen suffered from hookworm, and as historian Robert Saunders Jr. wrote, the poor state of health among Alabama Guardsmen "cut deeply in a culture that had long revered manliness, militarism, and the attainment of personal honor on the battlefield. But the fact was that many young males in the state simply did not measure up." While many Texans marveled at the physical characteristics of the state's soldiers, an Army study completed after the war argued that "northern middle and upper middle class men from suburban areas formed the healthiest potential army population."[48]

The president "drafted" the vast majority of the National Guard, including the 7th Texas Infantry, into federal service on August 5, 1917.[49] Officially, then, after that date, the soldiers of the 7th Texas were no longer National Guardsmen, but soldiers of the Army of the United States. For many of those men, the distinction may not have meant much. Furthermore, they were now going to be paid and still served with the men they had joined the regiment with. They would also be required to move into temporary camps until called to the major training facility of Camp Bowie, under construction near Fort Worth, and which they expected to open soon. Camp Bowie was one of thirty-two training camps built in the summer of 1917, sixteen each for draftees and federalized National Guardsmen. Work on Camp Bowie progressed slowly and the camp failed to meet its targeted opening date of August 15, 1917. Thus, each unit had to secure temporary encampments while awaiting orders to proceed to Fort Worth. Abilene offered free use of its Fair Park for the entire third battalion of the 7th Texas Infantry, which included the Abilene, Cleburne, Denton, and Fort Worth companies. Although the battalion did not consolidate there, Captain Wagstaff's Company I did take advantage of those facilities.[50]

In Cleburne, after the mustering in of Captain Underwood's Company L on August 5, the men were not allowed to return to their homes as they had done prior to being "drafted" into federal service. Local residents provided quilts and blankets for the soldiers, and a number of residents offered up their own homes so that seventy-eight members of the company had a comfortable place to sleep. The same was true in

Gainesville, where the local paper printed the cry: "Accommodate the Soldier Boys, Ye Good People of City," and "Be Patriotic and Make a Soldier Your Guest."[51]

In Donley, Hardeman, and Wise counties, the companies established temporary camps on local county fairgrounds. In Quanah, the soldiers took over "a large shed in the center of the stable grounds." In Crowell, Captain Graham's soldiers made a home out of a "new garage building." Captain Barton's soldiers in Amarillo named their temporary camp after Colonel Bloor, while in Denton County residents named Captain Roark's camp after Denton Mayor Paul Beyette. Although they had space, the companies remained short of supplies. While Denton residents provided some "comforts and blankets," some men were forced to sleep "on the ground or as best they can." Later, however, many of the Denton County soldiers claimed to enjoy their hilltop campsite because it was "well-drained and gets the advantages of all breezes." Indeed, the soldiers of Company M eventually had "shower baths and electric lights" to make their stay at Camp Beyette even more enjoyable.[52]

In Wichita Falls the soldiers moved into Camp Marlow, named in honor of J. B. Marlow, a local real estate man who offered a vacant house for the soldiers' use and who had been heavily involved in recruiting. After federal mobilization, however, the two companies moved out to Lake Wichita. The Wichita Falls soldiers remained short of uniforms and other supplies, and problems with sleeping arrangements forced some men to sleep in "canvas cottages" at the lake, others to sleep in "idle streetcars," while several resorted to sleeping on the ground. However, residents organized a "consignment of tents, cots, and blankets" to relieve such conditions, while in Amarillo, Captain Barton's Company A did not have enough cots to go around until mid-August. Likewise, most of the companies still had not received uniforms. In Gainesville, the members of Captain Tyler's company wore overalls because of the delay in the delivery of the uniforms, while Johnson County residents donated shoes to Company L, particularly "outing or tennis shoes ... since the boys do so much drilling and their feet must be kept in shape. Good socks will also be welcome." The men appeared to take their circumstances in good humor and the local paper wrote the men had learned the first rule of being a good soldier: "to make out with whatever comes along." When uniforms finally arrived, each soldier received one coat, two pairs of pants, two shirts, one service hat, and one pair of leggings and shoes.[53]

In late August, Wichita Falls residents reimbursed the officers of the two local companies almost $600 for purchasing supplies and equipment out of their personal funds. Leading citizens, however, increased the amount to $1000 not only to pay back the officers but to create a company fund "nucleus." Although inaccurate, rumors swirled that the city would become the training center for all National Guard soldiers in Northwest Texas.[54]

While officers recruited the 7th Texas and kept the men near their home communities, other National Guard regiments did not follow a similar pattern. Some National Guard regiments remained on active duty after the war declaration while others consolidated at state camps while still others came together from various locations. For example, after the war declaration, the state of Alabama kept its four National Guard regiments on active duty and consolidated them at Camp Sheridan in Montgomery. Then, the Alabama Guardsmen spent much of the summer guarding industrial and transportation facilities across the state, which introduced a different community dynamic from what the 7th Texas experienced, in that the Alabama National Guardsmen did not develop ties with local communities in the same way. Also, in many situations recruiters canvassed each state looking for recruits, who would then be sent to already existing organizations as replacements rather than joining a brand new unit such as the soldiers of the 7th Texas did. Along similar lines, the 15th New York Infantry, an African-American regiment from New York City, assembled at Camp Whitman near Poughkeepsie, then returned to New York City and soon started guard duty assignments at various locations. Another method of creating regiments occurred when officers established the African-American 372d Infantry Regiment by combining various separate battalions and companies from six states, a method which obviously did not result in the development of strong community ties like the 7th Texas.[55]

Once the soldiers moved into their temporary camps, officers implemented stricter control and started a training routine on a set schedule to help their soldiers prepare for life at Camp Bowie. For example, the soldiers of Company L had a 9:30 pm curfew in Cleburne, and the company appointed several soldiers to work with the city police to make sure the men observed it. In Denton, reveille sounded at 6:00 am and retreat at 7:30 pm, while in Quanah, Captain Wiley's soldiers could not eat breakfast until each had first "finished his run around the race track and had the hose turned on his perspiring body." The soldiers spent much of their waking time, however, in drill, which became a daily ritual after the men were mustered into service. As the *Wichita Daily Times* observed, "Time and Uncle Sam's drill masters will work wonders." In addition to drill, the new soldiers spent hours listening to lectures on "sanitation, personal hygiene, and military courtesy."[56]

During this period, a dynamic relationship developed between the communities and their companies. This relationship developed primarily by allowing local residents to watch the soldiers train. Thus, while Cleburne soldiers helped police the town, citizens watched the men drill. In Denton, the *Record-Chronicle* predicted that drill practice would draw the greatest interest, which it evidently did. In fact, sixty-nine years later, a longtime Denton resident recalled watching Captain Roark's men drill: "I seen them drilling right up on the square, you know, marching," and recalled that there was a "great big bunch of them, because I seen them there training on the square." Residents also watched their local units participate in mock battles. Cleburne's Company L held one on the grounds of Clebarro College to which the public was invited. Locals watched as eight squads of soldiers concealed themselves in a "battle line," which the remainder of the company then rushed. Witnesses described the battle as "fierce and interesting," and ending with a "hand to hand tussle." The defensive side apparently took the most prisoners and declared the winner, although the "offensive side" was "not the least discouraged." In Abilene, a crowd "which filled and overflowed the grandstand at Fair Park" and estimated at 3,000 people, watched Captain Wagstaff's Company I conduct a retreat ceremony followed by a changing of the guard. The company later marched through town to the music of the popular song "To Hell with the Kaiser."[57]

In Amarillo, Captain Barton's men marched eight abreast in a parade through town. Onlookers observed that the soldiers were "largely representative of Amarillo and particularly of the Panhandle." The men demonstrated their military prowess as "trench jumpers" by leaping several four-foot-wide drainage ditches filled with water. Evidently a few men did not make it across, and this caused a few laughs. Nevertheless, the parade ended in front of a local theater where Captain Barton inspected his men and then the company went into the theater where they "enjoyed two hours of unalloyed pleasure complimentary of the management." The soldiers also became familiar with a training tactic that would become all too common at Camp Bowie: hiking. Captain Tyler's Gainesville Machine Gun Company hiked sixteen miles to the Red River but received cold well-water and sandwiches at the hike's conclusion. In Denton, Captain Roark's men hiked from Camp Beyette to the business section of town to "toughen" their feet and show off the uniforms they had finally received. Company L received a nine-foot by five-foot American flag from county residents and on a rainy day marched four miles to the home of a prominent Cleburne resident, S. M. Hill, where Mr. Hill presented the flag and Mrs. Hill provided punch. After the presentation, they brought the flag back to Cleburne and planned to take it to France.[58]

Some individuals attempted to turn the training of the 7th Texas into a publicity stunt. For example, a "prominent publicity man" suggested that the Wichita Falls National Guard soldiers should march to Fort Worth instead of taking a train, a distance of nearly 100 miles. Company G's officers did not take the idea seriously and facetiously stated that it sounded like the perfect job for Company F. Company F's officers failed to embrace the idea and pointed out that their "natural modesty made them shrink from assuming the importance of publicity agents for the National Guard." The two companies, however, had not heard the last of that idea. Still, with all the hikes, drilling, and training, the soldiers still found time for leisure. In

Wichita Falls, when the soldiers had free time, they could be seen "deeply involved in the mysterious niceties of a poker game," while others read, and a few indulged "at rare intervals in the luxury of correspondence."[59]

Many towns made "comfort bags" for the soldiers, which included a number of useful items. The Bryan and Son drugstore in Clarendon placed an ad in the local newspaper offering their own suggestion for a "comfort bag," which included razors, soap, toothpaste and brushes, combs, tweezers, stationery, and an "indispensable" flashlight, among other things. In Gainesville, the men received laundry bags and a small sewing kit nicknamed a "housewife," while in Wichita Falls, families contributed "some article of bedding, comforts, blankets, etc." Generosity had its limits, however, as the *Amarillo Daily News* reported that there had not been a "generous response" to an appeal for newspapers, magazines, and books which in the soldiers' free time would "elevate them and afford amusement and instruction."[60]

While communities watched the companies train, locals contributed to the relationship, in turn, by holding celebrations in honor of the soldiers, invited them to church services, and brought them into their homes for meals. During a celebration in Cleburne, for example, local residents treated Company L to a "picture show party, then music by the Peacock Band, speechmaking by Senator [sic] [Willmot Mitchell] Odell and songs by the Red Cross girls." After that, the soldiers went to different "ice cream parlors and drug stores for a treat of ices, melons and cold drinks...." Red Cross girls waited on the soldiers, and "matrons, all in the colors, red, white, and blue" served as chaperones. The keynote speaker of the evening, president of the local United Confederate Veterans chapter, again stressed the connection between the former Texas Guardsmen and the state's past. He stated that as he looked into the "determined faces of these boys of Johnson County," he knew they would "never halt in the great fight for world peace" and would march through Berlin listening "to the strains of Dixie in the palaces of the arrogant and imperious monarch of Germany." In a final flourish, the speaker drove home his point: "remember that when you are far away in the service of your country ... that you went from Cleburne, and remember the history of that great son of the southland, this beautiful little city's namesake, Pat Cleburne."[61]

In Crowell, Captain Graham's soldiers attended a watermelon feast that lasted a full day. That evening, citizens held a talent show for the soldiers at the home of a local resident. After an instrumental piece titled "Preparedness" and several other civilian performances, one member of the company blew a number of bugle calls and explained their meaning to the audience. After that, two members of the company regaled the crowd with whistle, guitar, and fiddle music. A reporter for the *Foard County News* wrote that the "occasion will be long remembered by the soldier boys as well as the others who were present."[62]

In Clarendon, Captain Simpson's men attended church services "given especially for Company B," and the next week attended an "ice cream social" given by the Girls' National Honor Guard on the courthouse square. The square was decorated with "electric lights strung from tree to tree above the tables,"[63] and before the evening ended, the soldiers and the girls lined up and were introduced to each other. In Gainesville, the local chapter of the Workers of the World entertained Captain Tyler's men who also received an invitation to visit the public library where they could "look over daily papers, current magazines and maps of all foreign countries." Common to just about all the counties, the Machine Gun Company benefited from a massive picnic, in which the local paper called for "bread, cake, pies, roasted meats, salads, pickles, fried chickens by the score, melons, fruits, and anything you have that is good and refreshing for the hungry eatists." While Captain Lillard's Company H in Decatur did not have such a bounty, they ate a meal of "fifty chickens and forty cakes," courtesy of residents of nearby Alvord, who prepared the meal and then delivered it by automobile to Decatur.[64]

Wichita Falls organized a box lunch and dance for all military men in the city, not just the two companies of the Texas Guard. For this celebration, planners roped off a city street and an orchestra provided music for the festivities. The party also included a full program of speakers, including Maj. Alvin Owsley, one of the battalion commanders, and Mrs. Alfred Carrigan, the mother of Company F's Lieutenant Carrigan. Deemed a success by local residents, the *Wichita Daily Times* reported that the open air dance area was "brilliantly lighted" and "filled with the soldiers and their friends, several hundred being present to hear the program and to either participate in or watch the dancing." The Wichita Falls Guardsmen also wore their newly arrived uniforms.[65]

Sports offered an alternative training method, and many companies fielded their own baseball teams. The Gainesville company established two teams and invited the public to attend all of their games although the soldiers charged twenty-five cents admission. Gainesville's first game, against the town of Myra-Saint Jo ended in victory for the "Sammies," a common nickname for soldiers at the time, and the local paper claimed that the "grandstand" was "taxed to its capacity" with spectators. In Abilene, Captain Wagstaff's Company I anxiously hoped to "cross bats … with any aspiring organization here that can deliver the goods." Evidently, the soldiers had played each other but looked to expand against "outside talent."[66]

Like soldiers everywhere, the men of the 7th Texas used mascots as a way to further their cohesion and morale. In Denton County, Captain Roark's men ended up with a monkey, while the Gainesville machine gunners received an Airedale pup, which they promptly named "Texas." Out in Abilene, Company I received a registered Llewellyn Setter as their mascot whom they named "Judge Wagstaff" after the company commander's father. The local paper stated that the soldiers applied the name "in all seriousness, for the boys consider Judge Wagstaff one of their very best friends." Indeed, by the time the regiment arrived in Camp Bowie, the regimental mascots included "goats, wolves, eagles, badgers, monkeys, coyotes, pups, and bull dogs," and Gainesville soldiers claimed to witness a bulldog fight every day. Later, after being appointed guardian of the unit's mascot Texas, one soldier spent hours trying to teach the dog to stand at attention and salute Lt. Thomas D. Mitchell whenever that officer passed by.[67]

Of course, in any large group of young men, discipline could be a problem. Disagreements were commonplace but usually not serious. Sometimes problems arose when one soldier simply sought to convince his buddies not to take the rules of "soldier-life" too seriously. However, officers usually punished any breach in the rules rapidly. For example, in Cleburne, a group of soldiers who "broke ranks before breakfast" found themselves sweeping the sidewalks around the courthouse and picking up cigar and cigarette butts. County residents usually caught on that a fistfight had recently occurred in camp when they noticed soldiers sweeping in front of the courthouse. While no occurrences of fights were reported in Gainesville, the company officers encouraged the soldiers "to be gentlemen instead of ordinary rowdy soldiers." The most common problem seemed to be men who had enlisted in the company failing to show up at camp, most of whom likely preferred to take advantage of staying with nearby family and friends. While officers seemed to be fairly lenient about this at first, after units were drafted into federal service officers treated absences more seriously. In Wichita Falls, Captain Staniforth told the *Wichita Daily Times* that his "absentee" soldiers had three days to show up before he classified them as deserters. The paper passed on the news for any soldiers who might read it, that being a deserter in wartime was a "precarious" position in which to be found.[68]

While discipline did not appear to be a major problem for the company commanders, at least one serious breach occurred in Decatur, when Pvt. Harlen W. Bassett attacked the company's chief cook with a butcher knife, cutting him badly on the face and hands. According to the cook, Private Bassett entered the cooking tent and when ordered to leave, he grabbed the knife and attacked. The *Wise County Messenger* speculated that the cook would have been killed by Bassett if guards had not intervened in time. The guards locked Bassett in the guard house, and he was scheduled to be tried at Camp Bowie once the company arrived. What became of Harlen Bassett is not clear, although he was no longer on the roster of the regiment in Camp Bowie.[69]

The relationships between the local communities and the soldiers of the 7th Texas appeared to be genuine and communities often expressed their satisfaction with their local companies. In Decatur, the *Messenger* gushed: "Wise County is proud of Company H and its officers, and we know that no company will make a better showing than ours when the test of service comes." In nearby Gainesville, an editorial claimed that "Cooke County people everywhere cannot be too lavish with their praises, encouragement and manifested good cheer for these soldier boys who are certain to make good in their arduous undertaking ... they are our boys, therefore we should have a special fondness for them." Such feelings were usually reciprocated. When the Gainesville soldiers left for Camp Bowie, the company published a letter in the *Gainesville Daily Register* that read " 'all good things must come to an end' still holds good," and expressed appreciation for everything the citizens of the county had done for them, and was signed "Sammie," a nickname for soldiers. When the men departed, the editor of the *Daily Register* lamented, "Oh Cruel War, what a heartless monster thou art."[70]

It could be argued that August of 1917 was the most enjoyable time for the soldiers of the 7th Texas, in part because they were new to soldiering and remained relatively close to home and benefited from positive relationships with their local communities. Nevertheless, progress continued to be made on Camp Bowie, and the soldiers knew their time at home was coming to an end, although their feelings were mixed. In Amarillo, members of Company A expressed regret about leaving their families but were "eager to get to Fort Worth and over to France." In spite of all the food and friendship that Gainesville bestowed on its local Guardsmen, the men still cheered when Captain Tyler informed them they would be off to Camp Bowie in less than a week. Such an attitude was explained in a letter one of the soldiers, Joe Casey, wrote to his mother after arriving in France: "I had rather soldier here than in America. I would like to see all the folks and friends but don't get as homesick here as the camp, as I do not have time."[71]

Nearly all Texas National Guard units prepared for their move to Camp Bowie in late August or early September. At the camp, their training would continue and they would lose the local connection developed with their communities. Indeed, for the 7th Texas, the brief period in August 1917 while they waited to move to Camp Bowie served as the only time the regiment existed along the lines it was recruited: a Texas National Guard unit filled with Texas soldiers and commanded by Texas officers, all of whom were from the same or nearby communities. But, as the Texas summer extended into September, most of the units of the 7th Texas discovered the age-old military maxim of "hurry up and wait," as the Army's bureaucracy quickly made any movement schedule meaningless.

In Amarillo, the soldiers completed preparations to leave as early as August 25, and turned Camp Bloor into a "spotless model." When movement orders failed to come as expected, the men speculated anxiously as to when they would actually depart. Still in Amarillo five days later, on August 30, Captain Barton, perhaps in an effort to get their minds off of the situation, paraded his soldiers through the town and took them out to nearby Canyon, where the men enjoyed a picnic lunch provided by local citizens. In Gainesville, there was time for one final "farewell dance" as well as a final plea for "canned goods of any sort" as the Machine Gun Company prepared to depart.[72]

The soldiers of Cleburne's Company L had "big plans" for their arrival in Camp Bowie. The soldiers carried the flag they had been given as well as a twelve-foot banner identifying themselves as "200 strong from Cleburne." As the local newspaper observed, "Cleburne people have been delighted to have this splendid body of men here, and will have a feeling of great regret upon their departure." Captain Underwood expressed the soldiers' appreciation for the city's "many and repeated kindnesses," and the soldiers "broke into wild cheers of patriotic demonstration" until their train arrived, carrying troops from San Angelo. The *Cleburne Daily Enterprise* announced that Company L was "as fine a bunch of men as any county can offer to help establish the security of freedom." In Denton, the 3:00 am arrival of the train carrying soldiers from other North Texas areas such as Sherman, Bonham, and Paris, did not deter the soldiers from giving local residents "an initiation to the battle cries of the different companies."[73]

In Crowell, Captain Graham's soldiers enjoyed dinner on the courthouse lawn on their night of departure. After the meal, the "boys marched to the depot to take the east bound train" trailed by a crowd of several hundred county residents who "spoke goodbyes to their departing friends and loved ones." The writer of the article added that "it was not a pleasant thought that perhaps some of the boys were not going to return." On the other hand, the writer concluded, those who failed to return home "will be remembered by posterity as real patriots who willingly sacrificed their lives for the good of their country."[74]

In Quanah, Captain Wiley alerted his company to move at 10:30 pm. The soldiers formed up, "counted fours, and wheeled up Main Street." They marched past the courthouse to the "acclaim" of citizens who stayed up to watch them leave. The soldiers boarded their train and cheered as they steamed away. Several policemen rode along in case there were any "German sympathizers who might have been inclined to tamper with the track." A *Quanah Tribune Chief* reporter pensively wrote the next day that taking 150 soldiers born and raised in the area created a "big vacancy, and the town today does not look like it usually does. There are heartaches in many places, which it will take time to heal." While those left behind may have harbored such somber thoughts, the last words heard from Captain Wiley's soldiers as they departed were "Good bye, girls, good bye!"[75]

Of course, farewell dinners and cheering did not always mark the departures. For example, in Clarendon, Captain Simpson's Company B had their fingerprints taken and were given a final inspection by Regular Army officers. The soldiers of Captain Barton's Company A received a pep talk by thirty-five-year-old Congressman Marvin Jones, and took his "instructions and advice" well. In Wichita Falls, locals abandoned a plan for a large farewell for the departing soldiers in Companies F and G after Colonel Bloor and other officers told city officials the men were simply too busy with departure preparations. Nevertheless, several thousand residents of Wichita Falls watched their train depart about 10:00 pm, and "Wichitans gave their soldiers farewell in good spirits." In Decatur, Captain Lillard's Company H broke camp and waited all night for the train to arrive, which it did not do until 5:00 am. After the soldiers were gone, the *Wise County Messenger* perhaps summed up best the relationship between the companies and the communities they left behind: the paper joined "the thousands of friends and relatives of our volunteers" in congratulating the soldiers for their "rapid advancement," and hoped "for them a safe return to their homes after the alarms of war have ceased."[76]

The pattern of send-offs for National Guard companies and draftees was generally the same across the nation and was certainly not unique to the 7th Texas. However, send-offs were sometimes troubling, such as in Birmingham, Alabama, where members of the local United Confederate Veterans chapter participated in a send-off for black soldiers departing for training camp. In New York City, Army officers prohibited African-American Guardsmen from participating in several parades through Manhattan. Still, in most cases, local residents across the nation eagerly participated in send-offs and parades for departing soldiers. However, the way the soldiers of the 7th Texas developed relationships with local communities should be contrasted with draftees. While all may have received parades and send-offs on their departure, community relationships were not as well developed between draftees and their communities. For example, the draftees who comprised the Texas-Oklahoma 90th Division received a summons from their local exemption board and were shipped off to their training camp in San Antonio as individuals rather than as organized companies. Because of that, there was little organized activity for drafted soldiers to come together as a group much less to develop a relationship with the communities they hailed from, as the soldiers of the 7th Texas appeared to do. Those men remained in their communities as individuals until they were called up, the first group in early September 1917, and sent to their respective training camps. The fact that the 7th Texas remained in the communities in which its soldiers were recruited offers a unique perspective in the development of communal relationships between military organizations and local residents.[77]

Although all of the 7th Texas' companies left home with some sort of celebration and well wishing from local residents, one company experienced some negative feelings. In Clarendon, after Captain Simpson's men had departed for Camp Bowie, the *Clarendon News* published an editorial by "a parent" praising the company: "Our soldier boys are gone—gone to Camp Bowie at Fort Worth—perhaps their only stop till they go to the bloody trenches of France…" The writer then shifted focus and decried an "overflow of unkind, unjust criticism" that angered and wounded some soldiers and their families. The criticism insinuated that the company and its officers were "riff-raff" and that very few had any "social standing" in the community. In spite of such feelings among some residents, the *Clarendon News* insisted that Captain Simpson's company was "the very best of this country," and not one of them came from the "idle rich" or "pink-tea society." Regardless of such criticism, Captain Simpson thanked the citizens of Clarendon prior to his departure and wrote that "the kind treatment given us by the citizens of this country impels me as the commanding officer to give expression to these few words of public thanks." He also wrote that "the strongest feeling of good will has developed among the members of this company; good comradeship abounds." After parading through the town to the train station, the men boarded a train at about 7:00 pm that already carried Captain Barton's Company A from Amarillo. The train left Clarendon "to the accompaniment of cheers and hurried words of farewell," and arrived in Forth Worth at 9:00 am the next morning, having stopped only long enough to load Capt. Alonzo Drake's Company C in Childress.[78]

As the officers and men of the 7th Texas boarded trains across Northwest Texas and converged on Camp Bowie, Colonel Bloor could look back on the rapid organization of the regiment as a busy but successful time. While it is not clear that the regiment was "recruited in a record short period of time," as regimental chaplain C. H. Barnes believed, it remained a substantial accomplishment from an organizational standpoint. Of course, the men had little training and had much to learn before they could be called "soldiers." As the summer of 1917 came to an end, the Texas National Guard had recruited thousands of soldiers, among them the 7th Texas. Recruited over the summer and drafted into federal service in early August, each company spent the rest of that month in temporary camps where local communities feted and praised them. It is not too much to say that during this period local communities made those soldiers the center of attention, and when people thought of the war and how it affected their lives, many turned their thoughts to the dusty fairgrounds and parks where young men in overalls or bits of uniform marched and drilled as if they were great warriors. Little did any of them know that their time together as a regiment of Texas soldiers would not survive their first month at Camp Bowie, much less the war. The summer of 1917 was a time in which those soldiers were treated as heroes but had not yet known the horrors of war.[79]

2

A PORTRAIT OF THE 7TH TEXAS INFANTRY

An examination of the make-up of the 7th Texas Infantry from a socio-economic standpoint offers a useful composite portrait of its soldiers. This serves not only to broaden historical knowledge of those individuals, but also offers a starting point for comparing them soldiers with others in the state and other sections of the country. Who were those soldiers that Texans asked to uphold its military tradition? What were their lives like prior to the war? What occupations did they follow? Were they married, and did they have families? Answers to such questions bring these National Guard soldiers into sharper focus and point to representative characteristics of a World War I Texas soldier.

The fourteen counties mentioned in this study functioned as recruiting headquarters for fifteen companies of the 7th Texas Infantry. On arrival at Camp Bowie in September 1917, the regiment consisted of approximately 1,952 enlisted men. Research into the draft registration cards and other sources disclosed information on 1,096, 61 percent of the regiment. Across the counties, this amounted to 59 percent of each company. Because of a muster roll from July 1917, information was found on 99 percent of the Taylor County company. Company G of Wichita Falls had the fewest, with information gathered on only 42 percent of that company. Because this analysis was based primarily on draft registration cards, there are several reasons why data was not found on more than 700 soldiers of the regiment. First, some soldiers registered in other Texas counties or even in another state. For example, there was often no way to tell if a man who registered for the draft in Harrison County was the individual of similar name who later joined the company in Wise County. A misspelled name was another reason for failing to find information on a particular individual, either on the regiment's roster or on the draft registration card. In some cases, men registered in a neighboring county. When that occurred, the assumption might safely be made that the individual joined the company forming nearby. Finally, in cases with common last names, it was often not possible to tell beyond a doubt which individual joined a particular company. With that being said, the sample size of 61 percent still offered ample data to illustrate characteristics of the 7th Texas' soldiers. To illuminate those characteristics, it is worthwhile to examine several broad trends within the regiment, followed by a closer look at more personal characteristics. It should be made clear that the percentages used in this study reflect the number of soldiers for which data were collected, rather than the regiment in its entirety.[1]

The draft registration cards used for this analysis were the first of three registration cards used by the federal government. The style used for the June 5, 1917, draft registration required registrants to answer twelve questions and provide their age. The first three questions consisted of their name, address, and date of birth. The next set of questions concerned citizenship. The registrant noted if he was a natural-born citizen, a naturalized citizen, or an alien. Next, they wrote the town, state, and nation where they were born, and whether natural or foreign born. The next group of questions related to occupation, and called for the registrant's present "trade, occupation, or office," as well as their employer and the job's location. The next question asked whether an individual had any relatives "solely dependent" upon him for support, followed by questions about marital status and race. Finally, a registrant noted any previous military experience and what grounds, if any, he had to claim exemption from the draft. After the registrant signed the card, the registration officer would note cursory physical characteristics of the individual and then also sign the card. Registration officials tore off the bottom left corner of the form of African Americans in order to make those cards easier to identify.[2]

Based on the data gathered from the draft registration cards, five points can be made about the soldiers' social and economic characteristics. The first concerned age. Wars, of course, are fought by young men, and World War I was no different. As a whole, the average age of the soldiers in the regiment was twenty-three and a half years. Company B from Clarendon had the highest average age, at twenty-four, while Companies I and M the lowest at twenty-two years of age. A closer look at the age composition of the soldiers confirmed the regiment's youthful composition. For purposes of this analysis, the soldiers' ages were broken down into three categories: 23 and under, 24–26, and 27 and older.

However, the majority of all fifteen companies of the 7th Texas consisted of men twenty-three or younger. In fact, fully 667 of the 1,096 soldiers fell into this youngest category (61 percent). But, just 266 soldiers (24 percent) were slightly older, ranging in age from 24–26, and only 163 of the soldiers (15 percent) were 27 or older.[3]

Table 2. Ages.[4]

AGES	NUMBER	PERCENT
23 and under	667	61%
24-26	266	24%
27+	163	15%
Total	1096	100%

Although men could join the Texas National Guard between the ages of eighteen and forty-five, there were relatively few men close to those bookend ages in the regiment. Part of this is due to an anomaly in the sources as the first draft registration in 1917 did not require the registration of men under twenty-one or over thirty. However, evidence of men outside that age range who joined the regiment can still be found because some registered during the two later draft registration periods, either in June or September 1918, indicating they had been discharged from the regiment and returned to their homes prior to those later registration periods. In most of those cases, the men were either very young or very old, suggesting officers discharged them for being underage or for being unable to handle the stresses of military life, although such individuals could also have been discharged because of physical or disciplinary problems.[5]

On the other hand, the regiment's officers displayed age characteristics opposite those of the men. The average age for thirty-seven of the regiment's fifty-six officers was twenty-seven. Out of that group, nineteen (50 percent) were twenty-seven or older. Seven of the officers were in the 24–26 age group (19 percent), while eleven (31 percent) were 23 or younger. However, when combined, the two youngest age categories equaled 50 percent of the officers. Thus, although officers in the regiment tended to be older, half of those were younger than twenty-six and an even split existed between younger and older officers.[6]

If the 7th Texas was truly a Texas regiment, just how many of the soldiers were born in Texas? And if not born in the state, where did they come from? This analysis also considered how many of the regiment's soldiers lived in the central communities where each company kept its recruiting headquarters, or if they lived in more rural areas of their counties.

Of 1,081 of the regiment's soldiers, 817 (76 percent) were born in the Lone Star State, while 264 (24 percent) were born in other states and later moved to Texas. Of the soldiers not born in Texas, 89 (8 percent) hailed from the Upper South states of Tennessee, Kentucky, West Virginia, and Arkansas, while 81 (7 percent) came from states in the Lower South such as Georgia, the Carolinas, Mississippi, and Louisiana. This amounted to 170 of the regiment's soldiers who came from southern states, almost twice as many as the 90 men (8 percent) who came from Northern and Midwestern states, including Oklahoma. Additionally, at least three foreign-born soldiers enlisted in the 7th Texas, and probably more. Although just a fraction of the regiment, the three all came from Europe: England, "Russian" Poland, and Austria. The Austrian, Anton Strouhal, a twenty-eight-year-old surveyor, enlisted in Company C. As this small number of foreign-born soldiers attests, along with Texas natives and the southern immigrants, the 7th Texas reflected to a high degree the general southern background of the state and the region. Likewise, the soldiers' places of birth supports the idea that many residents of Northwest Texas migrated from the Upper South or the Midwest.[7]

The regiment's officers also displayed similar characteristics, as the majority claimed Texas birth. In fact, of the thirty-seven officers whose information was available, thirty-three (89 percent) were born in the state, leaving only four born elsewhere (11 percent). Of those four, two were born in Maine and Illinois, while the regiment's commanding officer, Alfred W. Bloor, hailed from Pennsylvania. Finally, one officer of the regiment, William H. Brownell, claimed Canadian birth, although he moved to Amarillo, worked as a railway clerk, and joined Captain Barton's Company A.[8]

Table 3. Place of birth.[9]

PLACE OF BIRTH	NUMBER	PERCENT
Texas	817	76%
Upper South	89	8%
Lower South	81	7%
North/Midwest	90	9%
Foreign	4	0.30%
Totals	1081	100%

Although the majority of the regiment came from Texas, more soldiers tended to live in rural areas or other parts of Texas rather than in the county seats of the fourteen counties that served as company recruiting headquarters. Still, a sizable minority, 445 (43 percent), lived in the county seats, while 579 soldiers (56 percent) came from smaller rural communities within each county or from a different region of Texas altogether. A handful of the men who joined the 7th Texas lived outside of Texas when they joined. Of those who did, almost all came from Oklahoma. Company D of Hardeman County tallied five men from Oklahoma, including Samuel M. Sampler, who would later receive the Medal of Honor for his actions in France. Wilbarger County's Company E had at least one man from Oklahoma, while Robert Farrington, a bookkeeper in Hollister, Oklahoma, joined the Wise County company, most likely because he had been born in Decatur. As might be expected, almost all of the men lived in Texas, although fewer than might be expected lived in the larger cities of Northwest Texas. Finally, the officers of the regiment again displayed characteristics opposite the men. In this case, the majority of the officers (72 percent) lived in the county seat of each company's location, while only nine officers (27 percent) lived in other areas of the county or the state.[10]

Table 4. Residences.[11]

RESIDENCES	
County Seat	Other
445	579
43%	56%

Another important characteristic was the type of work these soldiers did prior to their enlistments. In order to analyze the information, occupations were divided into several categories. The professional/business category included lawyers, accountants, clerical workers, businessmen, and anyone who might have undergone specific training for their occupation, such as a pharmacist. The second category consisted of skilled workers, which included carpenters, blacksmiths, railroad engineers, and any other job that required skill or some effort to master. Unskilled workers made up the third category, which consisted of occupations such as laborer, cook, or automobile driver. In other words, these were occupations that required no formal training and could be mastered with little practice. The fourth category consisted of farmers and farm laborers. Three other smaller categories were utilized as well: oil field workers, ranch workers, and the unemployed.[12]

Table 5. Occupations.[13]

OCCUPATIONS	TOTAL	PERCENT
Farming	468	45%
Unskilled work	190	18%
Prof/Business	183	17%
Skilled work	138	13%
Oil	25	2%
Ranch	11	1%
Unemployed	32	3%
Totals	1047	100%

The members of the 7th Texas Infantry primarily worked as farmers, as 468 (45 percent) members of the regiment pursued that line of work prior to enlisting, either as farming proprietors or hired labor. Numerically, the majority of the farmers came from Wise, Hardeman, and Wilbarger counties, while Fort Worth and Tarrant County, as might be expected because of their urban nature, counted just twelve men who farmed as an occupation. As for the clusters of counties, the average of the North Texas grouping of Wise, Cooke, Denton, Tarrant, and Johnson averaged 43 percent farmers. The second group, Wichita, Wilbarger, Hardeman, Foard, and Childress averaged 50 percent farmers, while Amarillo and Lubbock averaged just 23 percent. On the other hand, Taylor and Donley counties averaged 51 and 54 percent, respectively.[14]

The second largest grouping of men fell into the unskilled labor category, which accounted for 190 (18 percent) of the regiment's soldiers. This evidence suggests that the majority of the men in the regiment tended to fill jobs that were more physical and in many cases might have earned them less money than skilled workers. Taken together, farmers and unskilled laborers accounted for 63 percent of the regiment. Most of the unskilled laborers came from North Texas counties and in the larger cities such as Lubbock and Amarillo. After the unskilled group came the professional and business occupations. This category accounted for 183 of the regiment's men (17 percent), and included bookkeeping and clerical positions, although there were private soldiers such as the Supply Company's Allen Schultz of Post, Texas, who worked as an accountant; Company G's Thomas McCluer, who worked as an engineer for the city of Henrietta, Texas; and Company E's John Storey, a Vernon lawyer. Of all the counties, Potter County had, by far, the most men working in the professional and business category, with thirty-five while Wise and Tarrant counties had the next highest totals at seventeen and sixteen respectively. On the other hand, approximately 138 men (13 percent) filled jobs that might best be described as "skilled" labor such as carpenters and blacksmiths, while at least 25 (2 percent) men who worked in the oil fields of Burkburnett and Electra joined the two companies from Wichita Falls. Potter, Donley, and Taylor counties counted eleven (1 percent) ranch hands and stock farmers among their enlistees.[15]

The regiment also included unemployed men. As mentioned, some residents of Donley County grumbled that Captain Simpson's company consisted of the county "riff-raff." With that being said, just thirty-two men (3 percent) enlisted in the regiment who had no occupation at the time they registered for the draft, based on the available data. Those thirty-two men were also generally evenly spread out among the companies. Wise County had five, but most of the counties counted at least two or three unemployed men on their rosters.[16]

Table 6. Occupations as a percentage of each county.[17]

COMPANY	% FARM	% Prof/B
Co. A, Amarillo	21	42
Co. B, Clarendon	54	13
Co. C, Childress	68	16
Co. D, Quanah	62	11
Co. E, Vernon	63	13
Co. F, Wichita Falls	14	12
Co. G, Wichita Falls	27	10
Co. H, Decatur	56	19
Co. I, Abilene	55	20
Co. K, Fort Worth	20	27
Co. L, Cleburne	48	8
Headquarters Co, Foard Co.	65	7
Machine Gun Co, Cooke Co.	48	23
Supply Co., Lubbock	25	21
Co. M, Denton	43	15

This occupational data supports the assertion that a representative soldier of the 7th Texas was more often than not a farmer or unskilled laborer rather than a professional or skilled worker. Did the same hold true of the regiment's officers? As noted when discussing age, the regiment's officers displayed occupational characteristics very different from those of the majority of the enlisted men. In this instance, professional and business occupations typified the majority in the officer ranks. Twenty-three of the officers (68 percent) followed professional callings, while four men each worked as skilled workers (12 percent) or farmers (12 percent). Of those in the professional category, most served as lawyers with at least nine officers identifying themselves thus. Finally, three officers of the regiment (9 percent) described themselves as students, either at the Officers Training Camp or the University of Texas. While the majority of the regiment's soldiers worked with their hands either by farming or as an unskilled worker, the opposite was generally true of the 7th Texas' officers.[18]

By breaking down these general characteristics of age, residence, place of birth, and occupation, a clearer picture of these soldiers emerges. More often than not, a soldier of the 7th Texas was a native-born Texan who grew up in a rural area, was in his early twenties, worked with his hands, and was a reflection of the rural and agricultural land that he came from. On the other hand, while the regiment's officers also came from Texas, they were slightly older and more often than not worked in a professional or business capacity.

Another consideration in analyzing the composition of 7th Texas is to place the regiment within the context of the "Rich Man's War, Poor Man's fight" concept, an idea commonly explored by Civil War historians. Historians questioned whether the wealthy class caused the war while the lower economic classes bore the brunt of the fighting. However, recent works by historians Richard Lowe and Joseph Glatthaar show that the wealthier members of southern society as well as those with average wealth served their cause just as much as their less economically fortunate comrades, illustrating that the "Rich Man's War, Poor Man's Fight" was not altogether accurate.[19]

Historian Jeannette E. Keith examined that same concept as it related to World War I. In her book *Rich Man's War, Poor Man's Fight: Race, Class, and Power in the Rural South during the First World War,* she described how southern politicians used that concept to spur antimilitarism sentiments among the rural poor of the early twentieth-century South. Although her work deals specifically with draft resistance in the rural South, an area that included the communities of the 7th Texas Infantry, direct comparisons are difficult to make between those who resisted the draft and the Texas National Guard volunteers in this study. Nevertheless, the area of the state where National Guard officers recruited their men had its share of anti-war and anti-conscription sentiment, most notably with the Farmer's and Laborers Protective Union, and at least one man joined the 7th Texas simply to escape the draft.

Still, can the "Rich Man's War, Poor Man's Fight" concept apply to the 7th Texas? While the sources did not provide economic data, several useful points might still be made to enable such a comparison. First, the majority of the regiment's enlisted soldiers (63 percent) worked as either farmers or as unskilled laborers. Of course, those occupations may not imply a lower economic status, but that assumption might be made within reason. To bolster that argument, nine of the fourteen counties contained more farms operated by tenants than farms operated by owners, again an oblique indicator related to the economic status of individuals within the community. With that being said, 30 percent of the enlisted force also worked in professional, skilled, and clerical trades, occupations that could result in more income but not necessarily so. Also, only thirty-two members of the regiment's soldiers did not have a job at the time they enlisted while other men took significant pay cuts from their jobs in the Panhandle oil fields to enlist. Furthermore, the majority of the regiment's officers worked in professional occupations such as the law, and several came from prominent local families. From that perspective, then, the idea of a "Rich Man's War, Poor Man's fight" does not appear tenable regarding the 7th Texas Infantry. In other words, the regiment did not appear to contain a disproportionate number of soldiers from the lowest economic strata of the society, but consisted of individuals from a wider economic and social base. Thus, it is doubtful that the recruiting officers drew too heavily or purposely on the state's lowest economic groups to fill their companies. Indeed, a valid response to the "Rich Man's War, Poor Man's fight" concept might be to ask whether a young officer from a wealthy and powerful family would choose to enlist soldiers from the lowest economic strata of his community when his reputation and even that of his family rested on establishing the company and leading it into battle. Indeed, there is a distinct difference between county exemption boards that drafted undesirables and sent them off to the Army and who had no interest or responsibility in the outcome of a particular soldier's experience, and local officers who would have to lead their soldiers into war.

This point also ties into the work by historian Gerald Shenk, who explored the concepts of race and gender within the World War I draft in his book *Work or Fight!* While Shenk's work is also not directly applicable because it deals with the functioning of local exemption boards and the draft, Shenk's argument that the white community controlled society during this period could easily be illustrated by the 7th Texas. The regiment reflected the dominant society of the time, and as representatives of that society, officers would have wanted to recruit strong, virile men who displayed all the characteristics of white masculinity that Shenk describes, and which observers constantly noted in descriptions of the regiment's soldiers. Clearly, the 7th Texas Infantry reflected the society that raised it, supported the dominant white society of the time and illustrated Shenk's thesis that white society controlled the material world and marginalized those who did not fit those characteristics. If such was the case, would the company officers seek to enlist the poorest and less impressive members of society into a volunteer unit that supposedly represented the best the community had to offer?[20]

Although these general characteristics illuminate the soldiers of the regiment, there are several other more personal points that can be made about the regiment's soldiers. Those included marriage, number of dependents, prior military service, and reasons for exemption from the selective service draft. Based on the draft registration cards, only fifty-two (5 percent) enlisted members of the 7th Texas had married. Out of the fifteen companies, Fort Worth's Company K enlisted nine married men, while several companies had as few as two married men. Again, the officers revealed different characteristics: at least thirteen were married (38 percent), although the marital status of all fifty-six of the regiment's officers could not be ascertained. Nevertheless, 38 percent was significant when compared to the regiment as a whole.[21]

Although few of the regiment's soldiers were married, more than twice as many reported dependents that relied on them for support. Draft registration cards disclosed that 136 members of the regiment (13 percent) claimed at least one dependent. Decatur's Company H included seventeen men with dependents, while Clarendon's Company B claimed just three such men. Supporting the point that most of these soldiers were not married, ninety-five men (70 percent) who reported a dependent claimed responsibility for parents or siblings, as opposed to forty-one (30 percent) who listed wives and children as dependents. Not all of the married men claimed their wives as dependents. Thus, although an overwhelming majority of the regiment consisted of unmarried men, a fairly sizable portion had relatives for whom they were responsible. In the case of the officers, the dependent breakdown differed slightly. Fourteen of the regiment's officers claimed dependents (42 percent), although eight of the fourteen officers claimed wives and children as dependents as opposed to just two officers who claimed aged parents as their dependents.[22]

Table 7. Dependents.[23]

DEPENDENTS	NUMBER	PERCENT
Parents/Siblings	95	70%
Wife/Child	41	30%
Totals	136	100%

Experience served as another distinguishing characteristic of the regiment's soldiers. Obviously, men with prior military experience could be valuable to the regiment's leadership. Such men could join the regiment and immediately put their experience in training, organizing, and managing soldiers to use. In many cases, but not all, men with prior military service filled positions of responsibility. Overall, however, the 7th Texas was not an experienced regiment. Including the officers, only seventy-five men (7 percent) reported prior military experience on their draft registration cards. Experienced former soldiers were few in number and a rarity in the regiment. There simply were not enough men with military experience to go around. In fact, although the officers of Abilene's Company I had military experience, none of the men who joined the company claimed any prior military service. On the other hand, Company M in Denton enlisted ten men with prior military service, most of whom had served as non-commissioned officers. While the regiment included few veterans, the officers as a group had more experience, with well over half (68 percent) claiming some type of prior military service, again emphasizing the point that men with such experience filled positions of leadership in the regiment.[24]

Finally, while their motivations will probably never be known, a hint as to why some of them joined the 7th Texas might be revealed by their draft registration cards. Of those who registered for the draft on June 5 but later enlisted in the 7th Texas, 135 (12 percent) claimed a reason to be exempt from the draft. Denton and Wise counties each had seventeen men who claimed exemption, while the Taylor County company had just three. However, the point to be made is that 12 percent of the regiment initially highlighted a reason why they could not be drafted and yet later enlisted in the Texas National Guard. Although it will never be known what motivated these men to change their minds and enlist, several possible explanations might be suggested. First, they may have believed the rhetoric of the National Guard that they would serve with soldiers from their area and under the command of local officers. Serving in such an organization might have appealed to many men who wanted to serve but distrusted the draft. They may also have believed that their reason for exemption would not be validated by the local exemption or draft board and realized the National Guard was their best option. Others may have initially felt responsible for their dependents but later decided to enlist once arrangements had been made for their care, and some may have felt pressure from friends and colleagues. In a few cases, an individual clearly expressed the reason for joining the National Guard. For example, Clyde Beavers, a twenty-three-year-old Cleburne farmer enlisted in Company L, but on draft registration day he wrote on his card that he sought an exemption because he opposed the draft. Whatever the reason, those soldiers probably believed that they would be better off by enlisting in the Texas National Guard rather than waiting to be called up and sent off to a training camp among strangers. Even a number of men who later served as officers claimed exemption when they initially filled out their draft cards. Of twenty-six officers who registered, six (23 percent) claimed reasons for exemption. Of those six, four claimed dependents: two for wives and children and two for dependent mothers. Only one man, Sam Houston Owens, later the 1st Battalion adjutant, claimed exemption because he was a farmer and because he was in attendance at Camp Funston's officers training camp. The sixth was not readable.[25]

Table 8. Exemptions.[26]

EXEMPTIONS		
Medical	33	29%
Dependents	64	56%
Occupational	11	10%
Other	6	5%
Total	114	100%

For the enlisted members of the regiment, a number of possibilities explained why an individual might have sought a draft exemption, and 114 enlisted men claimed a reason for exemption from selective service when they registered.[27] The main reason those men requested exemptions was dependents, whether a wife, parent, or sibling, which mirrored nationwide characteristics. Sixty-four men (56 percent) who enlisted in the 7th Texas fell into this category. Second, a number of men requested medical exemptions. Interestingly, thirty-three enlistees in the 7th Texas, (29 percent), initially believed they had a medical condition which would preclude them from being drafted, or at least they hoped it would. In many cases, the registrant listed a generic condition, such as "weak eyes," "stiff joints," "stomach trouble," or simply "physical disability." In most cases, such conditions proved not to be serious enough to keep the men from later joining the 7th Texas. Although a registrant could claim an occupational exemption, few men who joined the 7th Texas did so. In fact, only eleven men (10 percent) sought such an exemption. Finally, six men listed other reasons for possibly being exempt from the draft. Those included one man who sought an exemption because his church opposed the war; at least two sought exemptions because of attendance at the Officers Training Course at Camp Funston in Leon Springs, and two who others believed prior military service should exempt them. Those two men, however, might have concluded their prior experience could lead to leadership positions in the National Guard and so enlisted in the 7th Texas. Regardless, prior military service was not a valid reason for claiming exemption from the draft. And as noted, one man claimed exemption because of opposition to the draft. Interestingly, the reasons why these men initially sought exemption from the draft matched the country on a national scale, in which dependents served as the primary reason for a draft exemption, while fewer received agricultural or industrial deferments. While certainly not a majority, a sizable number of men who enlisted in the 7th Texas initially sought a way to stay out of the military.[28]

It is possible to look at a number of characteristics of the regiment as a whole and draw several conclusions. The majority of the soldiers of the 7th Texas were in their early twenties and unmarried, although a larger portion of them than might be expected supported dependents, typically parents or siblings. Most of the regiment's soldiers also worked as farmers or as unskilled laborers, although a sizable portion held skilled and professional jobs, especially among the regiment's officers. Only a few members of the regiment had prior military experience, and generally, though not invariably, filled positions of authority. Also, a small percentage of men initially sought a reason for exemption from the draft but then later chose to enlist in the Texas National Guard. This portrait calls to mind historian Gary Mead's description of a "quintessential doughboy": a "white man in his early twenties, having little education and no previous military experience," a fairly accurate characterization. Likewise, an officer of the 7th Texas was generally older, and more likely to be married and have dependents. They more frequently engaged in professional or business careers and more often than not had some type of prior military service. While difficult to determine, how essential were these soldiers to the economic well-being of their communities? Comments such as those from Donley County residents who called Captain Simpson's Company "riff-raff," were unfair and not altogether accurate. Still, a sizable portion of these men worked as farmers or unskilled laborers whose contributions to the local economy were not indispensable. The answer will, unfortunately, probably never be known. Regardless of the individual economic value of these soldiers to their communities, the state recruited them to fight for the nation. Before they could do that, however, they had to be trained. They had to change from farmers, laborers, carpenters, clerks, and lawyers, into soldiers.[29]

3

CAMP BOWIE AND FRANCE

Although local communities treated the soldiers of the 7th Texas as heroes before the regiment had even left North and Northwest Texas, their arrival at Camp Bowie in the first week of September underscored their lack of training and unfamiliarity with Army ways. The companies from Potter, Donley, and Childress counties arrived first, followed by the companies from Hardeman, Foard, and Wilbarger counties. Eventually, the Lubbock, Taylor, Denton, Cooke, Johnson and Wise County soldiers arrived and all of the 7th Texas Infantry companies were in bustling Camp Bowie by September 11, 1917, the first consolidation of the regiment as a whole.[1]

Of course, the 7th Texas was only one small part of the Texas National Guard, which itself made up a fraction of the entire National Guard called to service for the second time in two years. When "drafted" into federal service on August 5, 1917, the 7th Texas consisted of 56 officers and 1,952 soldiers. At the time, the "combat arms" of the Texas National Guard, which included infantry, cavalry, field artillery, coast artillery, and signal corps, totaled 315 officers and 11,074 men, while the total Texas National Guard as reported by the state Adjutant General on August 5, 1917, consisted of 581 officers and 16,949 men. The 7th Texas amounted to 11 percent of the Texas National Guard prior to its arrival at Camp Bowie.[2]

Fort Worth's Camp Bowie served as the training camp of the Texas and Oklahoma National Guard. The federal government established it as one of thirty-two "cantonments" designed to train National Guardsmen and draftees in the rapidly expanding army. Sixteen of the camps housed draftees, those in the "National Army," while the remaining sixteen housed National Guard units. The War Department constructed National Army camps more durably because they believed those camps would be used for a longer period of time, while the Army constructed the National Guard camps in the south where the milder climate allowed guardsmen to sleep in tents. In determining the camp locations, Secretary of War Newton D. Baker deferred to his departmental commanders. In Texas, this was Brig. Gen. James Parker, commander of the United States Southern Department.[3]

Several leading Fort Worth citizens, including Ben E. Keith, L. J. Wortham, and Mayor W. D. Davis, organized a group to seek a training camp for Forth Worth as early as May 1917. Their proposal highlighted the city's "rail facilities," that it contained the two largest meat packing plants south of St. Louis, and that Fort Worth had the state's "best horse and mule market." The proposal impressed General Parker and he sent several officers for a closer look. The organizers "guided" the officers toward an area about three miles from downtown Fort Worth known as the "Arlington Heights addition." Arlington Heights Boulevard provided access to and from the city, and the area sat on a series of hills that offered good drainage. The committee also offered the Army additional acres of land west of Arlington Heights which could be used for a firing range and trench system.[4]

Nevertheless, delays held up the selection process and the Army did not notify city officials that Fort Worth would receive a camp until June 11, 1917, about the same time as the Texas National Guard began its recruiting campaign. While most observers expected that National Army camps would be ready by September 1, 1917, the War Department believed the National Guard camps would be completed earlier because they required less construction. However, many Army officers failed to appreciate the problems associated with building thirty-two "cities" and officers of the Cantonment Division of the Quartermaster Corps did not arrive in Fort Worth until mid-July to begin their work. Soon, the United States government signed a contract with the Thompson Construction Company of Dallas, the Army established quartermaster headquarters on July 23, and construction officially began on July 25, 1917.[5]

Although the camp was only "half completed," soldiers began arriving at Camp Bowie by the end of the first week of August. At the time, 40 miles of road had been laid and 150 buildings erected. Two weeks later, there were 900 buildings, including "mess halls, warehouses, bathhouses, and latrines." Although deemed capable of supporting troops by the end of August, the camp's construction was not complete until the end of October, and when the 36th Division finally departed for France in the summer of 1918, Camp Bowie consisted of nearly 3,000 buildings. The camp itself encompassed 1,410 acres, while the trench system near the town of Benbrook occupied 125 acres and the firing range 756. The government leased additional land near Weatherford in Parker County for an artillery range. The total cost for Camp Bowie was put at $3,400,000.[6]

When the "soldier boys" of the 7th Texas arrived, Camp Bowie was a thriving, busy place, filled with the sounds of construction as well as thousands of other soldiers arriving from across the state and Oklahoma. Senior Texas Guard officers Brig. Gen. Henry Hutchings and Brig. Gen. John A. Hulen arrived in late August, as did a number of Regular Army officers assigned to the division. Obviously, for many of the Northwest Texas Guardsmen, Camp Bowie offered quite a change. They could also see and understand that they were just one small part of a much larger organization, and many perhaps realized that they had taken their first step on the way to France.[7]

The arrival of Captain Tyler's machine gun company might have been typical of the arrival of most of the 7th Texas' companies. According to one member, Frank Duston, it rained much of the day they arrived and they slept in the "mess hall" the night of their arrival. Issued tents the next day, the soldiers spent the next few days "trying to get things straightened out." Other companies experienced this same confusion. Private Camilla Hanks of Abilene wrote that his company marched for three hours their first day before finding their camp site. The next day his company received mess kits while the 1st Oklahoma Infantry Regiment served up their first meal. Shortly thereafter they received tents, although they soon discovered there were not enough to go around and another company received their uniforms.[8]

The soldiers spent their first days completing the process of becoming United States soldiers, drawing equipment and uniforms, and becoming familiar with the camp. Most did not receive rifles. In fact, most did not receive a weapon until October, and some of the men performed drill and stood guard duty with sticks while the regiment's officers tried to decipher the intricacies of the supply system. One soldier wrote that Capt. Robert Wagstaff tried "awful hard" to get his company uniforms. The men seemed to appreciate his efforts as one soldier wrote "he sure is all right and all the boys like him fine." While this settling-in process continued, residents of North and Northwest Texas who helped recruit the 7th Texas soon began to appear at the camp. Many eagerly followed the progress of "their" local companies at Camp Bowie. For example, fourteen carloads of Gainesville residents made the trip in mid-September to see how Captain Tyler's Machine Gun Company fared. The company responded by creating a "register" for all Gainesville residents to sign during their visit. Another Gainesville resident visited the Machine Gun Company and reported that in spite of the rain that greeted the soldiers' arrival, they had "nice, clean, comfortable quarters … and an abundance of good eatables," and that it was "one of the best pleasures of his life" to have a meal with Captain Tyler's soldiers.[9]

On the other hand, Mrs. W. W. Coleman, a Wichita Falls resident whose husband oversaw the camp's plumbing, tried to bring a message of "cheer" to "each mother in Wichita Falls" after she returned to that city from a visit to Camp Bowie. She had sought out Companies F and G, and spoke to a "number of the officers and men," who all expressed their "complete satisfaction with the arrangements and asked that the folks at home be assured that they were well cared for and happy." According to Mrs. Coleman, the soldiers were "in a fine color," with "splendid appetites" and the energy to perform the most difficult tasks.[10]

The soldiers rarely lacked enough to eat. For example, a reporter from Donley County visited Camp Bowie in early October and described a typical meal for Captain Simpson's company. For breakfast the men feasted on bread and cream gravy with sugar and syrup. At lunch, the soldiers consumed sixty pounds of steak and fifty pounds of cabbage, as well as sweet potatoes, English peas, gravy, iced tea, sugar, and bread. For the final meal of the day, they ate roast beef and gravy, hominy, string beans, bread, and stewed apricots. The total cost for one day's meals for the company amounted to $18.28. A local resident who visited the company earlier wrote "there is no danger of anyone getting hungry if they are always as well fed as they were at this meal." While the men had quantity, they did not always have quality, as Sgt. Aubyn Clark of Clarendon wrote home that "Dad Cook says the reason a man gets so brave is because after he eats this Army chuck for six months he don't give a darn where he goes."[11]

While the soldiers ate well, they also underwent more physical inspections by Regular Army officers. This was the first point at Camp Bowie in which the integrity of the regiment began to disintegrate. For the soldiers of the 7th Texas, those physical inspections occurred less than two weeks after their arrival. As doctors inspected each company, men who were found unfit received a "Surgeon's Certificate of Disability," or SCD, and discharged. Few, if any, companies escaped those stringent physicals without losing some members. For example, Captain Lillard's Decatur Company lost twenty-four men. Even the regiment's sanitary, or medical, detachment had a number of men "turned back on account of physical disqualifications."[12]

The regiment started training almost immediately. Frank Duston reported that his company arrived on a Thursday and began drilling the next Monday. The daily routine, he reported, included seven to eight hours of drill and wrote, "I guess we will get more later on." By the time they had been in camp about one month, the 7th Texas had practiced many of the military arts of the early twentieth-century, including "grenade throwing, bayonet drill, the setting—and avoiding—of wire entanglements and the … art of digging themselves in." Other soldiers engaged in similar activities including "infantry methods, trench digging, trench raiding maneuvers … whole companies marching, semaphores signaling …" Indeed, the lack of rifles did not affect such maneuver training, although at one point prior to October, only six companies out of the dozens in camp had received their weapons and many remained without proper equipment or uniforms. The three machine gun battalions only had six weapons to train on as late as December, and the division did not receive all its equipment until March 1918, several months after the division commander testified about equipment shortages to Congress in December 1917. Such supply problems, however, were not unique to the 36th Division but were experienced in large measure by nearly all of the Army units in training for the war as the supply system struggled to accommodate the requirements of a massive wartime army.[13]

Shortly after their physicals, which began to dilute the original complement of the 7th Texas, the organizational structure underwent a more drastic change that had far-reaching consequences for the 7th Texas. Captain Steve Lillard's company from Wise County received orders to move to a new location in order to make room for a unit that was going to be consolidated with the 7th Texas: the 1st Oklahoma Infantry. While each company in the 7th Texas started out as a collection of local recruits with predominantly local officers, the Army started implementing organizational changes that had repercussions across most National Guard units in the country, including those at Camp Bowie.[14]

Most of the enlisted men in the 7th Texas were likely not aware that once they began their transition into the Army, it would be difficult, if not impossible for National Guard units to maintain their National Guard organization and designation. All National Guard units had to be assimilated into larger army organizations, such as brigades and divisions. In the summer of 1917, the Texas National Guard organized along the lines of an older Army model of a "triangle" division, which consisted of three infantry brigades of three regiments each. Based on the experiences of the European armies in the war and after three different studies, the Army's leaders decided to restructure the divisional organization, and implemented those changes in August of 1917 at the same time that the government mobilized the National Guard and drafted its personnel into federal service. This change in the structure of the division model resulted in two major changes: a new divisional numbering system and a new organizational structure. The new numbering system consisted of three components. The first encompassed the Regular Army, whose divisions were designated between 1 and 25. The second echelon encompassed the National Guard divisions, and division numbers between 26 and 75 were reserved for those units. The War Department used numbers 76 and higher for the "National Army" divisions, the draftees. In the new organizational arrangement, the Army designated the Texas and Oklahoma National Guard division the 36th Division, instead of the 15th Division as it was called according to the outdated organizational plan.[15]

Maj. Gen. Edwin St. John Greble, a West Point graduate and a regular officer, commanded the 36th Division. By all accounts Greble was a solid officer, although in 1917 he was fifty-nine years old, a fact which did not bode well for him as General Pershing generally sought younger officers for divisional command. Indeed, in the fall of 1917, Greble spent several months in France with a group of general officers, ostensibly to study conditions at the front, but actually so General Pershing could get a better look at them and decide who could or could not stand the rigors of trench warfare. While Greble may not have been aware of Pershing's ulterior motives, after returning from France, he focused on organizing, equipping, and training the division.[16]

Under the new organizational construct, Greble's division consisted of two infantry brigades designated the 71st and 72d Brigades, each with two regiments, "owing to the peculiar conditions relating to strategy, tactics, and the service of supply" of the war in Europe. The Army placed the 7th Texas under the 71st Brigade, commanded by the former adjutant general of Texas, Brig. Gen. Henry Hutchings. Hutchings had received his commission as a general officer in the National Army on August 20, 1917, as had his colleague and commander of the 72d brigade, Brig. Gen. John A. Hulen. Divisional field artillery, machine-gun battalions, engineers, and supply and sanitary, or medical, trains supported each brigade.[17]

General Hutchings's 71st Brigade consisted of the 141st Infantry and the 142d Infantry, while Hulen's 72d Brigade included the 143rd and 144th Infantry. Instead of having a large number of small infantry regiments as in the old organization, the new structure called for fewer, but larger, regiments, and that necessitated the consolidation of National Guard units. Unfortunately, the War Department miscalculated when it made its decision, not realizing that many National Guard units, including those of Texas and Oklahoma, were sorely disappointed to learn they would lose their state designations. While the War Department may not have placed much stock in the "state identities" of Guard units, such identities caused the Army a serious problem. In September of 1917, the War Department officially established the 141st, 143rd, and 144th Infantry Regiments by consolidating the existing Texas National Guard Infantry regiments. That action caused little grumbling because the units were all from Texas. However, that left the 7th Texas without another Texas infantry regiment to merge with, as it was an odd numbered separate regiment. For the War Department, the solution was simple: combine the 7th Texas with the 1st Oklahoma to create the 142d Infantry. As soon as the War Department issued that order, however, problems arose. While the consolidation made both regiments unhappy, it appeared that the 1st Oklahoma felt more strongly about the issue. The highest ranking Oklahoma officer at Camp Bowie and the former commander of the 1st Oklahoma, Brig. Gen. Roy V. Hoffmann, allegedly "protested" the arrangement "vigorously" to the War Department. The *Dallas Morning News* reported that the merger brought a "storm of protest" and that members of the Oklahoma National Guard "flooded the delegation in Congress seeking a reversal of the order."[18]

Because the state had just one infantry regiment, many Oklahomans believed it should remain unique. Many members of the 1st Oklahoma Infantry also believed they would completely lose their state identity while the Texans would not. Captain Alonzo Drake of the 7th Texas's Childress Company rebutted that argument by pointing out that the 7th Texas would no longer be unique to Texas either if combined with the Oklahomans. Regardless of how both units felt, the possibility that officers and men who had served together in the same local organization would be sheared away from the organizations some of them deeply identified with was not palatable to either group. However, because they had been "drafted" into federal service, they had truly ceased to be Texas and Oklahoma National Guardsmen whether they realized it or not.[19]

Several local newspapers across Northwest Texas commented on the proposed reorganization. The *Wichita Daily Times* pouted that the 7th Texas was at the whim of the Oklahoma National Guard's commanding general and commented that the 7th Texas "will become virtually an Oklahoma organization with the senior officers Oklahomans." However, the *Wichita Daily Times* also told its readers what it considered the major reason why the government merged the 7th Texas with the 1st Oklahoma: "The Seventh Texas is the pick of the camp at Fort Worth, and the men are considered the best material available," and "Texas companies have proven so desirable, they will be used to fill the gaps in the Oklahoma companies."[20]

While local papers followed the story, rumors swirled and the situation deteriorated. The War Department order for the reorganization was scheduled to take effect October 1, 1917, but the vehement protests caused the War Department to put the orders on hold at the end of September. That brought about "rejoicing" by some of the troops in the camp who believed they had won the fight to keep their state integrity. The delay was short lived, however, and by early October the War Department reversed itself and announced that the reorganization of the division would occur on October 15. This time, there was little that the soldiers could do about it.[21]

Colonel Bloor received the appointment as the commander of the new 142d Infantry. However, in a final gesture of protest of the consolidation, Lt. Col. Elta Jayne of the 1st Oklahoma, the new deputy commander, took a ten-day leave of absence. This left Colonel Bloor to work through a difficult situation on his own.

Bloor faced a tough challenge as the new commander of the Texas-Oklahoma regiment because the merger of the two units had seriously damaged the new regiment's morale and he had to figure out a way to ease the tension and make the transition as smooth as possible. Shortly after taking command, both Colonel Bloor and Gen. Roy Hoffman spoke to the assembled regiment. In his speech, Hoffman urged the Oklahomans to obey their orders, to be friendly with the soldiers of the 7th Texas, and to trust their new commander, whom he praised as "one of the best colonels in the American army." Bloor followed and welcomed the Oklahoma soldiers. He took advantage of their experience by asking them to help make the inexperienced Texans into better soldiers, stating "we want to make this the best regiment in camp."[22]

While Hoffman's and Bloor's forthright speeches appeared to help, more than 200 desertions occurred, mainly from the old 1st Oklahoma. Most of those men came back to Camp Bowie once their anger had cooled and they resigned themselves to the new arrangements. In an effort to be forgiving and yet to demonstrate his control, Colonel Bloor charged these men with being Absent without Leave (AWOL), and they were "tried and convicted by Summary Court and sentenced to be confined at hard labor for three months and to forfeit two-thirds of their pay per month for like period." Bloor then commuted the confinement portion of their sentences. After the war, the Oklahoma chaplain of the 142d Infantry, Captain Charles H. Barnes, wrote that "morale and discipline was stunned" and "torn to pieces" because of the merger. He wrote that "friction existed and it took alert commanders to keep it at a minimum." Barnes praised Bloor's leadership during the crisis, and pointed to his creation of a regimental football team as a way to bring the soldiers together and take their minds off the reorganization. The Texans and Oklahomans soon mingled together in their tents and "talked football." After the war, Barnes believed that the regimental football team served its purpose as the regiment "first and last was engraved on the minds of all … and was a powerful factor in restoring the morale and discipline." This reorganization and the disruption it caused within National Guard ranks should be contrasted with the organization of the 90th Division. As noted, many soldiers joined the National Guard with the expectation they would serve with friends or people from the same region. Conversely, they did not want to be drafted for fear of serving with strangers. However, that was not always the case, as illustrated by the Texas-Oklahoma Draft Division. Although composed primarily of Texas and Oklahoma draftees, the division's commanding general, Maj. Gen. Henry T. Allen, organized the division's two brigades into the 179th "Oklahoma" and the 180th "Texas" as a way to increase morale in the division during its training at Camp Travis in San Antonio. Ironically, then, some National Guard troops lost their state identities while some draftees maintained an affiliation with their home states.[23]

Most of the papers in Northwest Texas hardly noticed the merger once it occurred, and the *Wichita Daily Times* reported in early October that the 7th Regiment had become part of the 142d Infantry Regiment and that few changes beyond shifting several officer positions occurred. The paper observed that the Wichita Falls men appeared "well pleased with the consolidation." Although the reorganization turned out well in the end, some members of the regiment remained unhappy with the Army for eliminating some National Guard organizations. At the national level many National Guard supporters believed that the Regular Army frequently slighted the Guard and Guard officers. In fact, animosity existed between the Texas National Guard officers and some of the division's regular officers. Furthermore, at the same time as the consolidation, a contingent of reserve officers from Camp Grant in Illinois arrived, which further exacerbated the situation at Camp Bowie. Eventually, in an effort to put an end to continued political carping by supporters of the National Guard, the War Department issued General Orders No. 73 in 1918, which bluntly stated: "This country has but one army—the United States Army," and required all members of it to wear Regular Army insignia and all commissions, regardless of the component for which they were granted, would be recognized as Regular Army commissions. The order pleased Capt. Ethan Simpson of Clarendon who wrote to his wife from France that the order "was the wisest thing that has been done. It will do away with much jealousy and bickering."[24]

Combining these two regiments brought about a number of changes to the old 7th Texas and an entirely new organization from the commander to the individual companies, which now consisted of 250 men instead of 150. This required the companies to merge. For example, the regimental Headquarters Company consisted of Captain Wagstaff's Taylor County Company and the 1st Oklahoma Headquarters Company. Captain Graham's Foard County Company was then added into Headquarters Company as well. Likewise, Captain Merrill's Supply Company merged with the Oklahoma Supply Company. As was the case with all the machine gun companies, Captain Tyler's company joined the regimental machine gun battalion. Of the twelve infantry companies, the first six (A, B, C, D, E, and F) were created by combining the twelve companies of the 1st Oklahoma Infantry, while the remaining six companies (G, H, I, K, L, and M) were formed from the 7th Texas. Thus Company G consisted of the Potter and Childress companies; Company H the Hardeman and Donley companies; Company I from the Wilbarger Company and the "surplus of the regiment"; Company K contained both Wichita Falls companies; Company L combined the Wise and Johnson companies; and Company M consisted of the Tarrant and Denton companies. Of course, this consolidation and strengthening of the companies brought changes among the officers. For example, Captain Barton remained in command of Company G, while Company H remained under Capt. Ethan A. Simpson. Capt. William S. Key took over Company I. Key had commanded the Supply Company of the 1st Oklahoma, while the Company K commander was Wichita Falls Guardsman Captain Sneed Staniforth. Company L was commanded by Capt. Steve Lillard, and Company M by Capt. Noah Roark.[25]

The reorganization left some 7th Texas officers without a command. For example, Harry Baker of Vernon, Harold McGrath of Fort Worth, Homer T. Merrill of Lubbock, James E. Wiley of Quanah, Captain Alonzo Drake from Childress, who became regimental adjutant, and Clyde B. Graham of Crowell all lost command of the companies they organized. Those officers were attached to various companies, as were several lieutenants who were now considered "excess." Besides the company grade officers, the regimental leadership also changed. Although Colonel Bloor remained in command, the two regimental staffs consolidated. After returning from his leave of absence, Lt. Col. Elta Jayne of the 1st Oklahoma became second in command of the new regiment, rather than Lt. Col. John Jennings.[26] Two of the battalion commanders from the 7th Texas held onto their positions: Maj. William Culberson, who commanded the second battalion, and Maj. Alvin Owsley, who commanded the third. Command of the first battalion, however, shifted from Maj. Davis Decker to Maj. John Alley of the 1st Oklahoma. In total, the 7th Texas had fifty-six officers when it arrived at Camp Bowie in September. Forty-nine officers remained with the 142d Infantry, 89 percent of the original complement. While only a small loss, it was a loss nevertheless, and the first of many before the war ended.[27]

Those officers of the old 7th Texas who did not remain with the new 142d included the former executive officer, Lt. Col. John Jennings, and battalion commander Maj. Davis Decker. Lieutenant Colonel Jennings received assignment as second in command of the 131st Field Artillery, and Major Davis remained in Texas with the Texas National Guard, was promoted to colonel, but resigned his commission in 1918. At the company grade level, both Capt. Eugene T. Underwood and Lt. Earl Litteer, who raised the Cleburne Company, left the regiment, as did Lt. Thomas Newsome of the Wise County company and Lt. Gordon R. Porter of Wichita Falls. However, both lieutenants Litteer and Porter later re-joined the regiment in France. All of those changes hurt morale, and to many of those National Guard officers it was a "keen source of disappointment" to lose the companies they had spent time and money to recruit. Likewise, some soldiers expressed disappointment because they had joined a particular company to serve under its commander and suddenly found themselves "commanded by entire strangers." However, the divisional historian, Capt. Alex Smith, pointed out that from a "purely military standpoint" breaking up of "such connections" was probably "not a bad thing."[28]

Other changes following the reorganization further diluted the composition of the old 7th Texas, including the arrival of several contingents of draftees. The first group of nearly 2,500 men arrived in October 1917, to help fill out the division. These men arrived from Camp Travis and the majority came from Texas or Oklahoma, although the group included some Iowans and Minnesotans. Even though many were Texans, they generated friction because of their draftee status: "simply because they were drafted men in a division of volunteers, an animosity arose between them and their fellow soldiers which it took months of common association finally to eliminate." As a case in point to illustrate how these new men could overwhelm a unit and instantly change its dynamic, Company E once received an infusion of 203 draftees. In November 1917, reserve officers from Texas, who had been serving with another division, returned to Texas and joined the 36th. This also caused friction, because although "they were reserve officers, they were from Texas, and though they were from Texas, they were reserve officers." Finally, in May of 1918, the division received a second contingent of draftees numbering just over 6,000 which further diluted the core of the old 7th Texas and the other former National Guard regiments. That second contingent included 3,400 Oklahomans and 1,124 Texans, who managed to fit in more easily although they had received little training.[29]

As the commanding officer of a large number of former Oklahoma National Guardsmen, Colonel Bloor sometimes received direct correspondence from the governor of Oklahoma, A. L. Williams. For example, Governor Williams wrote to Colonel Bloor asking him to deliver Christmas wishes to the Oklahoma soldiers under his command. As the governor wrote, "I wish this letter to be considered a personal message from myself to every boy from Oklahoma in Camp Bowie," and letting them know that every "bit of man and woman power" was "squarely behind them." Colonel Bloor, ever the diplomat, responded that Lt. Col. Elta Jayne of the old 1st Oklahoma would read the message to the Oklahoma soldiers on Christmas Day, and that "the patriotism of the good people of Oklahoma is well known to the commanding officer for it is daily reflected by the soldierly attributes of her sons. The Oklahoma men of this regiment are real soldiers—what greater compliment can be paid them?"[30]

In spite of the turmoil caused by merger, the division continued to train and daily drill remained the priority. General Greble issued a standing order that "every man who wears the khaki must drill a full day on all days that drill work is prescribed." In truth, the regiment trained in a wide field of topics besides "drill." For example, the first month of training showed the range of things they studied including the articles of war, the obligations and rights of the soldier, and guard duties. Bayonet and target drills began in the second week of training, and in the third week soldiers received training in whistle and arm signals and first aid. At the conclusion of their first month, the curriculum included grenade and gas warfare training, although a gas chamber was not completed until January. As for bayonet drills, one sergeant claimed the soldiers were "practiced in the art of thrusting and parrying" and had learned "to plunge their bayonet into a human body with ease and to withdraw it quickly by much practice on the straw men set up at the trenches." Even map drawing was included in the training to help the soldiers scout terrain and find campsites. That training required them to indicate all "hills, hollows, ravines, streams, bridges, houses, trees, etc. ..." on their hand-drawn maps. The men received plenty of practice on their map skills as hikes of twelve miles or longer remained a common training feature. This training continued in ever more detail until the division left for France.[31]

The regiment spent days at the Camp Bowie trench system. The system included at least seven different trenches of varying sizes in which the soldiers practiced. They also held "endurance tests," in which soldiers spent as many as 48 hours in the trenches with no food and just one quart of water. Later, the men would crawl out and practice cutting and getting through wire entanglements. As one sergeant put it, "We're going to have some sure enough training in these trenches."[32]

Academic training also took up the men's time and covered a variety of subjects. For example, Colonel Bloor ordered 48 copies of the *Army Paper Work* manual, 750 copies of the *Privates Manual*, 232 copies of *Map Reading and Sketching for Non-Commissioned Officers*, 750 copies of the *Manual of Conversational French*, 106 copies of *Lessons in Visional Signaling*, and 7 copies of *Field Entrenchments*, among other works for the regiment's non-commissioned officer school. Each company also purchased its own textbooks. For example, Company D purchased thirty-five copies each of *First Lessons in Spoken French for Men in Military Service*, and *Le Soldat Americaine en France*. The division also opened schools at the camp to teach soldiers the "rudiments of French, mathematics, bookkeeping," and "other commercial subjects," with nearby instructors from Texas Woman's College (now Texas Wesleyan University) and what is now Texas Christian University.[33]

A significant number of the regiment's officers and men, from Colonel Bloor to the most junior officers and men, attended training schools away from Camp Bowie. Many of the senior officers, including Colonel Bloor, attended the Brigade and Field Officers School at Fort Sam Houston or the School of Fire at Fort Sill, Oklahoma. Upon completion of the course, some of the regiment's officers returned to Camp Bowie as division instructors, such as Lieutenants Bertram Bloor, Nat Perrine, and Daniel Blue. Bloor taught "automatic arms," Blue taught "grenades," but Perrine did not get the chance to expound on his knowledge of "field fortifications," as no regimental school in that subject existed.[34]

The soldiers faced dangerous situations on a routine basis at Camp Bowie because of the nature of their training. One officer of the 144th Infantry, Maj. Lloyd Hill, was hit in the leg by shrapnel from a shell that exploded prematurely, while another man from the 111th Engineers lost his right hand to a "smoke bomb" which also detonated early, and Pvt. Gus Alexander of Abilene's Company L accidentally shot himself in the forehead with a pistol in his tent. He lived for about one hour after the accident. However, the most serious training accident at Camp Bowie happened to men of the old 7th Texas. On May 8, 1918, a Stokes trench mortar shell exploded in Camp Bowie's trench system during a major divisional exercise, killing eleven men and wounding six others, many of whom were from Abilene, including 1st Lt. Alan J. McDavid, who had played such an integral role in recruiting and organizing Company I. The accident also killed several of the men that McDavid had recruited into that company. The explosion wiped out two gun crews, both of which belonged to Captain Wagstaff's Headquarters Company. Six men, including McDavid, were killed instantly, their bodies "terribly mangled." Corporal Alexander Hart was standing nearby and ducked when he heard someone shout "accident," which he heard seconds after the explosion. When he stood up, he turned and looked behind him and saw one of his friends, Euclid Simmons, on his back, "his head in a pool of blood, and a gaping hole under his jaw." At first, many thought the explosion occurred after a Canadian instructor witnessed a soldier attempting to "force a three-inch shell into a trench mortar." The instructor ran toward the gun crew trying to stop them when the shell went off. Other witnesses wondered if perhaps two shells ended up in the mortar. Whatever the theories, General Greble immediately convened an investigation board, and appointed General Hutchings as chair. The board's early reports concluded that the shell exploded because of an "unknown cause," although the board expressed confidence that the shell was not "defective." Of course, that suggested human error. In its final report, the board found that one of the gunners had accidentally loosened one of two safety pins on the shell, which armed it. When dropped into the mortar tube, the slight jar of the impact caused the round to detonate, killing the crew. Indeed, the accident gained such notoriety that even the *New York Times* carried a story about it.[35]

General Greble and some of his staff happened to be standing nearby when the explosion occurred, as well as several officers' wives. The guns had been fired throughout the day as part of a major exercise without any problems. Two days later, the *Abilene Reporter* wrote that Lieutenant McDavid was standing five feet from the mortar when it exploded and that he had been performing a salute, which he apparently did each time the crew fired the gun. McDavid had also been singled out by British instructors at the camp for his skill in handling the mortars and he was reported to be in high spirits on the day of the accident, excited at the chance to prove what his soldiers could do with the weapons.[36]

Although some of the men killed belonged to the 141st Infantry and were not members of the old 7th Texas, Taylor County suffered the greatest loss, losing four soldiers killed and three wounded. A few days after the accident, the people of Abilene mourned two of the dead soldiers, Cpl, William J. Ellis, and Pvt. Alfred J. Woodle. A group of soldiers from the 142d escorted the remains of their comrades back to Taylor County. After a church service both men received burial next to each other in the city cemetery, the escort rendered a 36-gun salute, and "Taps" drifted over the Abilene cemetery. Soldiers of the 142d Infantry also escorted the bodies of other men killed to their homes. Captain Wagstaff and thirty soldiers escorted Lieutenant McDavid's body to his hometown of Overton, in East Texas near Tyler.[37]

The author of the article in the *Abilene Reporter* covering the funerals concluded his piece by writing that he had chosen to "steal back to his office, and with doors locked, spend this hour in reflection, pondering over the significance of this first funeral service of two of our own Abilene boys." The writer believed that the dead soldiers "were our beacon lights to sacrifice and patriotism," and hoped they would inspire "every man, woman, and child of Taylor County" to "do his duty to win this war." The tragedy introduced one of the communities of the old 7th Texas to the reality of World War I before their soldiers had even left the state, much less American soil. Perceptive members of the community might have realized that many more funerals for Taylor County soldier boys might be held before the war ended.[38]

Throughout the period of training, Colonel Bloor and his staff remained absorbed with the complex task of overseeing the organization and proving their competence and professionalism to sometimes skeptical regulars.[39] Most of their tasks were administrative and involved approving or disapproving transfers, discharges, and taking care of training problems, personnel issues, and discipline. For example, the regimental staff handled all requests for leave from the officers of the regiment and the officers came and went throughout their stay at Camp Bowie. Among others, Captain Wagstaff requested and received two days of leave to return to Abilene "on account of important business," and Colonel Bloor's younger brother, Bertram, received leave for five days to "settle up with my tenants for the past year and to make arrangements for the coming year."[40]

Discharge requests did not receive the same level of approval, however, as the case of Pvt. Ellis A. Richardson of Company E illustrated. Ellis requested a discharge on the grounds that he was under age at the time of his enlistment. The company commander approved the request; Colonel Bloor forwarded it to the division, where it was summarily disapproved with the statement: "This man is now over 18 years of age" written on the request.[41] On the other hand, Pvt. Henry Montgomery received a discharge because his father had become "wholly dependent" on him.[42] As for transfers, company commanders endorsed them and forwarded them to Colonel Bloor's staff, who recommended approval or disapproval before forwarding them on to the division. Individuals sought transfers for a variety of reasons, including better chances at promotion, the opportunity to serve with a relative, or because they had specialized experience that could be put to use in a different organization. For example, Pvt. Jesse Alexander was granted a transfer to another company because of his status as "a full-blood Cherokee Indian" who could not "speak or understand the English language." He had friends in Company E who spoke both languages, which he believed would allow him to "learn my duties more easily." At least one officer of the original 7th Texas requested a transfer as well. Captain Homer T. Merrill, who organized the Lubbock Company, had lost his position with the activation of the 142d Infantry. He applied to General Greble for a transfer to the Aviation Corps, claiming "considerable experience with gasoline engines" and that he was "a fair mechanic." He also claimed "steady nerves" and was "very anxious to transfer" although no reason was given. Colonel Bloor, in his endorsement of the application, called Merrill "a very industrious young officer" and thought he could "render valuable service in the Aviation Section." General Greble approved Merrill's transfer and he spent the rest of the war at San Antonio's Kelly Field serving as paymaster, overseeing a payroll valued at $150,000 per month.[43]

On the other hand, Pvt. Waldo Burch lost his chance at a transfer because he talked directly to another unit and as his company commander wrote, without "permission from his commanding officer or without even apprising me of his wish for a transfer."[44] Two other men were turned down in their request for transfer to the Signal Corps because, as their company commander put it, "there is some mistake about these men possessing special qualifications for signal corps work, as they are both farm hands in civil life."[45] In some cases officers disapproved some transfers because individuals were more valuable in their current positions. For example, Company H First Sgt. Aubyn Clark tried to transfer to the regimental supply company, but Captain Simpson refused to allow it. Clark wrote home that Simpson had put on a good show when they discussed the matter with the battalion commander: "Captain cried like a baby when we were over at the major's and put his arm around me." Because Simpson claimed he could not run the company without him, Clark decided not to press for the transfer. Of course, men also transferred out of the 142d. For example, in October of 1917, Colonel Bloor's staff transferred a number of men who had "indicated their desire to join" the Ordnance Department. However, tying in with another issue that Bloor had to deal with on a frequent basis, not all of the men showed up to their new unit in a timely fashion.[46]

Absences without leave were a common infraction, and instances occurred from the beginning of the 7th Texas' time at Camp Bowie. One week after the regiment's arrival, Colonel Bloor secured the aid of Wichita Falls Sheriff George Hawkins in tracking down six men from the regiment. Even though soldiers committed these lapses in judgment, some felt guilty about what they had done and wanted to clear not only themselves but also make sure their home communities did not get a bad reputation. Such was the case of Decatur resident Pvt. Floyd G. Fowler, who published a statement in the *Wise County Messenger* refuting the insinuation that he had deserted from the Army. As Fowler put it, "I took a little trip to enjoy a little life." Claiming that he never took off his uniform, he wrote that he "was sorry that this report has gotten out that I am a deserter. I am going back to camp and make one of the best soldier boys Decatur has ever had."[47]

Colonel Bloor frequently sent sergeants to various parts of Texas and Oklahoma to bring back AWOL soldiers. For example, Sgt. Corley Smart of Company K went to Clinton, Oklahoma, to retrieve six men from Company A. In another instance, Sgt. Alvin O. White travelled to Slayton, Texas, not far from Lubbock, in search of Pvt. M. J. Foreman of Company G. White returned without the prisoner and informed Colonel Bloor that Foreman was in a Lubbock hospital with pneumonia, and that Foreman stood little chance of recovery.[48] However, most of those cases went smoothly, although the sheriff in Seymour, Texas, wrote to Colonel Bloor in September asking for a reward of $150 for the "apprehension, arrest, conveyance and delivery to your Lieutenant Colonel John D. Jennings" of three deserters from the 7th Texas. The sheriff claimed that Jennings told him he would "immediately send me the papers, upon which I might procure my money," but nothing had arrived. Bloor eventually sent the sheriff a voucher "in payment of your services." Most, if not all, soldiers who went AWOL received a trial by court martial when they returned. The soldiers who went AWOL over combining the two regiments were required to "drill during portions of the drill period and perform hard labor during balance of day." The AWOL soldiers also went on a sixteen-mile "practice march," with a prison officer and fifteen guards.[49]

Occasionally, one of the regiment's officers was charged with unapproved absences, as demonstrated in the case of Capt. Clifford Childers, a former member of the 1st Oklahoma Infantry. After Childers was charged, Bloor allowed him the opportunity to respond. Childers explained that he had planned to return before reveille on the morning of November 1, but that "circumstances arose that prevented it." He then wrote, "those circumstances were none other than a sudden decision to get married," followed by two days of apartment hunting in Fort Worth. Childers claimed that asking for leave would have "caused delay in the arrangements and probable defeat of the opportunity," as his "bride to be" would have departed for

Seattle. How Colonel Bloor responded to Childers's explanation is not known, but Childers did not continue to serve with the regiment.[50]

While AWOL cases took much attention, a closer look at the typical strength returns of the regiment illustrates the scope of the problem in a regiment of more than 2,000 men. In truth, the problem was not nearly as great as might be expected. For example, available personnel strength returns of the regiment for the week of January 28, 1918, through February 2, 1918, not only place absences without leave in context of the entire regiment, but also demonstrate the fluid nature of the regiment's time at Camp Bowie because of the near constant fluctuations in the regiment's personnel. First, during the week mentioned, the returns noted a total of 304 unauthorized absences across the regiment. However, when averaged out among the regiment's personnel the numbers were not as significant as they might appear. For example, on Monday, January 28, the regiment reported a total strength of 2,822 men, of whom 77 were reported as AWOL, just 3 percent of the regiment, the highest total for the week. For the rest of the week, the AWOL figures ranged between 1 and 3 percent of the regiment per day, not an unmanageable figure. It appeared that Company E reported the largest single number of unauthorized absences during that week, with thirty unauthorized absences reported on the evening of January 28, 1918, and thirty-five the next morning. Those strength returns also occurred at a difficult time in the regiment's training, when many of the soldiers believed they had been at Camp Bowie long enough and itched to get to France. As historian Jennifer Keene has noted, many soldiers were sympathetic to the fellow comrades who went AWOL, primarily because soldiers, in this regiment and others, were not aiming to desert, but just wanted to visit their families or have a good time before their departure for France. Still, the low desertion rate in the 36th and its regiments should be compared with that of the draft 90th Division in San Antonio, which maintained a low rate throughout its training period. Indeed, that division's AWOL rate was so low that General Allen received an official compliment from Secretary of War Newton Baker. Such a low desertion rate in the 90th belies the perception that draftee divisions suffered from poor discipline and low morale, which at least in this instance appeared not to be the case. Furthermore, it appeared that draftees could have as much or more esprit and morale than their former Texas National Guard comrades.[51]

Colonel Bloor also had his own difficulties in training a regiment of more than two thousand soldiers, and occasionally his superiors called on him to explain various infractions, although such problems did not reflect poorly on Colonel Bloor's leadership and managerial skills but instead illustrated the difficulty turning a group of men who had recently been civilians into skilled soldiers. Sometimes problems arose because of simple mental lapses, as when one of the battalions of the regiment failed to show up for scheduled training in the trench system. The battalion commander forgot about it, although for good reason, "his mind being occupied with the fire which occurred in this regiment at an early hour this morning." In explaining the officer's lapse to General Greble, Colonel Bloor wrote that he "regretted exceedingly this seemingly inexcusable failure to comply with instructions, and am sure it will not occur again."[52]

A clear example of the difficulties Bloor faced occurred on the night of November 8, 1917, when Capt. Noah Roark of Company M served as field officer of the day. Part of his duties required him to inspect the brigade area and file a report with the brigade commander, General Hutchings. Roark's report, written the next morning, began ominously by pointing out that five prisoners escaped from the 142d guardhouse the previous night. The report also described the lax attitude of the guards. At 2:30 am, Roark had visited the guardhouse and found the officer and sergeant of the guard absent. Roark stated that the sentry he did talk to "did not even present arms when I approached. He did come to Port Arms while I was talking to him." Furthermore, Roark claimed that the prisoners in the guardhouse "seem to consider their imprisonment as sort of a holiday," as they had "cards, dice, smoking tobacco, chewing tobacco and other conveniences for their enjoyment." Roark also drove an automobile through the brigade area at 1:00 am without being stopped by any sentries he passed. Roark noted that few of the sentries on duty could repeat the General Orders and even fewer could tell him what they were supposed to do in case of fire. When he asked one sentry why he allowed Roark to drive through the area without stopping his vehicle, the soldier responded that "he had only received orders to stop people on foot or horseback and had no orders with reference to people in automobiles." As if that were not enough, Roark reported that he arrived at brigade headquarters and found the sentry "sitting down on the running board of an automobile where he remained until I requested him to rise and assume the proper position." At the conclusion of his report, which clearly indicated a less than soldierly attitude on the part of the regimental guard, Roark did not recommend filing charges against the guards who allowed the five prisoners to escape because the guards could not see the men as they escaped as "there were no lights in the rear of the guard house."[53]

Roark forwarded the report to General Hutchings, who dispatched an angry letter to Colonel Bloor, writing that "Guard houses are not to be turned into pleasure resorts" and prisoners should not be given "sufficient entertainment to alleviate the mental anguish caused by separation from their comrades who may be then on the drill field." Hutchings wrote Bloor that "stringent measures will at once be adopted by you to correct the lax condition into which guard duty has been allowed to lapse in your command." Furthermore, Hutchings demanded daily written reports "as to the deplorable conditions now existing until such time as guard duty in this brigade can be looked upon with pride instead of with disgust."[54]

Colonel Bloor assured General Hutchings that the requirements of the "manual for interior guard duty are being strictly complied with and in addition thereto a Field Officer has been appointed to instruct the guard." Colonel Bloor ended by writing Hutchings that "Guard Duty has at all times been given special attention by me," and had made every effort to ensure the officers and men understood its importance. Although the soldiers caused some headaches for their commanding officer, most came to respect him. Members of Company K considered Bloor "Grade A," and Cpl. Archibald Hart believed their commander displayed enough athleticism that he "might have played the outfield alongside [Ty] Cobb or [Tris] Speaker." Such athleticism would serve him well in France.[55]

Of course, while the men trained, the city of Fort Worth beckoned. But before they could enjoy everything that Fort Worth offered they needed to be paid, and some of the regiment's soldiers became jealous when two Texas cavalry units received their pay while the 142d did not. Rumors swirled that the 1st Texas Cavalry was paid $40,000, while the 5th Texas Cavalry earned $73,000, surely a miscalculation. Just a few days later, however, soldiers of the 7th Texas finally received their first payday at Camp Bowie. A member of the company quipped in a letter that they expected to get "the cool dimes about Monday evening." However, even by September 21, some companies such as Captain Wagstaff's, had still not been paid and were desperate even to buy matches. As late as January 1918, the pay situation had barely improved, causing Sgt. Aubyn Clark to write a frustrating letter to his mother in Donley County: "Several of the boys went home last night. Perhaps you have seen some of them already. Don't know whether there will be any go tonight or not. They are all broke and no payday in sight. They are awful slow paying at this camp. I will look into the matter. And get eat up about it [*sic*]."[56]

As a general practice, 15 percent of each company in the regiment received town passes each night during the week after the evening meal, although they had to be back by 11:00 pm. A reporter for the *Clarendon News* described how a group of soldiers started their leave: "Those going to town are lined up and inspected, and only after each individual is found to be faultless as to dress and personal appearance, and has shown himself to be able to repeat the orders of the day, is allowed to enjoy his coveted trip to town." The men then climbed aboard a streetcar that took them "swiftly" to Main Street, where they were "emptied into that surging stream of humanity on pleasure bent that nightly rolls up and down that busy street" as the reporter described it.[57]

Much like the relationship the members of the old 7th Texas had with their local communities, the same situation developed, albeit on a larger scale, between

Camp Bowie and the city of Fort Worth, whose residents hatched numerous plans to entertain the thousands of Camp Bowie soldiers on leave in the city. For example, residents held "block" parties and opened their homes to any soldier who wished to "get acquainted." These block parties often included a street dance as well as card games and similar activities to help soldiers pass their time. Dozens of churches, the Young Men's Christian Association (YMCA), the Salvation Army, the Hebrew Institute, and numerous athletic programs offered more opportunities that the soldiers could enjoy when not training. The city also donated the use of Trinity Park to soldiers, and local horse shows and movie theaters offered free admission.[58]

While the officers frequently held dances, the soldiers found other ways to amuse themselves. Sgt. A. G. Poe won a contest by coming up with the most original name for the Camp Newspaper, *The Camp Bugler*, which won him money and a record player for his company. A number of Captain Tyler's Gainesville soldiers enjoyed watching a lieutenant try to ride a horse. The lieutenant was not well-versed in horseback riding and was thrown so high that he received "an aeronaut's view of Camp Bowie." True to their rural North Texas roots, one of the men "hopped onto the outlaw and showed the spectators how a Cooke County boy can ride a government broncho [*sic*]." Although the 7th Texas was an infantry regiment, they did receive their share of horses and mules, primarily for hauling supplies and heavier equipment. The machine gun company received "several teams of horses" and planned to use "its share of saddle horses." However amusing the men found the horses and mules, their enthusiasm did not necessarily take care of them according to government standards. After an inspection at the end of October, Colonel Bloor had to explain dirty harnesses and uncared for animals, writing that "a determined effort has been, and is still being made in this regiment to properly care for all animals, and to that end an officer is required to be present at stables and I make frequent personal inspections of corrals at stables and at reveille."[59]

Alcohol consumption caused problems for the division as a whole throughout its stay at Camp Bowie. Approximately 178 saloons in Fort Worth in 1917 offered their libations to soldiers, as did an increasing number of bootleggers. Although rumors circulated that "wagon loads" of drunk soldiers returned each night to Camp Bowie, conditions were not quite so bad, although officers arrested soldiers nearly every night. Of course, the 142d Infantry was not exempt from those vices. A number of the regiment's soldiers faced arrest for drinking and fighting, including one soldier who purchased a pint of whiskey for two dollars and who "was willing to plead guilty to drinking the whiskey," but remembered "nothing of the circumstances of the fight." The investigating officer, Lt. Clark Owsley of Denton, laconically wrote that "the only extenuating circumstance is that the accused appears to have been drunk." In another case, police arrested a soldier from the regiment for "affray and drinking" in a Fort Worth hotel, and in Dallas, a city detective charged two of the regiment's men with "attempted auto theft." During the Christmas break, a number of the regiment's soldiers went on a drinking binge in Dallas, causing Sergeant Clark to complain: "Well it was the same guy that does all the drinking for the whole company here. If any other boy was to do like he does they would be court-martialed."[60]

By February of 1918, General Greble instigated a "morality campaign" in an attempt to dramatically limit the sale of alcohol and stop prostitution. However, historian Lonnie White pointed out that Greble started his campaign not because of actual conditions, but because Secretary of War Newton Baker and Raymond Fosdick of the Commission on Training Camp Activities forced his hand by making cleaning up the areas around training camps a national issue. Eventually, Governor William Hobby got involved, claiming that "the traffic of liquor and prostitution among the peddlers of both has in the vicinity of certain army camps in Texas reached alarming proportions." He led the way in introducing legislation in the Texas legislature to ban the sale of alcohol within ten miles of any military camp in Texas. By late April of 1918, Fort Worth garnered a reputation as the "cleanest city morally in the Southwest."[61]

As in all training camps, sickness remained a problem, and the division suffered from the epidemic of Spanish Influenza and quite a few cases of pneumonia. Much of the illness began in October and continued through the winter. At its worst point, in November, the camp hospital reported 1,867 patients, although capacity at the time was 1,000, and normal occupancy was 800. As a result of such epidemics affecting thousands of soldiers at training camps around the country, the Surgeon General of the Army, Maj. Gen. William C. Gorgas, toured many of the camps to gauge the severity of the epidemic. He arrived at Camp Bowie in early December. On the day he visited the camp hospital, it held 1,440 patients. General Gorgas met privately with Governor Hobby, who also happened to be in Fort Worth, and then reported to the Chief of Staff of the Army, General Tasker H. Bliss, that over the previous month the camp had suffered 2,900 cases of measles and 409 of pneumonia, which resulted in 41 deaths. Gorgas' inspection resulted in the camp hospital receiving a new sewer system, hot baths, and more doctors and nurses, although the work was not completed until February. Furthermore, Gorgas wanted 3,000 more tents for the camp so that there would be fewer men per tent. Despite General Gorgas's efforts, Texas Congressmen James C. Wilson, John N. Garner, and Tom Connally expressed concern about the camp conditions. During Gorgas's visit, at least twenty-five men died of pneumonia in the camp, although none were reported from the 142d Infantry. The average age of the soldiers who died during his two day visit was twenty-two. Sergeant Aubyn Clark wrote to his older sister: "Don't get uneasy 'cause I will manage to let you know if I get sick or anything happens. I have not been in the hospital and I'll let you know when I go and I will also let you know how I progress and what my reason is for being there. I don't intend to have to go but we can never tell what will happen." Overall, from October to December 1917, the division lost 216 men to diseases, the majority in November. Of that number, 210 were from pneumonia or a combination of measles and pneumonia.[62]

The pneumonia epidemic, however, did not prevent General Greble from ending a medical quarantine of the camp on December 18, 1917, for those who had no contact with the sick soldiers and for authorizing a Christmas furlough for approximately 50 percent of the men at the camp, or 13,000 soldiers. As Christmas got closer, local papers reported that soldiers with furloughs left "as rapidly as they can get away from the camp and obtain railway accommodations." The soldiers who remained at the camp had "no home ties" or relatives living nearby in Forth Worth. The local paper took to calling soldiers with no families "orphans." Although thousands of soldiers could look forward to Christmas with their friends and families, 1,200 patients remained in the hospital, many of whom "were struggling to retain their hold on life." On Christmas Day, the *Dallas Morning News* reported that the camp was "almost deserted" except for guards and medical personnel. The paper reported that "the few soldiers who remained at the camp spent the time within their tents." However, the Young Women's Christian Association (YWCA) and the Isabella Cottage provided dinner for "many parents and their sons." Furthermore, just after Christmas, the local papers announced an improvement in the camp's health situation: the hospital had fewer than 800 patients and the death rate had declined from eight men per day to two per day.[63]

The training program resumed after the soldiers returned from the Christmas furlough, although they had an extra day off when a snowstorm prevented them from outdoor training. After they awoke to find four inches of snow covering the camp, they spent the day "tossing snowballs, shoveling snow, cutting wood and feeding the fires in the camp stoves." The men also expended energy in "bloodless battles, in which snowballs instead of cannon balls were used as ammunition." This spirit of play, however, masked a growing restlessness with their training.[64]

While many members of the old 7th Texas assumed that they would only stay at Camp Bowie for a few months before shipping out to France, such was not the case. As the training continued after the New Year, evidence began to mount that they were not going anywhere soon. Sergeant Clark wrote his mother that he did not believe they would be in camp much longer, but noticed in the newspaper that "Gen. Greble said it would take three months training yet to put us into shape. I think it will take all of that and then some but because we need it and must have it is sign that we will get it here." Local papers also reported on the soldiers' feelings about the length of their training. The *Dallas Morning News* wrote, "something that resembles a spirit of unrest now prevails in some of the units." For example, for many soldiers, in this case Company K, drill consisted of little more "than a hike out to the field, where the Company would dawdle through a few exercises, then sit around smoking and gabbing." General Greble must have been a close observer because he announced in the first week of February that drill would proceed "with all possible dispatch," after noticing "laxity" among his troops. To prove his intent, the general's order directed officers to "report those who do not know their drills that they may be gotten rid of."[65]

General Greble demonstrated his seriousness by issuing an order to the division in early February at 11:30 pm stating that a "supposed enemy was encamped at the Clear Fork of the Trinity River" and ordered the division to march there and "engage the enemy in combat." By 8:30 the next morning, the division, including the 142d Infantry, marched to meet the fictitious enemy. The soldiers hiked nearly twelve miles before engaging in a "sham battle" about 11:00 am, and then marched back to Camp Bowie that afternoon, the men feeling "a little cold." General Greble appeared pleased with the maneuver and made it known that "many such maneuvers will be tried out without any advance notice being given." Greble kept his word, as Corporal Hart recalled as late as the beginning of July, instructors woke them after taps and marched the men three or four miles "through the countryside." In spite of such efforts to keep the men focused on their training, the soldiers were ready to go and local opinion reflected that same sentiment.[66]

In early June the *Wise County Messenger* asked, "When is the Greble division going to France?" The editorial hinted that the soldiers of the division "want to go" but that senior officers of the division did not. While such statements had no basis in fact, the *Messenger* also reported that a French inspector stated that the soldiers in the camp were being "drilled to death" and that in his opinion the 36th Division had been "fit for France six months ago." At the same time, Sergeant Clark wrote home: "I hate to think the boys are of the disposition, I really believe they are getting tired of Camp Bowie." The same attitudes were expressed in the other Texas Division, the 90th, training in San Antonio. There, the draftees became excited at the news they were departing not because they wanted to get to France, but because they were simply tired of life at Camp Travis, engaging in drilling, maneuvers and parades until they were "ragged and worn."[67]

Much as they had done back in their Northwest Texas communities, the soldiers of the old 7th Texas participated in a number of parades and reviews. In one instance, General Greble selected General Hutchings's 71st Brigade, which consisted of the 141st and 142d Infantry, to parade in front of Governor Hobby and

Oklahoma Governor Robert L. Williams for the opening of the camp rifle range on November 21, 1917. As the *Dallas Morning News* reported, the "soldiers of the two states in company formation went swinging by ... with true military precision." The paper also estimated that as many as 30,000 people watched the parade and gave vent to their approval. After the parade, both Governor Hobby and Fort Worth Mayor W. D. Davis drew their own parallels with the military traditions of the state. Hobby said that "when I see the proud stride and flashing eyes of these young soldiers I am reminded of the heroes of San Jacinto," while Mayor Davis drew on his roots as a son of a Confederate veteran. Still, it pleased him to see "the sons of men who followed the Union flag and those who followed the Stars and Bars fighting side by side for a common cause." Again, officials expected great things from these soldiers simply because they were from Texas and followed in what many considered to be a distinct military experience.[68]

A review of the entire division occurred in February of 1918, although the most impressive one occurred in April of 1918. That parade was declared "a parting gift to the people of Texas and Oklahoma," although the division still did not know its actual departure date for France. For this massive parade, an estimated crowd of 150,000 and 225,000 people watched the division march through Fort Worth. The parade itself consisted of at least 25,000 men, 5,000 animals and 1,200 vehicles, and lasted for three hours.[69]

Finally, in June of 1918, General Greble ordered the entire division to engage in a "practice packing" of their equipment and the soldiers received new identification tags. The new tags had each soldier's serial number on it but not the unit, information that could be used by the enemy. The lack of unit information caused many soldiers to speculate on their imminent departure. However, the division did not receive orders to sail for France until July 2, 1918. Sergeant Clark wrote a final letter from Camp Bowie describing preparations: "Don't know just when will leave here but it looks like it will not be long off now ... I've packed all that we haven't in use now. And will have the men equipped with all that we can get here. The rest we will get at port and in France."[70]

As the soldiers prepared for their trip overseas, they learned that General Greble would not be going with him, the general having been informed in March that the War Department had declared him physically disqualified. Instead, he reverted to his Regular Army rank of brigadier general and remained at Camp Bowie in charge of a "development battalion." While General Pershing may have considered Greble too old for the rigors of the Western Front, it should be noted that Greble's counterpart in the 90th Texas-Oklahoma Draft Division, Maj. Gen. Henry Allen, was as old as Greble but was not removed from command by Pershing prior to the overseas movement. That, however, may have been because Pershing and Allen had served together on the Punitive Expedition to Mexico in 1916. Nevertheless, after consulting with General Pershing, the War Department selected Maj. Gen. William R. Smith to take the division overseas. Smith would lead the 36th Division through the war and back to Texas and Oklahoma in 1919. The new division commander started the war as a colonel in the coast artillery but had been rapidly promoted and most recently commanded the 62d Field Artillery Brigade of the 37th Division at Camp Sheridan in Montgomery, Alabama. Originally from Tennessee, Smith graduated from West Point, and was fifty years old, nine years younger than Greble. Smith received confirmation as a major general and was placed in command of the 36th Division on July 6, 1918. At that time, he was already in New York, preparing to lead the 62d Field Artillery overseas when word came of his new command. Instead of travelling to Camp Bowie, he remained in New York and waited for the division to arrive.[71]

Changes also occurred in the 142d Infantry that prevented more men from the old 7th Texas from going overseas. Another of the regiment's original officers, Capt. Noah Roark, who had raised the Denton Company and commanded the regiment's Company M, failed his overseas deployment physical and remained. Not only had the regiment lost several of its original officers, such as captains Homer T. Merrill and Noah Roark, but a number of others remained behind, their fate uncertain. Capt. Clyde Graham received his discharge from the 2d Pioneer Infantry on March 27, while lieutenants William R. Lockett and Robert A. Eubank were discharged on July 1 and 2. The Machine Gun Company recommended three men for Surgeon's Certificate of Disability on June 18, just a few weeks prior to departure, one of whom was an original member of the Machine Gun Company, First Sgt. William C. Culp, who had lost the use of his left arm and hand. The company commander also recommended that nineteen men be left behind for "labor and casualty organization," for reasons such as "unfit for MG work; no education; unable to learn work. Fit for Infantry," or "Unreliable; unable to learn MG work; fit for labor organization." However, none of those unfortunate nineteen men were from Captain Tyler's original Gainesville machine gun company. Nevertheless, those nineteen illustrated that the 142d had expanded well beyond the original complement of Texas and Oklahoma Guardsmen.[72]

Regimental officers also had to deal with last minute pleas from family members who did not want their relatives to depart. For example, in one case, Pvt. Robert A. Trimble of Wellington, Texas, with help from a lawyer, sought a discharge to assist his mother, who had been "compelled to earn her living by washing and ironing for other people and waiting on the sick." In addition, Trimble had a brother paralyzed in one hand and one leg and a half sister who was "very unwell being practically an invalid." Finally, Trimble wrote, "I assisted them when I was at home but when I volunteered to serve in the army I did not realize that they would suffer so much as they are." Although Captain Perkins recommended that Trimble receive a discharge, that did not occur and Trimble went to France with his unit. In another, Capt. E. W. Whitney, who had taken over the Machine Gun Company from Captain Tyler, received a letter from Mrs. Jesse B. Scott of Abilene dated June 22, 1918. In it, she asked Whitney to "assist in helping my child and I secure a discharge for my husband who is in your company." She continued: "Sir: I need my husband at home to help support myself and child very badly as my child is too young for me to leave and work myself." Unfortunately, there was little that Whitney or any of the other officers could do to answer such pleas as much as they might have wanted to help.[73]

The companies also had their share of administrative details to take care of prior to their departure. The Machine Gun Company offered a typical selection of tasks to be accomplished. Those tasks included winding down training and determining the training status of the company's soldiers, such as how many participated in various machine-gun courses. Furthermore, Captain Whitney filed a report on the experience level of the men in his company. In response to a query from Colonel Bloor, he reported that the Machine Gun Company only had one man who had less than one month of military training, no men who had one to three months, and 144 men who had more than three months service. Whitney wrapped up his administrative tasks, much as the other companies did, by making sure all debts incurred by the company were paid, reporting on men who were still absent and making recommendations for promotion or demotion concerning soldiers in his company, a task that occupied him even during the trip. Sergeant Aubyn Clark wrote a final letter from Camp Bowie on July 8, 1918, to his parents, "I will go and do what I can and when it's over I'll come back and try to be a better boy for the experience that I may get while in this thing. Whatever happens you may know that I did it for the country and people that I love."[74]

Each regiment took about four days to make the trip from Texas to the embarkation ports near New York City. The 36th Division travelled to New York during the most intense movement period in the war, July and August of 1918. For example, on July 13, one of the days that the division was travelling, the Army moved 41,000 soldiers on 77 trains. Most of the division travelled along the same route, although there were variations. The majority went east to Atlanta and then north to Jersey City, where the division made a final stop at Camp Mills before departing for France. One member of Company F, William T. Phillips, remembered departing Camp Bowie on July 12, 1918, and travelling through Arkansas, Tennessee, North Carolina, and Virginia before arriving in New York on July 15, 1918. Other units of the 142d, however, such as the Headquarters Company, followed a more northerly route, and at least one unit of the division actually travelled as far north as Canada.

One member of Captain Wagstaff's Headquarters Company, Daniel O. Blackmon, sent postcards home at several stops, including Little Rock on July 12, Cleveland on July 14, and Brooklyn on July 17. Corporal Archibald S. Hart mailed a postcard from Little Rock knowing that he could not be very specific about his location. Instead of continuing north toward Cleveland like Private Blackmon, Hart's unit arrived in Memphis at 2:00 am, where Captain Simpson of Company H marched the sleepy soldiers through the town to another train. Early the next morning, Hart saw a sign that read "Tupelo," and realized they were heading for Atlanta. At this point, Hart finally realized that they were no longer recruits going to training, but "troops on the way to war."[75]

After passing through Birmingham, Hart's unit continued on to Jersey City through Raleigh, Washington, DC, and Philadelphia, where there was a rumor that they had missed their transport by one day. While the officers in charge of the men found them quarters, Hart's Company K and other soldiers of the regiment got to swim, fifty at a time, in a local YMCA pool. Hart recalled travelling by barge to Brooklyn, where the company assembled on a "large weedy area on which a hundred or so tents had been pitched." While some of the regiment's soldiers spent three days in New York City, other units, such as Hart's, had only one night. Rather than sleep in the tents, most of the Company K soldiers slept under the stars. The next day, without any food, the men travelled to Hoboken where they received cocoa and sandwiches. After spending most of the day there, Lt. Joe Kell and Sgt. Corley Smart formed the men up and marched them onto their transport. As Hart recalled, as they crossed a narrow ramp he happened to look down and saw the dirty water of the Hudson River; otherwise he would not have realized "the exact time when Company K became sea-borne."[76]

A few men found time to send a note to relatives before they boarded their transports. In spite of all that the soldiers of the old 7th Texas had gone through, and all the changes that had occurred, there still remained a large core of men who had been there from the beginning in the summer of 1917. Many had been together for a year and while Company H's men boarded their transport, Capt. Ethan Simpson wrote briefly to his wife: "they are the finest company on earth," and he loved them as they loved him.[77]

With that, the 142d Infantry as part of the 36th Division left New York for France. Corporal Hart recalled nothing special about their departure, as many men considered Hoboken just another stop on their journey. The real departure, he wrote, had been from Camp Bowie. For the trip, the 142d Infantry occupied several transports. For example, the Headquarters Company, Machine Gun Company, Supply Company, the medical detachment, and the 2d Battalion, with companies E, F, G, H, sailed on the *Rijndam*. The 1st Battalion, including Companies A, B,

C, and D, sailed on the *Maui*. The 3rd Battalion, with companies I, K, L, and M, sailed on the *Lenape*.[78]

While many of the soldiers may have looked forward to the overseas journey, the question remained as to just how prepared the division was as it left for France. Although they had spent ten months at Camp Bowie prior to embarkation, the division was inspected between June 14 and 24, and the inspector assessed the division with the following terse comments:

> Many unfit officers owing to political combinations among the N.G. officers. Not enough regular army officers on duty with the division. 6,500 recruits with practically no training. Physical condition of men is satisfactory but their intelligence below the average. Training has been in general satisfactory. Discipline is barely good. All shortages of equipment to be supplied at Port of Embarkation. The division on the whole has made satisfactory progress.

As those comments illustrate, the animosity between National Guard and Regular Army officers continued even after the War Department sought to eliminate any distinction between the Regulars, Guardsmen, and draftees. Second, while members of the old 7th Texas had received months of training, the division, like many others, received thousands of replacements to fill its ranks, many of whom had little or no training. As noted above, the machine-gun company listed 144 men with three or more months of service. However, that does not indicate whether those men had three months or twelve months of experience. Interestingly, while the inspector noted the physical condition of the soldiers, he considered their intelligence and discipline to be below other units. Still, those comments point to the fact that the division was probably no better or worse in terms of training and preparations than most other National Guard divisions.[79]

The trip was generally without incident, although the ship's crews took target practice, and many soldiers experienced seasickness. Those aboard the *Rijndam*, which one soldier described as a "captured Dutch ship and they call it a mighty lucky ship," watched their escort ships fend off a German submarine. As Pvt. John T. Payne of the 142d Band recalled, "a little German sub got after us and believe me, you ought to have seen the ships scatter." Payne wrote that it was "a little exciting, but somehow I wasn't alarmed at it at all." While the soldiers on the *Rijndam* experienced that excitement, most dealt with nothing worse than seasickness. As William T. Phillips recalled, "Had a few storms and a lot of sick boys, myself included, but managed to get across the big pond." Private Hardy Wall of Company K wrote his sister that "we sure were some crowded and my but lots of the boys were seasick." With hindsight after the armistice, Wall concluded about the trip overseas, "We thought we were having a hard time, but we were in paradise considering what we went through since." Zack Salmon of Company M might have been the envy of his shipmates because he wrote to his father that he enjoyed the trip and had "plenty to eat and lots of good books to read. I didn't get the least bit seasick." Corporal Hart claimed that "social life aboard the *Lenape* couldn't be called dull," as there were "Yankee units and Mid-western units along with the Texans." Still, Company D's Dee McHaney might have expressed the general feelings about the trip, when he simply wrote his sister that "we were twelve days crossing the fish pond … I was sure glad to see dirt again."[80]

Thirteen days into the trip, Hart and his companions noticed the color of the sea had changed from a dark blue to green. Before long seagulls swirled about the ship, as did a French dirigible. Soon they could see a "hazy smudge" on the horizon which they shortly identified as France. That night the *Lenape* dropped anchor near Brest. On their way in, one member of the regiment recalled passing a "great fleet of fishing boats and saw great schools of a strange looking fish." This man, Lt. Roland L. Shine, recalled the passing fishing boats greeting their transport with shouts and cheers. He also noticed an American sailor on a hill signaling rapidly in semaphore, something Shine could only guess meant "welcome to France." That night, the soldiers remained on board the ship. Corporal Hart and a companion sat on a railing, letting their feet dangle over the edge, talked and looked at the "myriad lights of the city" that were "sprinkled variously from shore-line upward to what seemed in the darkness to be the crest of a towering mountain." The next day, July 31, 1918, the soldiers of the 142d Infantry debarked from the *Lenape.* They arrived twelve days ahead of the transport *USS Maui*, which did not dock in Brest until August 12, 1918, while the companies on board the *Rijndam* debarked at St. Nazaire, well to the south, on the same day as the *Lenape* reached Brest.[81]

Once the men arrived in France, many of the soldiers took the time to express themselves not only about the journey to Europe, but their perceptions of France. Lawrence Melton wrote his mother that he did not get seasick on the way over to France, but believed that possibility existed for the return journey. Ernest Britton of Cleburne expressed surprise that the ocean was "so wide as it is," and wrote that he was sick the first three days and "staggered around like a drunk man." He hoped "the ocean will go dry" before their return. The *Wichita Daily Times* reported on August 2, 1918, that the Wichita Falls soldiers had arrived safely overseas after Lieutenants Joe Kell and Gordon Porter managed to send telegrams from "an Atlantic Port," simply stating "the ship on which I sailed has arrived safely overseas."[82]

On one hand, Charles Meeker of Cleburne took a prosaic view of the trip, writing to his parents that he did not get seasick on the trip over and he wished they could see what he had seen, and to "watch the water day and night and to see the moon rise seemingly right out of the water…" He also described a fish or "substance" in the water that "looked just like the stars." On the other hand, when Lieutenant

Shine walked off the *Lenape*, he felt the urge to scoop up a handful of French dirt, only to realize that the "dirt looked pretty much like the dirt around the docks at Galveston, so I concluded then and there that, in as far as the earth was concerned, it was no different from that of my own country."[83]

Almost a year earlier, many of these soldiers had been members of the Texas National Guard with no training or uniforms, convinced by their communities that they were the best and bravest soldiers in the United States. They had arrived at Camp Bowie only to discover that the promises they had been made about serving with local friends in the National Guard could not hold up under the Army's bureaucracy. Along the way, they lost many members of their old regiment but they also became soldiers, spent months training, and finally made it overseas. Now that they were in France, those who remained of the old 7th Texas Infantry would continue the journey that they had started the year before in Northwest Texas. Everything so far had been preparation; now they would be put to the test and come face to face with life and death as soldiers in the Army of the United States.

4

"FIT TO GET DOWN TO SERIOUS BUSINESS"

The 142d Infantry Regiment, still containing a large core of men from the old 7th Texas Infantry and the former 1st Oklahoma Infantry regiments, arrived in France at a critical moment in the war. The German Army had launched a massive series of offensives beginning in March of 1918, which German leaders hoped would end the war before the influence of the United States could be felt too strongly on the Western Front. While German forces gained ground, by the summer the offensives along the Western Front had failed to achieve their strategic objectives, and the dynamic changed as the American Expeditionary Forces (AEF) continued to strengthen.[1]

As commander of the AEF, Gen. John J. Pershing struggled with the Allied leadership over whether or not American units arriving in France should be "amalgamated" into the European armies or used to build a strictly American army. For obvious reasons, Pershing desired the latter while the Allies pressed for amalgamation. By the time the 36th Division arrived in France, Pershing's goal had been realized with the creation of the First American Army. The question for Colonel Bloor and the soldiers of the 142d Infantry was how they were going to fit into this larger picture, and where and with whom would they fight on the Western Front? As they would learn, neither the 36th Division nor its four infantry regiments would serve with Pershing's First American Army in combat. Instead, Pershing would loan the American 2d and 36th Divisions to the French, where they would see combat in the devastated Champagne region east of Rheims. Before its first experience of combat, however, the 36th Division spent weeks at one of the

AEF's training areas undergoing a program meant to provide final preparation for service on the Western Front.[2]

After their arrival in Brest aboard the Lenape and the Rijndam, the soldiers of the 142d marched ashore and spent their first few days in France at the Pontanezen rest camp, near the barracks of the same name that dated from the Napoleonic era. Regardless of its historical significance, divisional historian Capt. Alex Spence recalled that the Pontanezen Barracks were filthy and "poorly equipped, badly laid out, worse regulated, and in the worst possible sanitary condition." While at least one soldier recalled sleeping on "chicken coop beds," for the most part the "rest camp" consisted of open fields near the barracks where the men made do with small tents that did not provide much protection from daily rain showers. Each unit of the division averaged a stay of seven or eight days at the camp before departing for the training area. Several important visitors toured the area while the division occupied the camp. In early August, the barracks of the 142d Infantry "buzzed with excitement" when word filtered down that General Pershing would visit. Senior officers selected Company K to provide an honor guard for Pershing's arrival and Capt. Sneed Staniforth of Wichita Falls ordered Cpl. Archibald Hart to form the guard. While Hart failed to recall anything memorable about Pershing's speech, his presence may have served to convince the soldiers that they were finally in France and on their way to the Western Front. Likewise, Pershing wrote in his memoirs that the soldiers of General Smith's division were "impatient when they could not be moved promptly to the front," which, he knew, tended to be the case with all newly arrived units, and these soldiers were no different. Additionally, the president of France, Paul Poincare, visited the division. Perhaps more interesting to the soldiers, however, was their first glimpse of German prisoners working on the docks at Brest.[3]

While waiting, many of the soldiers took the opportunity to write their families and convey their first thoughts on France. A Wichita County soldier, Pvt. John Butts, commented that "the Wichita boys with the Camp Bowie Panther Division, arrived in France in splendid condition, fit to get down to serious business and all of them most anxious to do so." On the other hand, Sam Jones, also of Wichita Falls, expressed a general sentiment when he wrote that France was "a beautiful country, everything looks different from the part of the good old U.S.A. I started from." Laurence Melton of Wise County, still in Captain Lillard's company, wrote his mother, "at last I am in France and doing fine." He also commented that "we are in an ancient city and there are lots of wonderful things to see … and there are lots of things that are amusing to a boy who never traveled much." Another Wise County soldier, Roe McBroom, wrote to his father that "I like this country fine, but it is queer; the buildings are strange looking structures, and the people wear wooden shoes." Many soldiers marveled at the wooden shoes worn by the French, causing one soldier to write his sister, "They say we get women's fashions from France. Well, the girls wear wooden shoes, so you will have to get you a pair."[4]

After a week, the division moved to Training Area 13, centered on Bar-Sur-Aube, a town of about 4,000 people that rested along the Aube River, some 120 miles southeast of Paris and just over 100 miles from the front. By the time the 142d departed for the training area, the regiment had swelled to 82 officers and 3,458 enlisted men, the division's largest regiment at the time, while the division itself totaled 965 officers and 25,922 men. The units travelled by rail, some through Versailles and Paris and others along a more southerly route, passing through Tours, Orleans, and Dijon. Many of the soldiers recalled the trip on the French locomotives, which some described as "toys" because of their small size. However, perhaps Bryan Autry of Company M put it best in the language that Texans could understand when he wrote his father that the railcars were so small they "would not hold as many cottonseed [sic] as Mr. Marshall's wagon you built for him."[5]

Laurence Boyd wrote to his family in Decatur that the tiny railroad cars, "40 and 8s" for forty men or eight horses, were certainly crowded, although "we have learned to overlook such little inconveniences as this" and instead focused on the countryside they travelled through and wrote that it was "simply beautiful. This is the season when the trees, flowers, shrubbery, growing crops, clover fields, etc. have on their best dress." Perhaps because he was a farmer, Boyd wrote that the local farms were small, and that seeing one on a hillside "with its small patches and many colors, looks like a large handmade quilt." He also noticed that the "small grain" was "cut and bound" by hand and threshed by a "horse tread mill thresher which looks very old timey to us who know of the modern machinery of America." A great number of the soldiers, including Capt. Ethan Simpson of Clarendon, and Roe McBroom and Travis Jones of Decatur, expressed amazement at the crops and how the French farmed and tilled their fields. Sergeant Aubyn Clark wrote to his brother that "the vineyards are thick as cotton patches in east Texas and the way that they are on the hillsides they are as pretty as can be, it's a pretty country, and if it was in America it would be cut up into parks and picnic grounds." In spite of the scenery, Company K's Archibald Hart recalled tempers flaring during the two-day trip, as the trains continuously stopped and started. Corporal Autry recalled that some men slept standing up, and those lying down were stepped on or had their faces "skinned by our hobnail boots." The overcrowding may have also led to the death of the regiment's first soldier in Europe. Company G's Pvt. Ed Strunce, sitting on top of a box car, was "knocked from the train and instantly killed" when the train passed under a low bridge.[6]

Once the regiment arrived at Bar-Sur-Aube, the companies marched to their various villages scattered around the countryside. When Corporal Hart's train carrying Company K arrived, Captain Simpson of Company H led the battalion march to the village of Nuismont, fourteen kilometers away. Some members of the regiment considered that march the most difficult they had made up to that point. The soldiers, obviously tired and exasperated after the train trip, were falling out and straggling and in the darkness many gave vent to their frustrations. Captain Simpson stopped the column of marchers and "berated the malcontents who in the darkness had felt safe voicing their profane objections." When they finally arrived at their village, Corporal Hart threw down his gear and went to sleep at the foot of a stone wall. Over the next several days, the companies, battalions, and regiment settled in and organized their living arrangements.[7]

Training Area 13 consisted of northern and southern sections. General Hutchings' 71st Brigade occupied the southern section, with brigade headquarters in the town of Bligny, while Hulen's 72d Brigade occupied the northern section. Within their section, commanders assigned each regiment, battalion, and company to a headquarters village. Colonel Bloor's regimental command post shared Bligny with General Hutchings, as did Headquarters Company, the medical detachment, and Companies C and D. The village of Urville hosted 1st Battalion Headquarters and Companies A and B. The 2d Battalion, Captain Perkins' Supply Company, and Companies E and F moved to Couvignon, while Companies G and H camped at Bergeres. Third Battalion and Company L were at Montmartin, Company I at Le Puits, Company K was billeted at Nuismont, and Company M at Meurville. The Machine Gun Company camped at the village of Le Val Perdu. None of the villages had more than a few hundred inhabitants, and the terrain was described as "hilly and fairly well interspersed with forestage."[8]

In each of these villages, besides wooden barracks, the soldiers found billets in stone buildings, such as houses, barns and some "vacant dwellings." A number of men in Company K lived in the Nuismont mayor's barn, but with threshing season in progress the barn was filled with dust from the day's work of a Percheron horse that walked a treadmill to power the threshing machine. Rather than deal with the horse's dust, Corporal Hart and others established a "pup-tent colony" outside. Laurence Boyd, in a letter home, wrote that his group was "quartered together in one building and are near a lake for bathing," while Travis Jones wrote that he was "billeted in a large barn, with plenty of hay to sleep on," and added, "I am just as well contented as I would be back at old Camp Bowie." Aubyn Clark wrote, "Have good quarters and excellent water tastes like panhandle well water and you know how good that is. Nothing better at any price." However, deficiencies existed, including a lack of bedding, clothing, and "fuel for drying clothes," and not each village had a

YMCA canteen to sell minor supplies. Many of the company headquarters occupied quarters similar to Captain Simpson's, which occupied a "nice little house on the main road in the village." In general, the living arrangements were not abysmal, although far from perfect. In addition, each unit appointed a "town major" to handle issues with local residents.[9]

As the regimental commander, Colonel Bloor occupied appropriate quarters. He lived in a "wonderful old chateau or castle" that belonged to a Paris judge. Richly furnished with paintings and tapestries, the chateau sat on land that included a hunting preserve and an artificial lake with a "built up beach." One of Bloor's staff officers had even shot a deer on the preserve.[10]

Once the companies settled in, they began final training preparations. While at Camp Bowie, the division, like others in the United States, had followed a course that stressed trench warfare. However, in France, the soldiers of the AEF received a full dose of General Pershing's training philosophy, which stressed maneuver or "open" warfare. General Pershing also assigned fifteen French officers and several teams of specialists to assist in the division's training. However, in a note to General Smith, Pershing wrote that "the training of American troops must remain in the hands of American officers." While Pershing admitted that valuable assistance could be gained from the French officers, he made it clear that "they will not be permitted by you to dictate methods of training" or "substitute programs for those provided" by AEF Headquarters. Much of the training consisted of field exercises on how to maneuver and how to attack machine-gun posts arrayed in depth, training which the division historian recalled as "intensive." In order to develop the ability to maneuver and advance quickly, endurance remained a fundamental aspect of training which the soldiers developed through numerous hikes. The training also included tasks such as live grenade training, bayonet drills, and day and night maneuvers with "strict march discipline." As Lawrence Melton of Decatur wrote his parents, "I am working hard over here but staying fat all the time; you can't kill a good man, so there you are." Sergeant Joe Casey got his first taste of the front while attending a gas warfare course and wrote home: "I have heard the cannons roar. The Americans are giving the Boches hell!" In some cases, platoons and companies were sent off for specialized training. For example, the signal platoon, the pioneers section, the intelligence platoon, the 37mm platoon, and the Stokes mortar platoon all traveled to various French towns for more intensive training in their specialties. The staff planned four major divisional exercises, although one member of the division later wrote that they failed to get the maximum benefit from the exercises because of a lack of artillery and equipment. At the division level, inspectors identified two glaring weaknesses during the training. First, officers in the advance elements failed to send back messages to the next higher echelon of command. Second, the division had difficulty maintaining contact, or liaison with other elements of the command. Both of those problems would surface again when the 142d Infantry went into combat for the first time.[11]

Laurence Boyd of Decatur described the daily hikes his company took, often with a full pack. Once a week they hiked all day. On one of these hikes, his company marched sixteen miles with a ten-minute break every hour and thirty minutes for dinner. On a different hike, his company left the road and "climbed a very steep hill and filed through the woods where the wild boar is occasionally found." Walking through these woods, Boyd imagined he was on a desert island. However, when he came to a clearing where he could see the valley of the Aube River with its houses, roads, and fields, he wrote, "the desert island dream was shattered."[12]

One soldier of the regiment, Joe Muldoon, wrote to his mother in September 1918 that "You must not worry about me for I am alright and have plenty to eat and we drill every day." Laurence Boyd echoed those sentiments writing that his unit worked "reasonably hard," and that "our food is excellent but we miss ice cream, cakes, etc…," as did Laurence Melton, who wrote that he was getting "plenty to eat and you know I am satisfied when I am well fed." Lloyd Moreland described a dinner one day that included "fish, beefsteak, French fried potatoes, eggs, fresh tomatoes, jam and coffee." Although the food was good, soldiers missed home cooked meals. Sergeant Joe Casey of Company L missed his mother's "chicken and good hot biscuit." To ease his craving, he and a friend bought a chicken and cooked it, but it did not taste the same. Sergeant Clark gushed to his brother "I would enjoy sitting down at the table and saying Papa pass the biscuits again, but Bill we have real biscuits once and a while, in fact our eats are good, fresh beef, fresh tomatoes…" Finally, in the excited chatter of young soldiers, Eugene Minor of Decatur, a member of Headquarters Company, wrote home about some of the Decatur members of the regimental band: "The band without an exception is in the very best of health. In fact, they are as fat as pigs, and Phil, Grady, Pug, Sam Man and others simply can't get enough. They are hungry all the time." Although the men appeared to eat well, supplies did not always come easy. For example, Company A's commanding officer wrote that his unit had received no fresh meat in four days and he had been forced to purchase small amounts of "mess supplies" in Bar-Sur-Aube, which made the "proper feeding of [the] organization extremely difficult." Captain Perkins, the supply officer, promptly retorted that Company A received fresh beef on September 10 and 14, and in the intervening three days received canned meat. Perkins wrote, "Co. A received their full allowance of the entire ration as issued by the Quartermaster and we hold their receipt for same."[13]

While they trained, they continued to soak in their surroundings. They saw more German prisoners, many of whom passed through the area on trains. Captain

Simpson came into contact with one group that had been told that Paris "had been blown off the earth" and that there were only "500 Americans" in France who were starving and whose return the United States demanded. As prisoners, however, they soon realized the extent of the American presence and told Simpson "we have been deceived, Germany is doomed." Besides prisoners passing through, a number of German prisoners helped work local farms.[14]

As they had since their arrival, many of the soldiers continued to express their feelings in letters home. Grady Woodruff of Wise County wrote to his sister that his town had "lots of pretty trees and flowers" although the town's streets were "narrow and dirty, and you can hardly tell which are stores and which are residences or stables." Still, Woodruff concluded that "in spite of all this beauty, though, everything seems so weird and mysterious that you are almost afraid to breathe." Private John Butts of Wichita Falls described France as "wondrously beautiful farming country," while Charles Meeker of Cleburne wrote that France was "a beautiful country but of course is quite different from ours, and that makes it all the more interesting." He told his parents that he wanted "to see lots more of the country before I return."[15]

In a long letter home, Laurence Boyd of Decatur described Training Area 13, commenting that "we are now billeted in a small village in the interior of France," and all of the buildings were of "stone slate or tile roof." Boyd also marveled at the presence of Dutch windmills "still scattered through the country." As for the French climate, Sergeant Wayne Somerville described August in France as "almost like late fall in Wichita Falls and the nights are similar to those of Nebraska and Colorado; it is all delightful and ideal training ground for the boys of Texas." Captain Simpson wrote to his wife about the French people they met, observing that the "little children hang around us saying 'good Americans' and hug our knees," while the old men "all tip their hats to us."[16]

With hard training, plenty to eat, and the excitement of being in a new place, the regiment's morale remained strong while in the training area. One member of Company L from Cleburne, Earnest McBroom, wrote home, "This is a fine place to be. A fellow can't help but be all o.k. so you needn't worry about us for we are all well all the time." Sgt. Sam Man of Decatur burst forth with an exclamation about the old Decatur Company after making a "flying trip" to Captain Lillard's Company L, and reported that "Co. L is still in the bunch and that everybody in the company is well and enjoying the best of health."[17]

Obviously, many soldiers developed bonds with their comrades after a year of training. Pvt. Lloyd Moreland wrote that "I am still in the same company and am with the same boys. They all seem like brothers." Sergeant Somerville of the medical detachment took the measure of his group of soldiers, writing that "the whole detachment seems to be increasing in wisdom and stature and becoming real sure enough soldiers," while Eugene Minor of Headquarters Company called his band mates a "jolly and happy bunch."[18]

Although quite inexperienced and ignorant of the real nature of combat on the Western Front, many soldiers expressed their bravado and often tried to reassure their families they would be fine. One soldier from Captain Lillard's company wrote "I think I will get to eat Christmas Dinner at home, as we are going to whip these Huns before that time." He also wrote his father that "This trip has been worth a million dollars to me, if I can get back safe and sound." Likewise, Sam Jones of Wichita Falls told his mother, "Now, I do not want you to worry about me for I am all o.k., and ready for anything that comes my way." Roe McBroom of Wise County, who transferred out of the 142d Infantry before it went into battle, told his father "don't be uneasy about me, as I feel like I will make it through all right," while another soldier, in a less than practical manner, wrote his parents: "Do not take my name in a casualty list as serious for I will cable if hurt. Our lieutenant's name has appeared four times and he has never been hurt." Lloyd Moreland of Clarendon was not quite boasting when he wrote home that "the war news is awful good. I think I'll be at home next year to help you all make a crop," while Travis Jones wrote his mother in Decatur not to "worry too much about your soldier boy. If anything should happen to me, you would know about it just as soon as possible. I feel just as safe here as I would if I were at home." He concluded his letter by telling his mother that he did not have the "least doubt in the world but what that I will be back in the good old U.S.A. by the time I am twenty-one years old. I wouldn't take a thousand dollars for my trip over here." Lt. Alfred "Pat" Carrigan of Wichita Falls carried a locket with his mother's picture in it, and after a church service he wanted to show the minister the locket "but did not get a chance." He wrote to his mother, "Don't worry about me, whatever God and headquarters say I will do."[19]

Some expressed thoughts about their presence in France, such as Charles Meeker of Cleburne, who told his mother that the French people seemed to think "we have come to redeem their country and bring back their loved ones. I know we have come here to help and I want come back home knowing I have had a part in helping a people who are so sorely distressed." He also gave his parents a gentle warning about his possible fate in combat: "I know you both will get along all right and that God will take care of you and me, so don't fear. All will be well at the end...." Sergeant Aubyn Clark made it clear why he was in France: "We are over here to whip the Kaiser and are going to do it up in proper style, and that pronto. When this little band go over the top he better hunt for his hole for things are to be popping out in front. We have the best bunch that ever came over to whip the rascal." Pvt. Lloyd Moreland told his parents that he carried the Bible they had given him, writing that he held it "dearer than anything I have with me," as it made him think about the "dear old father and mother that are waiting for me." He concluded by asking his sister to take care of his horses and wrote, "Gee but I would love to step in for a few days visit. But when I do come back home, I'm coming back to stay."[20]

Of course, not all of their time was spent writing pensive letters home. In spite of their busy schedule the soldiers also found time to relax. Some spent time at the local YMCA, such as Pvt. Sam Banks, while others sought out local French girls and places where they could obtain wine. A member of the division, Charles Ingram, wrote poetically about the prices of wine: "Say, wine is 40 cents per quart up and champagne, the kind that makes the drawing room lamp look like a flood of golden sunset and makes you see kind faced old cows standing in silvery streams of water—only $2.40 per quart." In the regimental headquarters village of Bligny, soldiers frequented three bars nicknamed "Dinty Moore's Place," "Ten Nights in a Barroom," and "Red Onions." Aubyn Clark claimed, "they have more wines here than you can shake a stick at but it is more like vinegar than our wine." As for French girls, Earnest McBroom wrote to his mother, "The French girls are sure thick and they sure do have some time. They give us all the wine that you can drink. What makes me mad, though, is that I can't understand what they say." On the other hand, Pvt. Sam Banks wrote "I haven't seen many pretty girls here yet. They all look alike to me over here and they don't look like the girls at home, ha ha," while Travis Jones of Decatur believed the French girls were "very bashful and it is almost an impossibility to get one of them to talk to you." However, once they left the training area and headed for the front, Joe Casey of Decatur wrote home that "there is no danger of my getting married, as the French girls are all gone from the place we are in now."[21]

Other types of festivities also occurred. Sergeant Clark wrote that they put on their own vaudeville shows, and "the people next door to the show grounds come out and take it in same as the soldiers." In another instance, soldiers from Headquarters Company befriended a French family who lived for a time in New York and spoke fluent English. Captain Simpson, Captain Staniforth, and several other officers relaxed by singing with a "quartet from Company K," and visited with a local French family whose daughter played the "Star-Spangled Banner" and the "Marseillaise" on the piano. The young lady played other pieces that Captain Simpson described as his kind of music: "soft, slow, and dreamy." Simpson wrote how "funny" it was to "see how anxious these people are to please the Americans and how hard they try to make us understand them, and vice versa." Indeed, after Simpson learned to repeat a particularly difficult French phrase, an old Frenchman joked, "Good, good, the commander will learn to speak French in two weeks."[22]

One day, an enlisted member of Company L managed to tag along with a group of officers on their way to regimental headquarters and then to Colonel

Bloor's chateau for an officers' dinner. At headquarters, the soldier heard "the latest news, which sure sounded good," and even found letters for himself in the mail room. Afterward, he strolled over to Colonel Bloor's chateau where "the officers were having a get together party," at which an English vaudeville troop performed. During the performance it started to rain and the soldier "took shelter with some of the headquarters boys, among whom were the top and mess sergeants." The "headquarters boys" provided him with a steak dinner, for which he was grateful enough to write home about. He then walked six miles back to his company village and was in bed by Taps. Later, that same soldier and five of his comrades were taken by an old Frenchman to a "cascade," that came out of the ground and flowed over a "series of rocky falls." Sometimes, the soldiers of the regiment took their rambles into places they should not have, and earned the ire of local residents. For example, on September 7, the division issued General Order No. 14, which stated in part, "Numerous complaints have been received from French citizens in towns and communities where the soldiers of this command are billeted, of trespassing over their fields and through their vineyards, and eating their grapes."[23]

While many of the soldiers had the chance to enjoy the countryside and their interactions with the local population, some noticed the strains under which the local French people lived and that conditions had steadily deteriorated through four years of war. In a letter home, Travis Jones wrote, "I certainly feel sorry for them and will be glad when this awful war is over so that the men can take care of them." Sgt. Wayne Somerville noticed that all the children who had lost their fathers in the war "wear a black apron—little boys and girls alike." Somerville may have recognized their sacrifices, but in a way indicative of the southern culture he had grown up in: "They are making sacrifices and adopting a standard of living that the average Negro would think pretty tough."[24]

While the soldiers continued training, one member of the old 7th Texas became a pawn in old-fashioned Texas politics. Capt. Steve Lillard, who raised the Wise County Company, became the focus of a political smear campaign by members of Charles F. Spencer's congressional campaign, headed by his brother French Spencer. Both Spencers and Lillard hailed from Wise County, and the Spencer brothers' father, Richard, had served as County Judge at the turn of the century.

According to French Spencer, Lillard approached Spencer while Spencer was a member of the Texas legislature and asked him to speak with Governor Ferguson on Lillard's behalf to secure him a commission in the Texas National Guard. Spencer did so and Lillard received his commission, a not uncommon occurrence at the time. However, according to Spencer, Lillard approached him again after impeachment charges were filed against Ferguson and suggested that if Spencer voted to acquit the governor, Lillard would be promoted to major and Ferguson and his allies would line up support for French's brother Charles Spencer to go to Congress "with such an overwhelming majority as no other candidate has ever received." In other words, if Lillard secured Spencer's cooperation, Ferguson planned to reward both men.[25]

Apparently, French Spencer rebuffed Lillard, who angrily left the meeting. After that, French Spencer charged that Lillard tried to undermine Charles Spencer's campaign for Congress. As French Spencer wrote in the *Wichita Daily Times*, the "attacks upon Charles in this race is bottomed upon my failure to bow to him [Lillard] and trade off the right of the people that he may be furthered in his attempts to be made a major." While the accuracy of Spencer's charges is unclear, many residents of the area came to his defense, including his parents, who printed their own response to French Spencer's allegations. It is also unclear how much Lillard knew about the controversy while in France. However, the *Wichita Daily Times* devoted a full page to French Spencer's charges and the rebuttal by Lillard's parents. Nevertheless, the issue highlighted the complaint from regular officers of National Guardsmen receiving promotions as political favors rather than on merit. As events would prove, Lillard had more than enough ability to lead soldiers in combat.[26]

Finally, in spite of the training, food, and camaraderie among the soldiers of the regiment during the course of their training, things were not well from a medical perspective, at least according to the conclusion of the regiment's chief medical officer in a report submitted to Colonel Bloor. In his report, the surgeon pointed out that the soldiers' clothing and equipment, which had been "barely adequate at the beginning," had diminished "in quantity … and in quality" over time. That situation, combined with the fairly rigorous training of the soldiers in all weather conditions and the "widespread tendency on the part of line troops to disregard sanitary and hygienic regulations," led to a corresponding increase in illness among the regiment, particularly some cases of influenza and pneumonia.[27]

To prevent the outbreak from getting worse, the regiment implemented "the most vigorous anti-epidemic measures" in the villages of Bligny, Le Puits, and Montmartin. The "anti-epidemic" measures included isolating sick soldiers in "improvised infirmaries." Although the regiment was never free from disease while in the training area, the regimental surgeon could at least claim such measures achieved "an abatement of the epidemic," and cases "were reduced to a relatively inconsiderable number prior to departure" from the training area.[28]

Other medical concerns for Colonel Bloor and his staff included "defective bread issues" that caused intestinal sickness, ensuring the availability of "adequate bathing methods" and that "vigilant care was exercised in [the] sterilization of water." Obviously, staying clean could be a problem. Pvt. Jewel Young wrote home that he had everything he needed but "a bath and some clean clothes." He also mentioned that "some of the boys here have also spoken of the shortage of water for bathing purposes." Finally, officers closely supervised the "type and care" of latrines, and Bloor implemented "strict policing measures" regarding sleeping areas and kitchens. In mid-September, the medical detachment received a full allotment of its combat medical supplies, an indication the regiment might soon to move to the front.[29]

The regiment also dealt with more transfers, both in and out of the unit. Perhaps the most significant transfer was that of the regiment's brigade commander, Gen. Henry Hutchings, the former Adjutant General of Texas. Hutchings failed to impress General Smith during a series of maneuvers and Smith reported Hutchings' lack of proficiency to the AEF Inspector General, Major General A. W. Brewster. Shortly thereafter, Smith, with the concurrence of Brewster, recommended to General Pershing that Hutchings should be relieved. Pershing agreed and removed Hutchings from command of the brigade on August 29, 1918. Hutchings arrived at the reclassification center at Blois, where he was offered a position at the rank of major, a significant demotion. Hutchings refused the offer, received a discharge from active duty, and returned to Texas, leaving France on October 1, 1918, a week before his brigade went into combat.[30]

Brig. Gen. Pegram Whitworth replaced General Hutchings. Whitworth, a Louisiana native, called Tacoma, Washington, home. Whitworth graduated next to last in the West Point class of 1894, although he later earned three Silver Star decorations in the Spanish-American War and in the Philippines. Prior to being appointed brigadier general and assuming command of the 71st Brigade, he had served as commander of the 362d Infantry Regiment of the 91st Division and had arrived in France just a short time before the 36th Division.[31]

Changes also occurred at the regimental and company level. Lt. Colonel Elta Jayne, the Oklahoma Guardsman who had served as the deputy commander of the 142d Infantry, was replaced by Lt. Col. Irving Phillipson, a Regular Army officer who had served with the division in various capacities since its formation at Camp Bowie. In addition, Majors William Culberson and Alvin Owsley moved from the regiment to the division staff, with Culberson appointed division inspector and Owsley as division adjutant. At the company level, Capt. Alonzo Drake, who had raised the Childress Company and later served as regimental adjutant, also went to Blois for re-classification.[32] While the changes were not overwhelming for the 142d Infantry, in total the division sent forty-five officers to Blois for discharge or reclassification, 68 transferred to other units for various reasons, and 80 officers and 86 non-commissioned officers went to various AEF schools and training courses, including Company I's commander Capt. Robert Wagstaff and Company K's Lt. Joe Kell and 1st Sgt. Corley Smart.[33]

Finally, another indicator of the loss of original members of the 7th Texas Infantry can be seen in the number of officers who remained with the regiment when it went "into the line." As will be recalled, the 7th Texas arrived at Camp Bowie with fifty-six officers. After the merger with the 1st Oklahoma Infantry, forty-nine officers of the old 7th Texas transitioned to the 142d Infantry. By the time the regiment completed its training, travelled to France, and prepared to enter the line, the Army's bureaucracy had taken its toll. At the end of the first week of October 1918, only twenty-six (47 percent) of the 7th Texas' original officers remained with the regiment. This of course, included Colonel Bloor, who remained the only regimental commander of the 36th Division to stay with his regiment throughout the war.[34]

Besides those mentioned, other 7th Texas officers no longer with the regiment at this point included Capt. William Tyler, who raised the Gainesville Machine Gun Company as well as two of his three lieutenants, Horace Jennings and Thomas Mitchell; Capt. James Wiley of Quanah; Capt. Harry Baker of Vernon, and Lieutenants Jim Bomar and Lester Burns. Finally, Capt. Harold McGrath of Tarrant County, and Lt. James Stiff, who had received a commission from Major Decker the previous summer in Denton, no longer served in the regiment, although many remained in the Army.[35]

However, several of the officers who raised companies still led their companies and would lead them into battle, several of whom would play significant roles in combat. Those men included Capt. Thomas Barton of Amarillo; Capt. Ethan Simpson of Clarendon, who raised the Donley County Company as well as Captains Sneed Staniforth and Duncan Perkins, the two Wichita Falls officers who raised companies F and G of the old 7th Texas. Staniforth commanded Company K, while his friend Perkins commanded the Supply Company. Capt. Steve Lillard of Decatur still ran Company L, and Capt. Robert Wagstaff commanded Company I, although in attendance at the School of the Line. Several lieutenants from the original group remained, including Sam Owens and Robert Armstrong of Company G, and Lt. Bert Davis, who still served with the Machine Gun Company. There was Lt. George O. Thompson, who shifted to the Headquarters Company and commanded the Stokes mortars platoon, while Lt. Nat Perrine and Lt. Daniel Blue moved over to Company B. Lieutenants William Murphy and Stayton Hankins of Quanah remained with Company H. Wichita Falls officers Lt. Joe Kell and Lt. Alfred Carrigan were with Companies H and L respectively, while Lt. Ed Sayles of Abilene carried on with Headquarters Company and commanded the 37mm gun platoon. Colonel Bloor's younger brother, Bertram, also stuck with the regiment, serving as the unit's operations officer. Lieutenants Young Yates and Clark Owsley remained, Yates with Company M and Owsley as the regimental gas officer. Finally,

Lieutenants Gordon Porter and Earl Litteer returned to the regiment. Porter joined Barton's Company G, and Litteer, who helped recruit the Cleburne Company with Captain Underwood, commanded Company A as the regiment prepared to move into the line.[36]

While about half of the officers remained with the regiment, such was not the case with the enlisted men. In fact, the number had decreased significantly. When the 7th Texas consolidated at Camp Bowie in September of 1917, there were over 1,900 men from North and Northwest Texas in the regiment. One year later, as they prepared to go into the line, approximately 615 original members of the 7th Texas Infantry remained, about one-third of the original complement. That was a far cry from the oft-quoted National Guard recruiting refrain that a man would serve with soldiers from his area. Of course, discharges and transfers, duty at AEF training schools, and illnesses whittled away the number of men remaining. Although many still considered the 142d a "Texas" regiment, the original members had dwindled considerably.[37]

Finally, nearly 2,000 soldiers transferred out of the 36th Division to other units. Those transfers impacted all four regiments although the 141st Infantry lost 700 men, far more than the other regiments. Many of these soldiers were sent to the 42d "Rainbow" Division. At least two original members of the 7th Texas transferred with the hope of getting to the front quicker. One of them, Roe McBroom, wrote to his father, "I have transferred to the Rainbow Division, Co. K, 167th Infantry. I am sure glad I made the change, for a fellow always likes a change." However, three weeks later, the *Wise County Messenger* reported that two Decatur boys, Roe McBroom and Newt Young, were "tiring of [the] inaction that their regiment was being subjected to back of the fighting line in France, joined up with another regiment, one that was moving to the scenes of hostile acts." The paper pointed out that "the joke is on the boys, for in a short time after they went up with another regiment, their [original] regiment was ordered into action." The division also received 783 former members who had been left at Camp Bowie because of sickness or because they were absent without leave when the division left for France. Perhaps this group included Earl Litteer and Gordon R. Porter, the two officers who lost their positions during the regiment's consolidation, but had rejoined the regiment when it went into the line. Illustrative of the bond between the remaining Guardsmen, Capt. Sneed Staniforth of Wichita Falls attempted to secure the return transfer of an original member of his company, John Beasley, at the time assigned to the 164th Infantry. Beasley wrote his old commander that he wished "to get back to old K Company. Will you please make an effort to get me back?" Unfortunately, before the transfer could be made Beasley was sent to the 32d Division.[38]

A sure sign that the regiment prepared to move to the front occurred when all sick soldiers were evacuated to Camp Hospital 42 at Bar-Sur-Aube. One soldier in that group, Victor Nobles of Decatur, remained behind while recovering from an illness. In a letter home, he told his sister he would never be in the infantry again and wrote: "the company left me behind. I sure hated to see them go," in part because he would be separated from his brother, but also because of the bond he had with his fellow soldiers: "I would have wanted to go with them anyway on account of the other boys." Company commanders made final preparations, which included documenting the number of gas masks in their units, how long they had worn the gas masks each day in training, the number of unserviceable rifles, the religious preferences of their men, and the number of men needed to bring each company to full strength. In summing up the division's stay at Bar-Sur-Aube, the division historian wrote that morale was good, and "their confidence" was "amazing." As he wrote, "they had come to France to whip the Boche, and it never occurred to any of them that they would not do it." On one hand, the division, including the 142d Infantry, received grades of "fair" in combat maneuvering, "above average" in rifle and bayonets, and "excellent" in gas defense. As Captain Spence believed, the division's "strength lay in its splendid personnel." On the other hand, the division remained weak in map reading, maintaining liaison with other units, and suffered from a lack of experience among the division's officers.[39]

The division received its movement alert order on September 23, 1918, about a week before completing advanced training at Bar-Sur-Aube. Nevertheless, leaving early caused some surprise among the division's officers as most units were normally sent to a quiet place in the line. Three days later, on September 26, the same day that Pershing's First American Army launched its major offensive between the Meuse River and the Argonne Forest, the 36th Division left Training Area 13 and travelled almost due north toward Champigneul, between the towns of Epernay and Chalons. Although the distance was less than 100 kilometers, the trip took an average of nine hours because of the circuitous route of the trains. Once there, General Smith located his headquarters in the village of Pocancy. This location placed the division south of Rheims, where, instead of being assigned to Pershing's First Army, the division joined the French Group of Armies of the Center (GAC), and went into reserve.[40]

According to the division machine-gun officer, Lt. Col. Harry Hawley, the journey north illustrated the confusion the division operated under and the difficulties in working with soldiers of other nationalities. As Hawley wrote in his diary, "We will probably go into the lines within a few days, east of Rheims, without transportation and poor liaison between our G.H.Q. and the French." Furthermore, the division's arrival in the Pocancy area was not well coordinated, there having been "no preparatory plans of any kind" made "in expectation of the arrival of the division." Indeed, the lack of details on billeting caused Hawley to complain that the soldiers were "suffering greatly, due to the excessive and unnecessary marching with heavy packs."[41]

Division historian Captain Spence believed that the 2d and 36th Divisions were assigned to the French out of a sense that the war could soon be ended and the two divisions might help prevent a German withdrawal and hinder the effectiveness of the enemy's forces. Because of that, Spence believed that using incompletely trained divisions such as the 36th was a necessity. More specifically, Pershing assigned the 2d Division to the French because of its experience, while the fresh 36th Division was simply close at hand near the Champagne front, an accurate assessment.[42]

Although GAC commander General Paul Maistre maintained tactical control over the division, the French Fifth Army assumed responsibility for supplying and equipping Smith's division, which it badly needed. According to division machine gun officer Lieutenant Colonel Hawley, the Fifth Army leadership would not let the division enter the lines until it had been properly supplied, an attitude he considered a French "commentary on the American G.H.Q. who sent us here." The French Fourth and Fifth Armies together provided Smith's division with at least 300 horses and mules, 75 rolling kitchens, Stokes mortars and signal pistols, while the GAC provided an additional 200 horses and 100 carts. However, because the French Fifth Army would not control the division in combat, that organization "was not particularly interested in the division's affairs," which made getting supplies and equipment that much more difficult. Although they did manage some equipment, Captain Spence wrote that the division's officers were frantic with "worry and apprehension" on getting what they needed in time. Lieutenant Colonel Hawley wrote that the machine gun troops had one pistol for every ten men and that the machine gun ammunition they received was stamped "For Practice Only. Not to be used for combat purposes." In his words, the "equipment questions is simply terrible. We are told the equipment is not in France." More specifically, the 142d Infantry prepared for combat with shortages of fourteen water carts, five combat wagons, three medical carts, 154 draft animals, and all of its rolling kitchens. In addition, inventories of each company uncovered uneven stores of supplies and equipment. For example, Company K had 2,800 rounds of .45 caliber ammunition on hand, but not a single one of the sixty-seven .45 pistols they were required to have. Additionally, the American First Army offered few additional supplies or equipment because of its combat operations in the Meuse-Argonne. The 36th Division waited just to the west of the Argonne Forest, on the other side of which the American Army engaged in a brutal struggle. While the American First Army advanced east of the Argonne Forest, the French Fourth Army advanced west of the Argonne. They planned to meet north of the Argonne, and continue their advance from that point.[43]

According to General Smith, General Maistre originally planned to assign the 36th Division to the French Third Army, but in the fluid situation he assigned the division to the French Fourth Army, at the time headquartered at Chalons and under the command of General Henri Gouraud. The division's stay in the Pocancy area was marked by "uncertainty and uneasiness" because of their proximity to the front. The men could see the "continuous flash of guns on the nightly horizon," blacked out their windows, and listened to the "continual whirring of airplanes." In a letter dated from this period, one member of the 142d Infantry, Private First Class Alton C. Poe, wrote home that "Don't think mamma it will be very long now before I will be fighting," while Sergeant Clark penned a five-page letter on October 2, writing "Have plenty of work to do and expect plenty of fighting soon, before you get this letter. And the sooner the better. Am getting rather anxious to get in and get my feet wet."[44]

On October 4, 1918, General Gouraud, through General Smith, transferred control of General Whitworth's 71st Infantry Brigade, consisting of the 141st and 142d Infantry Regiments as well as the 111th Field Signal Battalion, to the French 21st Army Corps, at the time engaged in combat operations north of the French towns of Suippes and Somme Suippes. Smith chose to deploy the 71st Brigade because it was closer to the front than the 72d and could move more quickly. The brigade received the task of relieving the American 2d Division north of the Suippes area beyond the town of Somme-Py. The Suippes area was approximately fourteen miles to the northeast of Chalons, and Somme-Py was nine miles beyond Suippes. The relief would take place near the town of Saint Etienne-a-Arnes, which was just over five miles north of Somme-Py. Just north of Somme-Py was a small hill named Blanc Mont, a major strong point in the Hindenburg Line. At the beginning of October, the 2d Division had relieved the French 61st Division and taken over the left portion of the line of the French 21st Army Corps. On October 3, the Marine Brigade of the 2d Division attacked German positions on Blanc Mont. In spite of heavy casualties, the 2d Division captured the hill and pushed north toward Saint Etienne. On October 5, Maj. Gen. John Lejeune, the commander of the division, requested relief for his exhausted soldiers and Marines. General Gouraud then released the 36th Division for action, and although it had no combat experience, Whitworth's 71st brigade was ordered into the line. At the time, the brigade consisted of 247 officers and 5,955 men.[45]

Route to the Front.

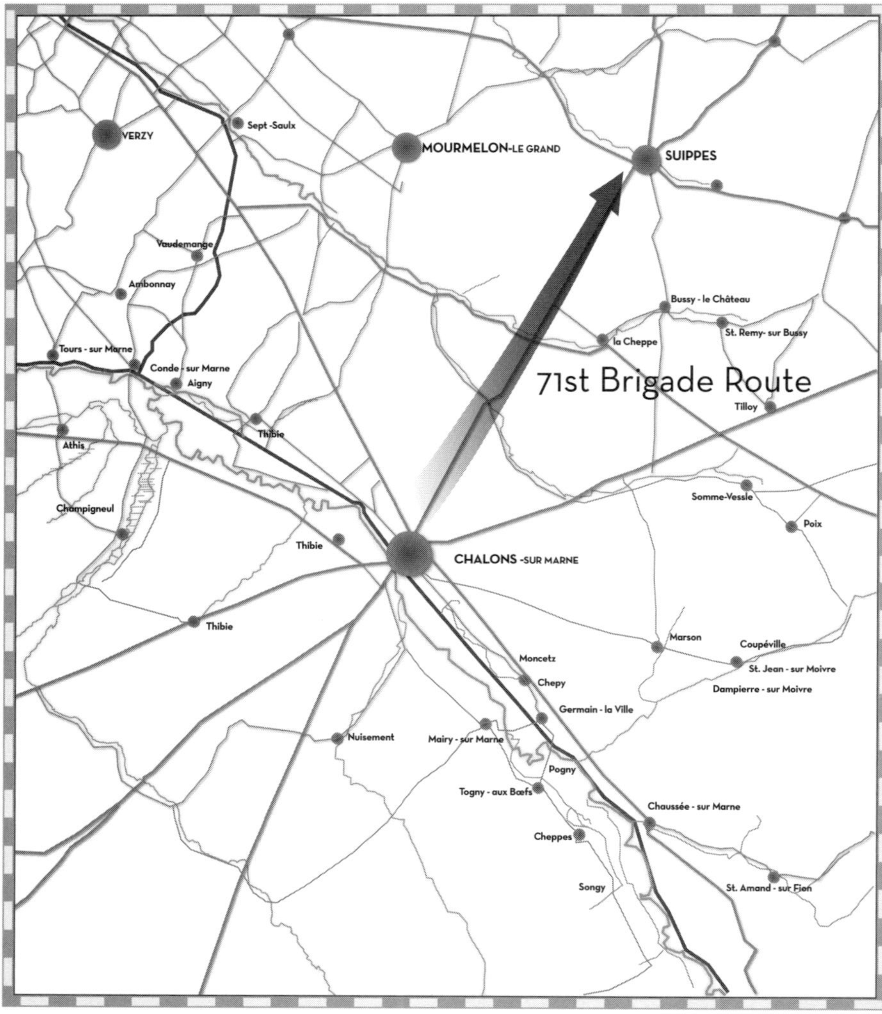

Route of the 71st Brigade toward the front, October 5, 1918, from Group of Armies of the Center Reserve to Somme Suippes.

On October 4, after receiving the orders to send one brigade forward to assist the 2d Division, and after piling their personnel gear in areas to be guarded by the regimental band, the 142d Infantry rode in trucks to Chalons and from there to Suippes. Captain Barton of Company G recalled loading his company after dark and riding with no idea where they were going. As Barton recalled, they "drove all night and at daylight on the morning of the 5th we arrived at Somme-Suippes." From Somme-Suippes they marched about four kilometers south and went into a rest camp of "dugouts, shacks and tents" in the chill, damp weather. The 142d Infantry arrived at Suippes still short of equipment, particularly combat wagons, water carts, and draft animals, and none of its rolling kitchens had arrived. As the regiment moved closer to the front, General Whitworth, his regimental commanders Colonel Jackson of the 141st and Colonel Bloor, as well as Major Preston Weathered of the 132d Machine Gun Battalion, sought situational awareness in an attempt to understand the concept of operations and fit the brigade into the larger scheme of operations. At 8:00 pm on the night of October 5, 1918, General Lejeune called Whitworth, Bloor and Jackson to the 2d Division command post. General Lejeune assumed tactical control of Whitworth's brigade for the relief, making the brigade no longer technically under the control of Smith's 36th Division. Additionally, Lejeune appointed one of his brigade commanders, Brig. Gen. Hanson L. Ely, over the entire front, which eased the pressure on Whitworth so he could focus only on his brigade's sector. Lejeune appeared pleased with Whitworth's brigade but worried that the soldiers were "entirely lacking in combat experience." Lejeune hoped that the brigade would share time with his front line units in order to get accustomed to the front "before being called on for offensive operations." To help the new brigade, the relief orders called for two battalions of the 2d Division to remain at the front along with the 2d's machine gun battalions, 37mm guns, and Stokes mortars, which would remain with the 71st Brigade for twenty-fours. Furthermore, the relief was even more difficult because one brigade prepared to relieve an entire divisional front. Nevertheless, in the course of Whitworth and Lejeune's meeting, the soldiers and Marines discussed the "best avenues of approach" to the front as well as the location of the main supply dump and what equipment the Marines could provide. Based on the maps available, the Marines, Whitworth, and Bloor decided to place the ammunition and supply dump at a point about two kilometers south of the town of Somme-Py, also the planned rendezvous point for the Marine guides to take the 142d Infantry into the line. The meeting lasted until nearly 3:00 am on the morning of October 6. General Whitworth then ordered Bloor and Jackson to have their men ready to march toward the front by 8:00 am.[46]

Later on the morning of October 6, Colonel Bloor started his regiment from Suippes toward the rendezvous point south of Somme-Py. Most of the regiment moved along a trail next to the Somme-Py–Suippes road, and reached the rendezvous point about 3:30 pm. On the way, Captain Barton designated one platoon in each company to fire at enemy airplanes should any appear. According to Barton, this was the first indication "the men had of our close proximity to the firing line," and the clues to the approach to the front became more recognizable

Route to the Front.

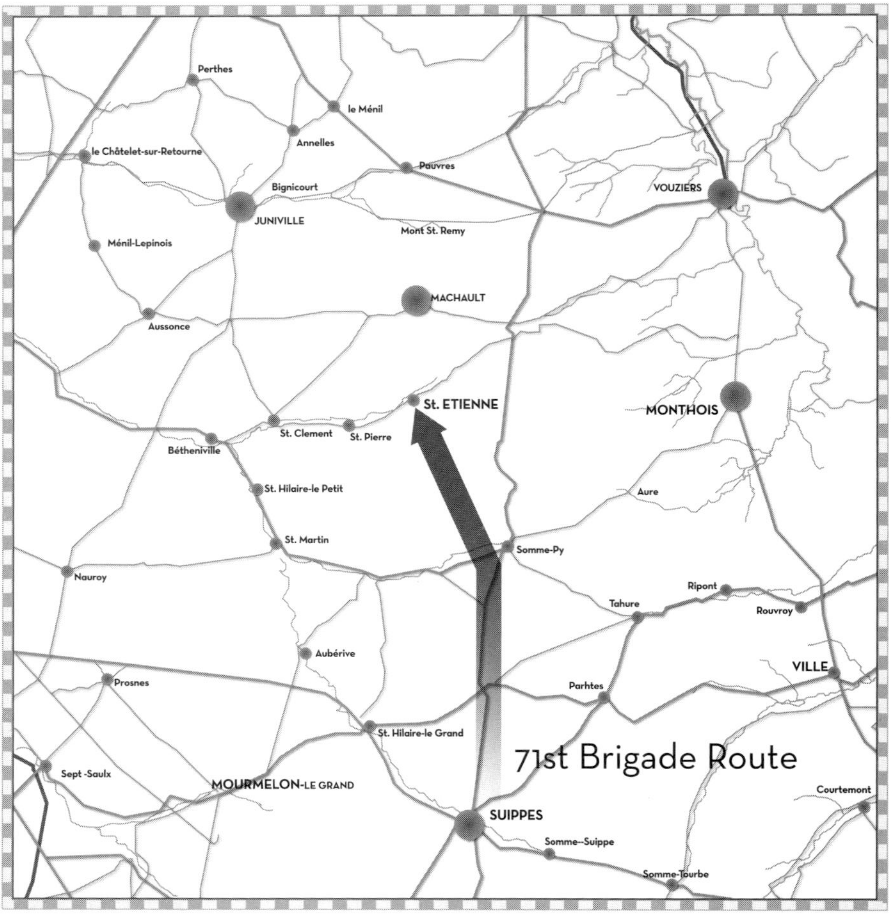

Route of the 71st Brigade toward the front, October 6-7, 1918, From Somme Suippes to Saint Etienne.

as they passed through the old Hindenburg Line and began to see dead Germans and Frenchmen along their route. As the soldiers passed north of Souain ridge, they heard the guns again and saw observation balloons "hanging like huge, solemn sausages midway between heaven and earth." Still, many of the men doubted they were actually approaching the front because Blanc Mont ridge cut off their view of the ground, and the soldiers they could see performed activities "with a lack of excitement verging on monotony." Still, the regiment marched through that surreal world and arrived at Somme-Py without any straggling. Their movements had not passed unnoticed however, as German intelligence summaries that day reported "increasing truck train traffic" along the Suippes–Somme-Py road. When the soldiers arrived at Somme-Py, they discovered that the Marines located the ammunition and supply dump closer to the town than expected, which, according to Colonel Bloor, required "large carrying parties and rendered obtaining of ammunition and supplies more difficult," as groups of soldiers had to gather the material and move it to the rendezvous area. In addition to the 200 rounds of ammunition they already carried, Captain Simpson recalled handing out additional bandoliers of ammunition to his men. He was nervous about being so near the ammunition dump, later writing that if an enemy shell happened to land nearby he knew he would be killed and his body would "explore about one hundred different parts of the surrounding landscape at one and the same time." Even the single water pump at Somme-Py proved dangerous as the Germans shelled the area around it when the supply company attempted to draw water. They managed to collect only half the water the regiment required.[47]

Once Colonel Bloor settled the problem with the supply dump and ordered his soldiers to eat and rest, he received a summons back to the 2d Division Command post, again with General Whitworth. When he arrived at the command post at 4:00 pm, he was given a copy of the just-issued Field Order No. 39, the "relief" order for the 2d Division. The order stipulated that the relief would start that evening and end by 3:00 am the morning of October 7. Now certain that the regiment would be put into the line, Colonel Bloor tried to get maps of the area north of Somme-Py for his battalion and company commanders. Unfortunately, the maps were in sections with nothing to glue them together. The Marine staff worked on new maps, but Bloor did not receive copies until near dark. As he later pointed out, the maps did not have critical information and "most of the company commanders didn't preserve the maps." The division assigned code names. General Whitworth's headquarters became Colorado 24, while Bloor's 142d Regimental Headquarters was Colorado 31.[48]

Even without accurate and reliable maps, Colonel Bloor knew that his regiment would occupy the left side of the front, with the 141st to their right. The Marine guides, he found out, could be met at the Somme-Py church at 5:00 pm on the evening of October 6. Bloor dispatched an officer to meet the guides at the church and returned to his regimental command post. However, as so often happens in war, the simplest plan went awry and the Marine guides, travelling in a truck instead of on foot, drove past the officer waiting for them. Other guides took shelter in a dugout when Somme-Py was hit by an artillery barrage and then mistakenly attached themselves to the 141st Infantry. Not until 8:00 pm did Marine guides arrive at Bloor's command post. The Marines had forgotten what regiment they were to guide into the line. When Bloor discovered these particular Marines occupied the left-hand sector of the front, he surmised that these were his guides and quickly assigned them to each of his three battalions. By 9:00 pm, the regiment completed its supply efforts, dropped off personnel records that had inadvertently been brought forward, and prepared to move. Colonel Bloor ordered the men to leave their blankets behind under guard and the 142d Infantry began its journey to the front, on the final leg of the journey the soldiers of the old 7th Texas started thousands of miles away in North Texas and the Panhandle.[49]

5

THE WESTERN FRONT, OCTOBER 6–13, 1918

As the 142d Infantry marched north out of the French village of Somme-Py, they passed a group of Marines walking south, away from the front. One of those Marines recalled passing "full strong companies of National Guardsmen. They went up one side of the road; and in ragged columns of two's, unsightly even in the dim and fitful light, the Marines plodded down the other side." The Guard companies "gibed" at the Marines as they passed on their way to the front, "singing and joking as they went. High words of courage were on their lips and nervous laughter." The only response came from a few Marines, who said to each other, "Hell, them birds don't know no better … Yeah, we went up singin' too, once—good Lord, how long ago! ... They won't sing when they come out … or any time after … in this war."[1]

As the regiment wended its way toward the front, Colonel Bloor made his way to the command post of the 6th Marine Regiment, the unit being relieved, to meet with its commander, Col. Harry Lee. He arrived about 11:00 pm on the night of October 6. There, the two officers conversed and waited for the relief to occur. At about 1:30 am, Maj. William Culberson, the division inspector, showed up and reported to Colonel Bloor that the Marine guides had gotten lost with at least six companies of the regiment. The guides had taken the road to Medeah Farm instead of the Somme-Py–Saint Etienne road. Culberson worried about the lost companies and suggested that Bloor should personally guide them in. Colonel Bloor refused to do this, not being familiar with the front, particularly at night. Furthermore, Colonel Lee told Bloor that he expected to receive attack orders on the morning of October 7. Thus, Colonel Bloor wanted to study the maps and gather all the information he could about the situation at the front. To help, Colonel Lee provided more guides and Culberson led them to where the lost companies waited. Culberson later received the Distinguished Service Medal for his actions. By 3:00 am, Bloor and Lee received word that the front line battalion of the regiment had completed the relief. Shortly thereafter, Lee and Bloor received the coded message "13 children were in bed," indicating that the "balance of the regiment," except Headquarters Company, had reached their positions. After the armistice, Colonel Bloor found out that while all the companies had managed to get into the lines by dawn, they had not all been in position at 3:30 am as reported. Still, by this point, both colonels realized that orders to attack in the morning were not forthcoming and they would have a short reprieve. Interestingly, based on information from a captured soldier, German intelligence officers also expected an attack on October 7, and even a tank attack on October 8.[2]

As Capt. Thomas Barton recalled, his Marine guides realized they were lost about 2:00 am and halted his company along a road intermittently shelled by the Germans. After talking with some French officers of a nearby artillery unit, the battalion "cut across country" and "after travelling in several different directions came to another road." At this point, Captain Barton recalled that no one knew where to go, but after more "reconnoitering and argument" they halted along another road at 4:30 am. While the Americans were stopped, the enemy shelled the area and Barton's company lost one man killed and two wounded in just a few minutes. Barton moved his men down the road to get away from the shell fire, and recalled that "it was fast approaching daybreak and everyone was nervous and anxious to get somewhere out of sight before daybreak." While waiting, Sgt. Maj. Allen Beville of Clarendon "moved up and down the line, laughing and joking and keeping the men closed up." When shells landed nearby, Beville laughed and told the soldiers near him, "Steady, fellows, that bird did not have our address on it." Again after "considerable argument among the guides, they started forward with my company, one platoon at a time to relieve the Marines...." Barton realized that dawn was breaking and they still had a kilometer to go before reaching their position in the lines, which they did by 5:30 am. If Barton had a difficult and anxious time trying to get to the front, Captain Lillard's Company L, moving to reserve position, also marched all night until "some officer in a Cadillac car found us and finally got us to our destination at daylight." Somehow, Captain Simpson found humor in the situation when his men were marching along a dirt road and a French artillery battery opened up about fifty yards away from the road: "Every one of us thought German shells were after us. In the twinkling of an eye that road was vacant and the ditches at the side were packed closer than any sardines were ever packed into a can."

When they realized what happened, Simpson recalled Lt. John Boyce disgustedly saying, "We are damn fools, that is our own guns." Evidently, the nervousness of the men combined with the echo because of nearby Blanc Mont ridge caused them to fail to distinguish between friendly and enemy artillery fire.[3]

As daylight on October 7 approached, rather than get caught in the open, Bloor's Headquarters Company retraced its steps to Somme-Py to try again after nightfall. Once Bloor realized they had returned to Somme-Py, he decided to bring them in during daylight because rainy and foggy weather prevailed and Bloor believed the poor visibility would allow the company to reach their positions "in comparative safety." Nevertheless, Headquarters Company did not make it to Bloor's command post until "late in the afternoon." After the battle, Bloor considered the delay in the arrival of his Headquarters Company the most "serious injury that was done to the regiment through the inefficiency of the guides," for obvious reasons: Headquarters Company was responsible for locating each company and battalion command post, marking routes to them, and identifying communications wires. Bloor also pointed out that dressing stations could not be located close to command posts either, because of the failure of Headquarters Company to locate all of the command posts before the attack. Also on October 7, Bloor called up the 37mm cannons and the Stokes mortars, which was waiting at Somme-Suippes while the infantry got into position.[4]

Captain Perkins's Supply Company struggled to keep up with the infantry, and arrived at Somme-Py about 3:00 am on the morning of October 7 after marching from Chalons to Somme-Suippes and then on to Somme-Py. At one point, French officers ordered Perkins's men to leave the main road due to "congestion." However, two kilometers north of Somme-Suippes the wagons bogged down in mud and he ordered the supply train to cut back to the main road, this time dismissing the protests of the military police and finally arriving at the regimental area. Once there, Perkins spent October 7 setting up Colonel Bloor's kitchen, which was "established in a hole in the ground until the night of the 11th." They also attempted to get food to each battalion, including corned-beef and tomatoes, the latter serving as a substitute for water. Perkins also managed to secure a number of water-carts, although they found it exceedingly difficult to get water at Somme-Py because of the number of soldiers trying to use the single water pump.[5]

Likewise, Lt. Ed Sayles, in charge of the 37mm cannons and Lt. George O. Thompson, in command of the Stokes mortars, struggled northward on the seventh along with the Supply Company. They watched German "sausage" balloons drifting along the northern horizon. Sayles remained convinced the regiment was heading for a quiet sector and told a member of his platoon, "When we go in, it won't be for anything but a little training." As they marched from Somme-Suippes to Somme-Py, his attitude changed as he saw "flashes of light far ahead" and a steady glow on the horizon, presumably from fires started by artillery shells.[6]

As they moved closer to the front, Sayles saw red, green, and white flares shooting into the sky and in that dim light saw a "skeletal forest of shattered tree trunks, winding rows of chalky earth from deep trenches, piles of rocks, and ghosts of walls." Besides seeing flashes of light, he could now hear the "thunder" of the guns. When they finally reached Somme-Py, Sayles described the little town as a "struggling village of shattered buildings straddling a shallow stream." Village houses were marked by "dirty grey stone, battered walls, gaping doors and windows, [and] splintered timbers." While there, he received a meal consisting of "cold beans on a thick slice of bread and a cup of coffee." When he sat down to eat it, however, he unknowingly rested his back against a dead French soldier, "his face and hands as blue as his clothing."[7]

North of Somme-Py, Sayles's platoon came to an intersection targeted by German artillery. Supply wagons raced across the intersection after each explosion, while others moved forward to await their chance. Things only got worse for Sayles and his men as they plodded northward. Sayles saw his first dead American, then more dead French soldiers, and finally "piles of Germans lying on their backs." The detritus of war surrounded the bodies: broken guns, ammunition belts, machine gun tripods, gas mask canisters, and helmets. Finally, after hours of trudging through torn, muddy ground, Sayles and Thompson arrived at Colonel Bloor's regimental command post, their weapons arriving several hours later.[8]

The soldiers on the line spent October 7 organizing their positions across the four-kilometer front in foggy weather with poor visibility. Desultory shell fire and machine-gun fire continued and enemy aircraft occasionally fired on rear areas. The experience of Captain Barton's Company G serves as an example of what the other line companies experienced as they familiarized themselves with their positions along the front. Barton reported that on arrival, his soldiers found no trenches but rather "little holes which the men had dug for themselves." According to Barton, this "necessitated my men having to dig in under shell and machine gun fire, with the German lines not over a hundred meters distant." One original member of the old 7th Texas, Zach Salmon, was "resting easy" in his fox hole when a shell landed right in front of him and tore his rifle apart. He later wrote that the next day he had to "go over without any gun," although he quickly found one and was "shooting for all I was worth." During the day, some soldiers of the regiment caught their first glimpses of the enemy as they saw German soldiers moving about, quickly crossing from one wood to another, forming occasional skirmish lines, and carrying wounded comrades. Company G held their position throughout the day without any communications or instructions and "without any food or water other than what little water the men still had in their canteens." As afternoon dwindled away, Barton sounded like a veteran, reporting that the Germans "gave us their usual afternoon barrage and I had one man killed." Indeed, according to the regiment's deputy commander, Lt. Col. Irving Phillipson, the shelling on that first day was "the most severe" he experienced while in combat, although division machine-gun officer Hawley wrote that in spite of the shelling, "the morale of the men seemed to be excellent and they displayed none of the greenness supposed to be incident to inexperienced troops." At one point during the day, a group of German soldiers filtered through the confused front lines, although a combined group of Marines and soldiers captured a large number of them.[9]

By the evening of October 7, Colonel Bloor had effected a front line relief under difficult circumstances, with no maps and lost guides. His command post, which was in an old German trench "twenty feet underground and reached by two sets of stairs opening in the trench, and facing to the north," was in full operation. Lieutenant Sayles realized that the Germans most likely knew its location and might shell it. Sayles concluded that a single shell "could be dropped into the trench at the mouth of [the] dugout," effectively sealing it off. Inside, the command post was dim and lit by "flickering candles" that illuminated the "timbered walls, hung with equipment." Wooden bunks, "crowded with regimental officers," were built into the sides of the dugout. Across from the bunks the officers' equipment, helmets, and packs, were piled up. Thick layers of tobacco smoke filled the command post, as did the odors of "tallow … damp woolen clothing, greasy food, and human bodies." Sayles commented that in the candlelight, "faces were only recognizable when they came into the dim light."[10]

Although no attack occurred on October 7, Colonel Bloor was "morally certain" the regiment would attack the next day, October 8, and he wasted no time in continuing preparations. This was a tense time for the commander of an untried regiment, and so far Colonel Bloor had done an exceptional job under the circumstances. When General Lejeune of the 2d Division learned that the 71st Brigade was to attack on October 8, however, he protested to the French 21st Corps commander, Gen. Stanislas Naulin, and asked that the brigade be given several days to acclimate to the front. In ordering the attack, Lejeune declared that Naulin expected "the impossible." Nevertheless, Naulin ordered the attack to proceed and exclaimed, "Tomorrow will be another great day for the 21st Corps!" During the preparations for the upcoming attack, Bloor received a boost with the arrival of a French tank officer to coordinate the use of tanks for the attack. Bloor assigned the tanks to the assault battalion, in particular to Captain Barton, and the French officer reportedly told him that the tanks "should lead the line."[11]

Saint Etienne.

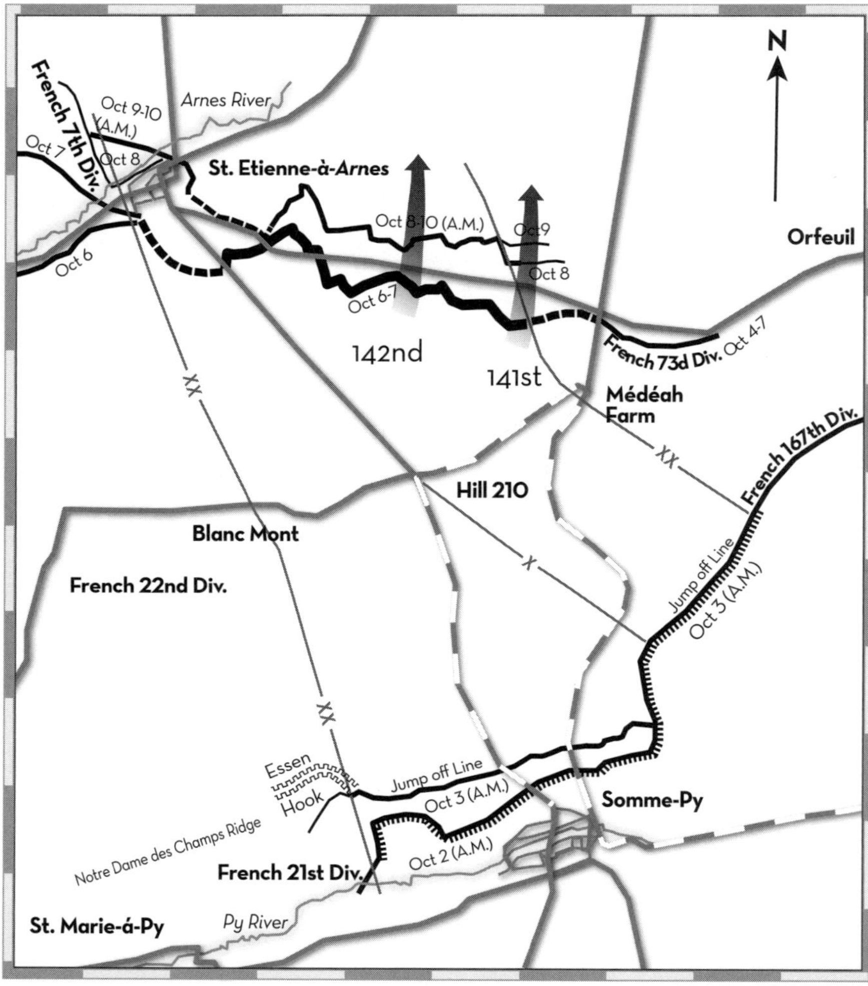

The Battle of Saint Etienne, October 8–10, 1918. The first combat action for the 142d Infantry and the soldiers of the old 7th Texas.

The terrain facing the 142d had been fought over for the last four years. The area in front of the regiment consisted of flat, open ground "covered with old German trenches and wire." Through this area ran the Arnes River and beyond that was a "ravine" in which the Germans had built a number of "fireproof dugouts." Finally, the ground sloped up to a wooded height which was controlled by the enemy. On the west, or left, of the regiment's line, rested the town of Saint Etienne while to the east ran a range of low hills from which German artillery commanded the area. Finally, a slight hill just southeast of Saint Etienne was called Hill 60 on the regiment's maps, although it would later be nicknamed "Barton's Hill." Who controlled the town of Saint Etienne remained unclear, and Colonel Bloor expressed concern that German troops might move into the town during the night and attack his left flank during the advance. If Germans occupied the town and the cemetery just to its east, they would have a wide field of fire from the southwest to the northeast and could easily fire into the left flank of his regiment. He had been told several times that French soldiers possessed the town, and each time the report turned out to be false. Thus, Bloor doubted a report he received on October 7 that claimed the French again occupied Saint Etienne. To ease his mind, he pressed Colonel Lee of the 6th Marines to send two companies into the cemetery east of the town to guard his regiment's flank. Colonel Lee, who had come to Bloor's command post, agreed to the proposal. At the same time, Colonel Bloor received a summons to the brigade command post but waited until the officer in charge of the two Marine companies arrived and received his orders from Colonel Lee. Bloor also asked Colonel Lee to secure copies of the 2d Division attack order for him. According to Lieutenant Sayles, the two colonels conversed at the end of the dimly lit dugout, where an old blanket hung from the ceiling to afford them a little privacy.[12]

With this coordination completed, Bloor proceeded to General Whitworth's brigade command post, leaving his own around 7:00 pm on October 7. It had started to rain and the roads were "congested with ammunition trucks, tanks, ambulances, artillery, [and] ration wagons." Germans also shelled the road so Bloor, in his motorcycle side car, did not reach Whitworth's command post until nearly 8:30 pm.[13]

When Bloor arrived, Whitworth told him, Colonel Jackson of the 141st, and Colonel Weathered of the 132d Machine Gun Battalion, that the division "contemplated" an attack for the morning of October 8. Whitworth had just returned from a meeting with General Smith and he issued verbal instructions and promised that written orders would be issued as soon as he received the divisional order. The colonels received more maps of the Saint Etienne sector, although Bloor was dismayed to find that those maps were also in sections and that it took four to make a complete map of the sector. Colonel Bloor left the brigade command post at nearly 10:00 pm, after leaving a runner to wait for the divisional order, but did not reach his own command post until nearly 1:30 am on the morning of October 8. By this point, Colonel Bloor had been actively engaged for over twenty-four hours. There would be little time for rest over the next several days.[14]

Bloor immediately called his three battalion commanders to his command post. While awaiting their arrival, he received word that Colonel Lee's Marines had entered Saint Etienne and were in the cemetery east of town. Bloor also received five copies of the 2d Division attack order, which stated that "the enemy, in an attempt to protect his withdrawal from the vicinity of Rheims, is resisting the advance of the Franco-American troops north of Somme-Py." The attack would take place at 5:15 am, and the order called for the brigade to advance north toward the town of Machault. Bloor's battalion commanders arrived slowly and the last one did not arrive until almost 4:00 am. Bloor gave each a map of the sector and explained the attack. While Bloor briefed his battalion commanders, other preparations continued, including the establishment of an ammunition dump that held small arms ammunition as well as rifle and hand grenades and flares. However, Colonel Bloor later reported that the assault battalion went into action without receiving any grenades, and Captain Spence recalled that the supply dump was not fully operational until October 9.[15]

After briefing his battalion commanders, Bloor essentially had done all he possibly could to prepare his regiment. Preceded by an artillery barrage from the 2d Division artillery brigade, his regiment, with the 141st on its right, planned to advance two kilometers beyond Saint Etienne. From this point, the success of the attack depended on the will and the abilities of the regiment's front line leaders and the soldiers who crawled from their dugouts and trenches and moved toward the enemy lines. Unfortunately, because of the delays in getting orders, some soldiers did not even realize that they were about to attack.[16]

Captain Barton, assigned to lead the assault battalion, recalled the frantic preparations on the morning of October 8. He received an order to report to the battalion command post at 4:50 am only to find that Maj. William J. Morrisey, the battalion commander, had not yet returned from Colonel Bloor's command post. Morrisey arrived shortly and told Barton and the other three company commanders, Captains Will Pearce, Carter Hannah, and Ethan Simpson, that the attack would occur at 5:15 am. Barton looked at his watch and said to Morrisey, "Major, I cannot make it; it is 5:11 now." As Barton recalled, Morrisey told him to get back to his company as soon as he could. Finally, Morrisey told his company commanders: "I have no maps but you attack in this direction," and waved his hand and said, "leaving St. Etienne on your left." Captain Barton believed these instructions were "rather indefinite," as he had "dodged" shells and machine gun fire to and from the battalion command post, and it became "rather hard to tell what 'this direction' was." Captain Barton was not even sure of the location of Saint Etienne, writing later "there was nothing ahead of me that I could see except a woods."[17]

Captain Simpson's Company H waited next to Barton's company in the line. As the night of October 7 dwindled away, Simpson managed to scrounge some coffee and beans from a Marine officer, which he shared with his first sergeant Aubyn Clark "while the shells screamed overhead to explode 200 yards in the rear" and "machine gun bullets would thud into the earth a few feet in front of us." It was about 1:00 a.m. About every half hour, a "star shell would flare up to illuminate the earth as if every object was in the glare of a calcium light." Simpson and Clark spent a few minutes discussing their homes, their loved ones, and "what we might do in case we were spared in the battle coming the next day." Also during the night, one of Simpson's sergeants, Star Johnson, an original member of the regiment, was blown out of his fox hole by an artillery blast and "badly shell shocked." Simpson had Johnson join him in his fox hole the rest of the night so he could keep an eye on him. Simpson also sent out several patrols and, with a Marine, ventured toward the German lines. On that patrol, the two men spotted two Germans and the Marine fired a shotgun at them before he and Simpson hustled back to their own lines. After this, Simpson received his summons to battalion headquarters like Barton to gather what details he could about the impending attack.[18]

What little information the Americans possessed revealed that the enemy lines extended about two miles along a road between Saint Etienne and Orfeuil to the east. The Americans were south of the road, with the 142d on the left and the 141st on the right. On the left, in Colonel Bloor's sector, enemy machine-gun nests and snipers were as close as one hundred yards. This area was generally open, with small clumps of trees and brush, which concealed German machine-gun positions arranged to support each other when attacked. The Germans had strung belts of barbed wire through the woods and across open areas. To the left of the 142d Infantry was a battalion of 2d Division Marines as well as the French 7th Division, while the French 73rd Division occupied the line to the right of the 141st. Between the 141st and 142d Infantry, where there was a noticeable gap, an original member of the regiment, Lt. Young Yates, commanded a platoon and several machine guns. He assumed responsibility for maintaining liaison with the 141st, whose positions were nearly six hundred yards to the rear of the 142d. Without protection, this gap would allow the Germans to enfilade the 142d Infantry as they waited to attack.[19]

The German 195th, 213th, and 17th Divisions faced the Americans and French to the north of the Saint Etienne–Orfeuil road. While the Army considered the 17th "one of the best" German units, all three had been weakened by combat and division intelligence estimated that approximately 5,000 Germans occupied the area opposite Whitworth's 71st Brigade. As the regiment found out, the Germans still had good morale and plenty of ammunition and artillery. The Germans also expected an attack in that area, having observed many of the previous day's preparations and marked the arrival of French tanks in the area. Indeed, it did not take long for the German intelligence service to find out that a new division had entered the line. Later, captured German officers expressed surprise that an untested unit had been put into the line across from what they considered well-constructed and well-defended positions.[20]

In the 142d Infantry, Maj. William Morrisey's 2d Battalion led the assault. It included companies E, F, G, and H. Company G was commanded by Capt. Thomas Barton and Company H by Capt. Ethan Simpson. They were designated as the assault companies, to be followed by Companies E and F, under Oklahoman captains Pearce and Hannah. Going over the top with Captain Barton that morning were other former 7th Texas officers Lieutenants Sam Owens, Gordon Porter, and Robert Armstrong. With Captain Simpson were Lieutenants Stayton Hankins and William Murphy, both of Hardeman County, and Joe Kell of Wichita County. In addition, the attack order assigned two companies of the 132d Machine Gun Battalion to the assault battalion, and two to the following battalion.[21]

Captain Charles T. Kuhlman of Waco commanded the 1st Battalion, next in line to follow the 2d Battalion. First Battalion consisted of companies A, B, C, and D, companies made up primarily with members of the old 1st Oklahoma. Captain Earl Litteer commanded Company A, and Company B now included Lieutenants Daniel S. Blue and Nat Perrine, all three former 7th Texas officers. Finally, the 3rd Battalion, commanded by Captain A. M. Greer of Beaumont, included companies I, K, L, and M, and served as the third line in the assault. Company I was commanded by Lt. Rudolph E. Fried because Captain Wagstaff had not returned from the AEF School of the Line. Captain Sneed Staniforth commanded Company K, which included Lt. Andrew Y. Beverly of Foard County, who had enlisted in the old 7th Texas, but earned a commission and was back with the regiment. Captain Steve Lillard of Wise County led Company L of the 3rd Battalion. Wichita County's Lt. Alfred H. Carrigan served as his second in command.[22]

By the time Captain Barton returned to his company command post, it was 5:25 am, ten minutes past the scheduled attack time. Approximately 100 meters in front of his position was "the edge of thick pine woods, which we knew from our own observation and what the Marines had told us, was full of machine guns." Barton pointed out the edge of the woods to his mortar officer and "asked him to use his trench mortars freely." The officer, probably Lt. George Thompson, replied that he had only nine shells, and Barton told him, "Use them, as we will never need them worse." In consultation with two lieutenants from the Machine Gun Battalion, he pointed out where he believed "the enemy machine guns were located" and asked one of them, "to give them all he had." Barton then directed all of his Browning automatic riflemen and infantry to converge on that point. Finally, he called on another officer of the old 7th Texas, Lt. Gordon R. Porter, and placed him in charge of the platoon nearest the German position in the woods. He told Porter the instant "the enemy fire slackened to rush his platoon." While making these final arrangements, the "rolling" artillery barrage started, meaning that every minute the barrage would shift 100 yards farther north. As the artillery began, the sky lit up with "flashes from exploding projectiles," and with smoke and dust. These rolling barrages were meant to provide protection to advancing troops, who would stay a certain distance behind the barrage and advance behind it. However, after the battle, the soldiers realized that the barrage overshot the most forward German defenders and failed to help the attacking troops. Major Morrisey may have had misgivings about the number of enemy they were facing, later writing that in the early morning darkness, "flashes of machine guns were visible all along the enemy front, showing that he had many more guns that we had suspected."[23]

As soon as Captain Barton noticed a slight reduction in the enemy's fire, and believing this was his "golden opportunity," he jumped up and ran forward into what one member of the regiment described as air filled with "whizzing, whistling, screaming, bursting instruments of death." Captain Emil Horner of Company E recalled that his men dashed forward "in short rushes," and to Horner it seemed "there was not a square foot of air space through which bullets were not flying." In spite of the fire, Barton wrote that "every man went forward with a single bound and before the Germans had time to realize what we were doing we were on top of them." Across the line, the assault battalion moved, followed by the second battalion 800 yards behind. In the woods to his front, Captain Barton and his men discovered four dugouts. Barton saw Lieutenant Porter clearing out the first one with his platoon, so Barton and the rest of the company pressed forward and captured the other three dugouts, which netted between fifty and sixty German prisoners. Out of seven officers in the company, three were wounded in that first opening struggle, including Porter.[24]

Porter, who had been told by Barton to rush the woods when the enemy fire slackened, had moved from "hole to hole" until he was on the left of the line, where they received machine-gun fire from the right front. The fire struck two men in the head near where he lay. When Barton's machine guns opened up on the woods in front, which Porter estimated were sixty yards away, he advanced toward them with "a number of men from my company." After securing the first enemy dugout, Porter advanced with Barton and the rest of the soldiers, but he saw a German machine gun position on his right and wrote that "evidently he didn't see me so I walked right on the two of them." The two Germans surrendered to Porter, who later recalled: "I turned the gun around and I could see Germans in advance and I operated the enemy machine gun on those people." This occurred while Captain Barton was still gathering prisoners from the dugouts in the woods. While he was using the machine gun, more soldiers came up to his position and pointed out another machine gun to Porter's right front. Porter left the machine gun and ran to another strip of woods, where he took three more prisoners before being wounded. In Porter's estimation, his wounding occurred thirty to forty-five minutes after going "over the top." Another member of the old 7th Texas was not so lucky. Private Lloyd W. McGowan, who had moved out as part of an advanced sniper party, was shot and killed by an enemy sniper himself. McGowan had joined the company back in Amarillo in the summer of 1917.[25]

While Porter was wounded and McGowan killed, Captain Barton continued forward, capturing an estimated 150 additional prisoners beyond the woods, which the Germans started to shell with gas. Continuing forward, Barton realized that he had soldiers from every company mixed in with the assault battalion but saw no other officers. He moved toward the left, looking for Captain Simpson. Instead, he found Lt. John T. Fulcher of Granger, Texas, who commanded the "remnant of H Company." From Lieutenant Fulcher, he learned that Captain Simpson and Lieutenants Murphy and Hankins had all been wounded. Before long, Barton received word that Capt. Willis Pearce of Company F had been wounded, and Capt. Carter Hannah of E Company had been killed. This left Barton as the only remaining company commander in the battalion. Since the five messengers sent by Barton to contact the battalion command post were either killed or wounded and unable to communicate with Major Morrisey, Barton took command "of the entire firing line" and operated it like one large company, having the men dig in along the St. Etienne–Semide road.[26]

Captain Simpson's Company H had gone over the top next to Barton's company that morning. Simpson however, was quickly wounded, shot in the left side and the left hip by what he believed to be a German soldier operating a machine gun "from a platform located in a tree." After being hit, however, Simpson managed to shoot and kill the German machine-gunner. Along with Simpson, both of his lieutenants from Quanah, Stayton Hankins and William Murphy, were also wounded. Simpson recalled that an American soldier ordered a group of Germans to carry him to the rear. When one of them refused to work because he claimed to be an officer, an American soldier asked the German, "You devil, do you refuse to carry the captain?" When the German repeated that he would not work, the man shot the German prisoner in the head. In his letter, Simpson claimed not to remember the soldier's name or what company the man belonged to. Nevertheless, the assault continued and one original member of the old 7th Texas, Cpl. Samuel Sampler, advanced under severe machine-gun fire. He spotted a German machine gun position, and armed with captured German hand grenades rushed forward on his own and threw three grenades at the machine gun. The third one found its mark. It killed two German soldiers and caused twenty-eight Germans to surrender to Corporal Sampler.[27]

Besides many wounded officers and soldiers, Captain Simpson's Company H lost a number of original members of the 7th Texas, including 1st Sgt. Aubyn Clark of Clarendon, whom Simpson had shared his meal with on the night before the assault. Clark went over the top and advanced about seventy-five yards before being "struck in the breast by at least two machine gun bullets" and died "almost instantly." When Simpson heard of his death, he wrote "I have lost the truest, best friend I ever had. He cannot be replaced." Sergeant Bergen Waldrop was wounded on the morning of the assault and told to go to the rear; he refused and shortly after was "struck by a large shell and killed instantly." Likewise, Sam Price was killed "almost instantly" by a machine gun bullet, while Pvt. Alton C. Poe tried to advance across an open space within range of a machine gun. Sergeant Joe Wilson saw Poe try to take cover, but Poe was struck in the head and neck and killed. Corporal Roy Warren of Quanah took cover behind a tree but was shot in the shoulder. When he tried to move he was hit by a machine gun bullet and died a few minutes later. Private James Russell lay in a shallow hole when he was hit by a piece of shrapnel in the right temple. He "murmured something" his comrades could not understand and died. Thomas Bland of Quanah was killed, as was James Blanks of Clarendon, who also refused to go to the rear when wounded and was killed shortly thereafter by machine gun fire. Corporal Charles Heneise, from Clarendon, hit by machine gun fire, tried to get up, but was struck again and killed. Private Floyd Alvey, also of Clarendon, was hit "directly by a shell about the left knee," and lived for just a few more minutes while Pvt. Thomas B. Blevins stayed with him.[28]

In the assault, Company K lost Sgt. Robert E. Moss, hit in the head by a piece of a shell near Blanc Mont. Finally, Cpl. Amos Childress lost his life when targeted by an enemy sniper, who shot him once in the left side and then in the head. Company M also lost several original members of the company early in the fighting. Corporal Roy C. King raised his head to fire at the enemy and was struck by a bullet "over the right eye." Company M's Sergeant Arthur O. McNitzky went to the front, although as the mess sergeant he was told that "he had no business up here" and to go back. McNitzky refused, saying "I've come too far to go back, and besides it's open season and don't cost anything to kill 'em. I'm going to have my share." McNitzky advanced with the company and sought shelter at the edge of a hole, where a witness recalled that he worked "his rifle at his utmost and had fired about fifteen shots when a bullet struck him in the forehead, killing him instantly." Sergeant Ollie Calvert and Cpl. Warren T. Sweeney of Denton County were charged with escorting German prisoners to the rear when they were caught in an artillery barrage and took cover in a roadside ditch. According to Sweeney, a piece of shell the "size of a man's thumb," struck Calvert in the chest, killing him. After the barrage ended, Sweeney continued escorting the prisoners to the rear and had to leave Calvert's body in the ditch. Fancher Reagan, who had been the first man to join Captain McGrath's Tarrant County company in the summer of 1917, was killed by machine-gun fire on the crest of Hill 60 southeast of Saint Etienne. Finally, mechanic Freddie Butler, of Denton, along with Lt. Oscar Baker and another man, sought cover from machine gun fire. Lying behind a small ridge, Baker told the two men to "lie low as the Germans had found us." The other man, Tom Collier, yelled at Butler to lie down just as Butler received a "volley of machine gun bullets through his legs, and as he pitched forward, his body was riddled."[29]

Another soldier who found himself at the front was Bryan Autry of Denton, a member of the battalion intelligence section who did not have to join the assault. He volunteered as a runner and delivered a message to one of the companies just before the attackers went over the top. When he arrived at the front, he heard the captain of the company urging his men forward. Deciding to join the action, Autry advanced with the company and saw several of his friends "shot down by my side." He stayed in the lines until October 10, when what he described as a "lucky hit was all that saved me from being blown into bits of nothing." Another member of the 142d Infantry, and a veteran of the old 7th Texas, Cpl. Harold Turner of Seminole, Oklahoma, led a group of scouts, runners, and Signal Corps soldiers. Enemy fire eventually whittled their number down to four men, and they took shelter about twenty-five yards from a German machine-gun emplacement. When the machine gun shifted its fire, Turner leaped up, vaulted a belt of barbed wire in his path, and charged the position alone. He was later credited with capturing fifty Germans and four machine guns.[30]

In spite of a steady machine gun fire from the left and right, as well as a "constant barrage" of artillery, Barton pushed his men forward to the road which ran east-west through Saint Etienne. Here, he halted them and had the soldiers dig in. About three hundred meters ahead of Barton's position was a line of trenches, which he sent men to scout. The trenches were deserted, but they found more American soldiers who were part of Capt. Steve Lillard's company of the 3rd Battalion.[31]

According to Captain Lillard, his battalion went over the top at 5:35 am. Like Captain Barton, he had been shown a map, had the regimental order read to him, told to keep Saint Etienne on his left, and then improvised. During the advance, Lillard noticed that the first two battalions had drifted to the right, while his own 3rd Battalion drifted left. This put his battalion on a course toward Saint Etienne, no longer under the Marines' control. The battalion suffered from a machine gun being operated either in the town's church steeple or on the roof of a nearby house. Lillard's men were also delayed by machine gun fire and wire entanglements until Lillard sent sergeants Kelly Nail and Chester Roberts with a platoon of soldiers to silence machine guns on the left, an action that resulted in the capture of 17 German machine guns and 112 German soldiers. Nail, who escaped unscathed, later counted twenty-five bullet holes in his uniform and two in his helmet, although he would later suffer from gas inhalation. A group of soldiers not recognizable to Lillard silenced the machine guns on the right. As Lillard's company moved forward, the old 7th Texas lost one of its officers. Lieutenant Alfred Carrigan of Wichita Falls stopped at the wire entanglements to "pull one of his men, who had been hit, from the wire." Carrigan had trouble extricating the wounded soldier and called for help. Immediately afterward he was shot in the neck and killed. James McFadden, a member of the Cleburne company, got caught in the wire and was struck by machine gun fire that riddled his body. Corporal Monte Dunaway of Decatur made it through the wire entanglements only to be cut down by enemy fire. Despite those casualties, Captain Lillard's Company L and parts of Company I pressed the attack and rounded up over two hundred prisoners. Lillard moved his soldiers forward into the graveyard on the edge of Saint Etienne, which the Marines had supposedly secured. In the cemetery, Cpl. Lloyd Smith from Decatur, already wounded and told by Lillard to go to the rear, refused and was hit in the head by shrapnel and killed instantly. Another Cleburne resident, Pvt. Orla Shirer, was killed near the graveyard while trying to deliver messages.[32]

By this point, Lillard noticed that his soldiers advanced in little groups, without cooperation, and in the words of another officer, the "number of men who had penetrated as far as the town was amazingly small." Lillard stopped the men and "established a line along the road." He knew they had advanced beyond the other battalions but wrote after the fact that stopping the soldiers "was only done in order to reorganize the men, with a view of withdrawing them to a position in our rear which could be maintained; or if the troops on our right came up we could advance with them." At that point, Captain Barton's soldiers linked up with Lillard's group, and Barton, as the senior officer, took command.[33]

Both officers knew they sat in an exposed position as the 141st on their right had not kept pace with the advance. Barton sent one officer to try to locate their sister regiment and another man to find Major Morrisey and then to report their position and status to Colonel Bloor. He told the man to ask Bloor if a battalion could be "thrown on our right and to make arrangements to get us ammunition as quickly as possible." While in their advanced position, Barton and Lillard's men were subjected to at least six artillery barrages and received enemy fire from the right rear. Both Barton and Lillard received slight wounds and were given first aid in a dugout, where they also conferred about the best course of action, all the while hoping that the 141st Infantry would advance along the right and come even with them. While they talked, the Germans counterattacked to get around the exposed right flank, killing Lee Finley of Decatur. According to Barton, they had two choices: stay where they were and probably be captured; or fall back to the edge of the woods and Hill 60 where, he wrote, "we knew there were an abundance of German machine guns and plenty of German ammunition."[34]

The two officers chose the second option and withdrew their men about 200 yards, where they discovered 3rd Battalion commander Captain Greer with men from Captain Staniforth's Company K. After pulling back farther, the soldiers under Greer, Barton, and Lillard dug in on top of Hill 60 and waited for night. Wanting additional support in case of a German counterattack, Captain Barton coaxed a company of Marines forward while Captain Whitney and the Machine Gun Company arrived. As Barton later wrote, "This made the world look brighter."[35]

The area where Barton and Lillard holed up for the night earned the nickname "Barton's Hill" by members of the regiment. At this point, Barton estimated that losses in the 2d Battalion from the day's attack were close to 60 percent and little could be done about that now. Lieutenant Sayles also tried to maneuver one of his 37mm cannon to Barton's men. On the way, he passed Lieutenant Carrigan's body, which lay in "an opening of barbed wire near the road." Because of the number of dead officers he had seen, Sayles took everything that identified him as an officer off his uniform. While those soldiers consolidated their position, others had lost contact with their companies from the very beginning and fought almost alone during the day. One of those men was Corporal Hart of Company K, who had started on the far left of the regimental sector and had become separated from his unit. Realizing he was on his own, he decided to become a sniper and took a shot at a German soldier about 400 yards away. While the man dropped to the ground, Hart had no idea if he had hit him or not.[36]

While the battle continued, Colonel Bloor tried to keep up with the fighting and to maintain situational awareness. Although the attack was well under way by 7:30 am on October 8, it took that long to get a message to Bloor that the attack had even started. As the day progressed, messages took longer to get to him. Nevertheless, in difficult and trying circumstances, Bloor found ways to keep himself apprised of the action and, he hoped, influence it. For example, he established an "advance information center," under Lt. Temple Black near where the 2d Battalion command post had started the morning. Runners, instead of having to make it all the way to the regimental command post, could stop at the information center, where messages could be relayed by telephone. Unfortunately, the information center was exposed and within six hours only three of its fifteen men had not been wounded. At Colonel Bloor's request, General Lejeune provided two companies of the 2d Engineers as support troops to shore up Bloor's regiment. On the night of October 8, Colonel Bloor placed them at the extreme left of the regimental sector.[37]

The constant rattle of machine guns filled the evening air of October 8 for the men on Barton's Hill, who also feared a major German attack in the morning. The night sky was constantly lit by German flares, and the cries of wounded men were occasionally heard. Lieutenant Sayles recalled that "all during the night, runners and signal platoon men, stringing wires, were passing so close to our holes as to cause the dirt to slide down our collars." While this went on, Captain Perkins's Supply Company continued to try to get food and water to the soldiers. Captain Perkins found three wine casks between Somme-Py and Saint Etienne and filled them with water. One, however, still contained red wine, which Captain Perkins reported "the boys" drank first when they got it to the front. However, Colonel Bloor would not allow the Supply Company to take rations to the front lines, so Perkins established ration dumps at each battalion command post, and then guides were sent to each company to lead them to the food. The danger of going to the ration dumps was apparent the next day when Cpl. Roland Polk of Quanah was "struck by a shrapnel and instantly killed" while returning from the ration dump. Those who made it back with their rations drank tomato juice and had a loaf of soggy bread. One man had a can of corned beef, which had been previously opened, and "though it had some dirt in it, it went fine."[38]

The men became increasingly nervous as dawn on October 9 arrived, but apart from some scattered automatic rifle fire and a few artillery shells, no enemy counterattack materialized that frost-covered morning. The brigade spent most of the day trying to reconsolidate and reorganize after the previous day's fighting. The entire line was badly disorganized and each unit attempted to sketch its position in an effort to make some sense of the location of the front lines. However, in looking at the sketches as they came in, the regimental intelligence officer, Captain P. E. Barth, realized that "no one in the line knew where they were." For the men on Barton's Hill, the day passed with nothing "of special interest" except for a "terrific barrage later in the afternoon." Perhaps this was the barrage that killed Pvt. Andrew Floyd, another Amarillo soldier. This barrage might also have been the one that killed Pvt. Sam J. Ford of Crowell, and Pvt. Thomas L. Minor of Company K, hit by shrapnel in the arm and the body while working on a new defensive position. Evacuated to the rear, he died on October 11. This same barrage also cost the life of Pvt. Willis Goodger of Denton, who shared a hole with two others. Several shells landed close enough to shower the men with dirt, and after a particularly close call, one of the men said, "How do you like that one, Goodger?" Goodger did not reply and after looking at their comrade he found that a piece of shrapnel had "torn a hole through his head."[39]

While the soldiers on Barton's Hill waited the day out in anticipation of German attacks, Colonel Bloor received an order to advance his regiment, as General Whitworth believed that the 141st Infantry had advanced beyond the 142d, a severe miscalculation. Nevertheless, Bloor sent Captain Greer's 3rd Battalion forward from the slope of Blanc Mont, as well as a 37mm cannon from Lieutenant Sayles's platoon and several mortars. Bloor stayed in contact with the attacking forces by telephone. The attack, however, bogged down rapidly after an advance of just 200 yards. Lieutenant Sayles of the 37mm platoon watched the assault. As he later wrote, "a line of men was crossing the flat before us. The shells were falling amongst them. Some of the men were running and dropping into shell holes. We could see them throw the dirt out and hug the bottoms of the holes." When he had the chance, Sayles peered out of his own hole and watched a number of soldiers of the regiment "in shallow 'fox holes', huddled on their knees, their faces held close to the ground." Sayles proved a quick study on distinguishing nearby artillery shells from those that landed father away. He noticed that "a cloud of dust and smoke would follow a burst of dirt where the projectile struck." If he heard the explosion of the shell "just as the dirt spurted up, it was close enough to make it safer to duck the piece of shell that zinged through the trees and fell into our fox holes as hot as a coal fire." On the other hand, if the spurt of dirt was followed by the smoke before he heard the explosion, "then the shell fell too far away to bother."[40]

After Greer's battalion dug in, patrols went forward and confirmed that the 141st was not in front of the 142d. Additionally, Captain Barton received a map that showed the 141st ahead of the 142d, which he knew to be incorrect. Nevertheless, later that night the 142d received orders to relieve the Marines and engineers who had advanced to a line in front of Saint Etienne, although they did not complete the relief until nearly 1:00 am on October 10, after the men slipped single file into Saint Etienne. Greer's men who had dug in when their attack failed that morning were withdrawn in the evening by Colonel Bloor, although most of those men had already filtered back to Barton's Hill on their own. Indeed, two platoon leaders who went to the battalion headquarters to gather information returned to their positions to find that most of their men had "melted away." However, Capt. Steve Lillard discovered a group of soldiers from Company I and Company M under Lt. Rudolph Fried about 150 meters to the right front of Barton's men on Hill 60. They remained in those positions for the rest of the night and then made their way back to Hill 60.[41]

During the night of October 9–10, the 71st Brigade received intelligence that the enemy had withdrawn during the night. To verify this, General Whitworth ordered Colonel Bloor to advance "to gain contact." The morning of October 10 was again cold, with frost covering the living and the dead, as Lieutenant Sayles remembered. The commander of the 144th Infantry Regiment had moved into Colonel Bloor's command post earlier in the evening, and Colonel Bloor made a trip to the front lines that morning. However, the attack for that morning was called off when General Whitworth went to General Lejeune's command post and argued that the brigade was "badly disorganized and thoroughly exhausted." That changed little along the front as artillery fire and sniping continued and patrols went out to maintain contact with the enemy and to keep in contact with French troops on the flanks. At one point that day, Captain Lillard was described as ambling "along as unconcernedly as though he were strolling on the campus of Decatur Baptist College." Although Lillard "bore a charm on his life that day," the Germans unleashed a withering barrage of high explosives and gas shells that prevented the brigade from continuing to advance, although an expected German counterattack never materialized. The barrage, however, swept away another member of the old 7th Texas. Several men from Company M, including William Q. Curtis of Fort Worth, went to regimental headquarters to fill a number of canteens. On their way back, they came under shell fire and ran about 200 yards to regain the shelter of their hole "before the bombardment became too heavy." Corporal Andrew Leonard recalled that as they climbed into their hole, "a one-pounder shell exploded about fifteen feet to our right and a piece struck Private Curtis at the intersection of his neck and shoulders which killed him instantly." The artillery barrage created a "rather tense situation," and in order to ease the pressure on his men, Captain Barton tried to get an artillery barrage to silence the German guns. Barton sent Lt. George O. Thompson back to Colonel Bloor's command post to point out on a map where they wanted the barrage. This again exposed problems with brigade headquarters about the presumed location of the 141st. It would not be until later that day that higher headquarters agreed on the true position of the 141st, even after three officers of the 142d Infantry made a 3:00 am circuit of the lines to verify the position of the regiment, for which they were recommended for the Distinguished Service Cross. Eventually, Colonel Bloor ordered the barrage on his own responsibility, knowing full well that no American troops occupied the area. In order to sketch a more accurate map of the regiment's positions, two soldiers, Cpl. Roy D. Blair of Barton's G Company and Pvt. Levi N. Cox of Simpson's Company H, crossed "a heavily shelled area and penetrated through the village of Saint Etienne," which was also being shelled with chemicals. Cox was an original member of the Donley County company and Blair was an original member of the Gainesville Machine Gun Company. Later, the 141st Infantry finally confirmed their position was incorrect on the map; according to Barton, "instead of being a mile ahead of us they were one mile behind us."[42]

After the attack on October 10 was called off by General Whitworth, Colonel Bloor received orders to continue reorganizing his regiment. Later that afternoon, the 71st Brigade was released from control of the 2d Division and returned to General Smith's command. General Smith planned to put the 72d Brigade into the line next to the 71st Brigade, but after being briefed by General Whitworth on the condition of his brigade, changed his mind. By 5:00 that evening, General Smith issued the order relieving the 71st Brigade from the line. The soldiers of the 141st and 142d held in place while General Hulen's 72d Brigade moved up and took over their positions. At the same time, news arrived that the French divisions on both sides of the 36th Division were advancing. This caused confusion as the 71st Brigade was suddenly ordered to move forward and maintain contact with French troops on the flanks and with German forces in the front. Nevertheless, the new regiments accomplished another difficult relief, and the 144th took over the front of the 142d. With the relief complete, Captain Barton wrote that he "stood in our trenches and watched them cross this shell pitted flat and go up the hill beyond the creek for two miles before there was a shot fired." During the relief operations alone, the 71st and 72d brigades lost 18 men killed and 178 men wounded. In the 142d, two men lost their lives and fifty-four were wounded.[43]

While the 72d Brigade took over the front line positions, the Germans fell back from their positions in a general retreat to the Aisne River, less than twenty miles to the north. The 72d Brigade received responsibility for maintaining contact with the retreating Germans while the 71st Brigade remained in place to be "reorganized in depth in their present positions … and prepare to advance and support the 72d Infantry Brigade." While the 72d pushed forward, Colonel Bloor moved his regimental command post closer to Saint Etienne to manage the reorganization and resupply of his regiment. The men were intermingled and the remaining officers went from group to group trying to get men in their proper organizations, all the while exposed to the danger of long-range harassing fire from German artillery. Nevertheless, Colonel Bloor took advantage of the respite and allowed his soldiers to rest until the morning of October 12, although he expressed concern that Saint Etienne was "heavily laden with mustard gas" and ordered all troops to stay east of the town and "under no circumstances" to enter the village. However, the regimental gas officer found the town safe and soldiers received permission to move into it. Lieutenant Sayles arrived in the town to find dozens of soldiers using the town's well to shave and wash up. Other men lined up at a French wine cart filled with water, even though it "tasted strongly of the sour wine that had once filled the wooden keg." As the soldiers filtered through the town, many were pleased to see friends who had made it through the fight, but they soon quieted down. Some of the soldiers "were smoking, sitting on the ground; others stood in the sunshine, waiting, silent." As Lieutenant Sayles recalled, "I had come into the line with twenty men; two had been killed and three wounded. We were only three days in. And now were merely catching our breath before we should move forward again." That evening, fourteen rolling kitchens and five water carts arrived. As if to signal the end of the fighting, the town received a final burst of ten enemy shells. And then, as rapidly as it had started, the first combat action of the 142d Infantry Regiment ended. The soldiers who had joined more than a year earlier from North and Northwest Texas came face to face with combat and seen the death and destruction wrought by modern weapons. They had lost some of their friends and comrades, but more would be lost before the war ended.[44]

With the fighting over, it was time to count the cost. The assault battalion of companies E, F, G, and H lost seventy-three men killed, including nineteen men from Barton's company and twenty men from Captain Simpson's Company H. In the 3rd Battalion, Captain Wagstaff's Company I lost eleven men, Captain Staniforth's Company K lost eight, Captain Lillard's Company L lost sixteen men killed, and Company M lost nine soldiers. The 1st Battalion, comprised of members mainly from the old 1st Oklahoma Infantry, lost forty men in the fighting around Saint Etienne. The medical detachment, Headquarters Company, and Machine Gun Company lost a total of nine additional soldiers killed. In total, the 142d Infantry lost 8 officers and 111 men killed and 20 officers and 358 men wounded on October 8. As for those wounded in the fighting after that, Colonel Bloor later reported that the regiment, which went into action with 58 officers and 1,715 men, suffered 26 officers and 540 men wounded, 32 percent of the regiment. The 71st Brigade as a whole reported more than 1,600 casualties in the three days fighting around Saint Etienne, with 1,300 on October 8 alone. Although Brig. Gen. Henry Hutchings had been relieved of duty prior to the fighting, he still maintained a connection with the brigade. His son, Maj. Edwin Hutchings of the 141st, accompanied the assault battalion in that regiment and lost his life after advancing three hundred yards. Two of Captain Barton's fellow company commanders in the assault battalion of the 142nd, Captains Carter C. Hannah and Capt. Willis E. Pearce, both died, one in the fighting and the other from wounds he received. Both Ethan Simpson and Sneed Staniforth had been wounded. Indeed, Captain Staniforth's wounds led his friend Captain Perkins to write home that his survival was "doubtful," although he did survive. Lieutenant Daniel S. Blue received a wound in the arm during the fighting. However, of the original officers of the 7th Texas, only Lt. Alfred Carrigan had been killed. Two officers of the old 7th Texas, Thomas Barton and Steve Lillard, displayed courage and initiative and proved themselves to be strong leaders. Within several weeks, both Barton and Lillard would serve as battalion commanders and one would lead the 142d Infantry's final assault of World War I.[45]

With the pause in fighting, Colonel Bloor reviewed the performance of his regiment. He claimed that with the "exception of the trench system in front of Saint Etienne, my troops had cleared their sector of the enemy, as far as the intermediate objective, at 10:30 o'clock in the morning" of the first day of fighting. He singled out the performance of the regiment's aid stations and Captain Perkins's Supply Company. Overall, he believed his soldiers displayed the "dogged resistance and bravery of tired men in the face of terrible casualties inflicted by all the arms of modern warfare." While Colonel Bloor rightly praised his soldiers, the divisional historian later wrote that the "courage of both officers and men bordered on recklessness and probably resulted in unnecessary loss of many lives." There was also a bit of malingering, but the brigade medical officers attributed most of it to "mere nervous excitement," or "temporary fright" from mistaking high explosive fumes for poison gas. However, the malingering, or straggling, may have been more prevalent than Bloor let on. Corporal Hart discovered a group of stragglers hiding in a German dugout but did nothing about it, considering it better that "skulkers" stayed out of the lines where their cowardice might cause more deaths. Likewise, Captain Lillard noted some of his men who joined another unit. Although Lillard was nonchalant about it, those men might have indeed been stragglers. Finally, as mentioned, when two platoon leaders returned to their front line positions, they found that their men had simply "faded away" on their own, and later, members of the 2d Engineers, in support of the 36th Division, reported they had "picked up stragglers and forced them to go to their organizations." Based on that evidence, it appeared the Texans, who were expected to uphold the military traditions of their ancestors, were no more immune to fear and straggling than other AEF soldiers. Last, Bloor strongly critiqued the artillery support: "the visible and tangible support rendered by the artillery supporting me amounted to very little." Likewise, the perceived boon of having French tanks in the initial attack turned out to be an illusion, as the tank officer Bloor met in his command post was killed and "those tanks not crippled by the enemy's fire were withdrawn." Overall, Bloor appeared to stand the test well as the regimental commander. Based on the limited information available, he made the correct decisions, assumed responsibility for the regiment's actions, knew that his place was in the command post, and did his best to maintain communication with his front line troops and knew their locations as best he could. Nothing more could be expected from an untested regimental commander. With that being said, Bloor also bore responsibility for failing to get orders to his battalions in a timely manner, and the first message to brigade headquarters that the attack had been launched was not sent until 6:55 am, more than an hour after it started. In addition, Bloor appeared to have a much better feel for the positions of his companies than the 141st Infantry, whose messages were plagued by such conflicting information that General Whitworth ordered Colonel Jackson to ascertain personally his regiment's positions. However, the Army later considered the attack by the 71st Brigade to be a failure, and a recent historian argued that the "green troops" of the brigade "were not ready for the challenge," an assessment that was perhaps not altogether fair as Bloor and many of his officers and men proved to be capable leaders and his regiment performed as well as might be expected for its first time in action.[46]

The Germans also had their own opinions of the fighting around Saint Etienne. After noting the buildup of forces in the area, German intelligence fully expected an attack on October 8. As their intelligence report for that day summed up, "the main attack of the enemy, which was expected by the Army, commenced this morning with full strength." The Germans also captured a copy of the 71st Brigade's attack order, and knew its objectives. From the German perspective, the attack had failed because of a "tenacious resistance in defense and a revived combative spirit in counter assault." Describing the American attack near Saint Etienne and Orfeuil, German sources claimed that attack broke down and could not develop "because of our annihilating fire." When the fighting ended on October 8, the Germans claimed that the front line remained virtually intact, except for "small local losses." After capturing six members of the 36th Division during a night raid, the Germans realized they faced a new unit. When no major attack occurred on the ninth, German intelligence attributed it to the "heavy defeat" for the Americans on October 8, which prevented the continuance of the offensive. While the Americans certainly did not collapse the German lines, the attacks by the 71st Brigade were not quite as disastrous as contemporary enemy reports made them out to be. The 142d suffered from a lack of planning and preparation. Lack of time, more than anything else, might have played the larger role in the overall ineffectiveness of the attack. The regiment would learn its lesson.[47]

Although October 8–10 marked the first combat experience of the remaining soldiers of the old 7th Texas, the war continued. After the 72d

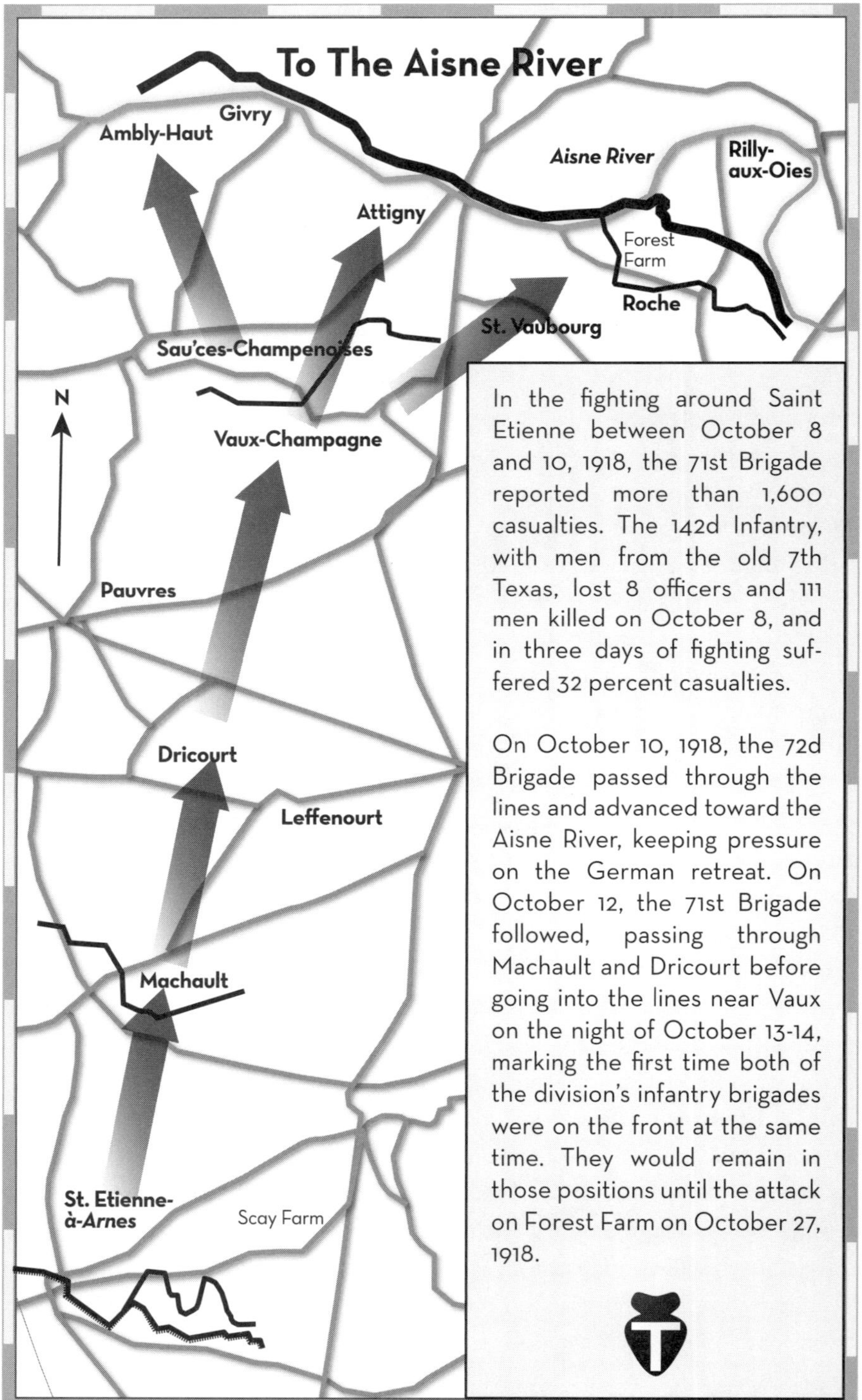

In the fighting around Saint Etienne between October 8 and 10, 1918, the 71st Brigade reported more than 1,600 casualties. The 142d Infantry, with men from the old 7th Texas, lost 8 officers and 111 men killed on October 8, and in three days of fighting suffered 32 percent casualties.

On October 10, 1918, the 72d Brigade passed through the lines and advanced toward the Aisne River, keeping pressure on the German retreat. On October 12, the 71st Brigade followed, passing through Machault and Dricourt before going into the lines near Vaux on the night of October 13-14, marking the first time both of the division's infantry brigades were on the front at the same time. They would remain in those positions until the attack on Forest Farm on October 27, 1918.

Brigade took over the front, General Whitworth's brigade followed General Hulen's 143rd and 144th Infantry regiments in a general advance against the Germans, who completed their retreat to the Aisne River in cold and damp weather. Many of the men suffered during the advance because they did not have tents and blankets, but still continued the pursuit. On October 13, the 142d Infantry started out again to keep up with the advance. Eventually, they reached an abandoned German camp and took a break. A field kitchen caught up with the column of soldiers and gave many of them their first hot meal in five days. The men feasted on a small amount of "coffee, bread, jam, and beans," and ate raw turnips found in the German camp. The break allowed some of the soldiers to tease Captain Perkins of the Supply Company, who was "standing with his foot on the hub balancing a cup of coffee on his knee." Lieutenant Thompson asked Perkins why he had not brought the field kitchen to the men when they first went into action, and one of Perkins's men joined in, telling Thompson that Perkins had "crawled under the kitchen when the shells fell on the road; he set his breeches on fire and we couldn't come up."[48]

That evening, as the regiment camped near Dricourt, some soldiers found sleep hard to come by because of the quiet. They had become used to the constant sound of artillery and machine guns and the silence made them restless. The next day, the regiment continued and by dusk approached the new front lines near the village of Vaux.[49]

Colonel Bloor also moved his command post to Dricourt, approximately seven miles north of Saint Etienne, and then to Vaux, and his regiment went back into the line beyond Vaux Champagne in front of the city of Attigny, which rested on the Aisne River. On the night of October 13–14, the 71st Brigade moved to the right of Hulen's 72d Brigade, and for the first time the entire 36th Division was in the line together. The 142d occupied the left side of the brigade sector, and the line between the 142d and the 143d of the 72d Brigade was approximately one hundred yards west of Attigny. Eventually, the regiments were aligned so that the 141st occupied the left side of the brigade sector and Colonel Bloor's 142d the right. This put the 71st Brigade near the point east of the city where the Aisne River made a horseshoe bend to the north, creating an area on the south side of the river that the Germans had strongly fortified. Some of the brigade's positions were only sixty yards from German strong points in the bend of the river. The horseshoe bend, known to the Americans as Forest Farm, was one of only two points south of the Aisne River still held by the Germans in that sector, and American and French officers expressed concern that the area could be used as a "bridgehead" to attack General Gouraud's French Fourth Army. Many officers believed that if the French or Americans could get into that area, they could outflank the German defenses in Attigny. To prevent just such an occurrence, the Germans fortified the bend with a trench running across the entrance of the mile-and-a-half-wide horseshoe, protected by numerous logs and at least three belts of barbed wire, with three strong points interspersed with supporting machine guns. Intelligence assessed at least sixty machine guns in the horseshoe bend of the Aisne River facing the 71st Brigade.[50]

As the 36th Division and the 142d Infantry settled into their positions along the southern bank of the Aisne River, the 142d Infantry had experienced combat for the first time. While facing odds because of the lack of experience as well as a poorly coordinated attack, the soldiers from North and Northwest Texas had been bloodied by a determined enemy. Although their first battle was not a success, they would translate the lessons learned at Saint Etienne and apply them with significantly better results at Forest Farm. Before that occurred, however, the 142d Infantry watched and waited for the enemy who sat just across the Aisne River.

A typical Texas National Guard recruiting poster from the Wichita Daily Times, *June 19, 1917.*

Colonel Alfred Wainwright Bloor. Colonel Bloor, an Austin attorney, commanded the 7th Texas Infantry, Texas National Guard, and later the 142d Infantry Regiment during World War I (Photo from C. H. Barnes, History of the 142d Infantry of the Thirty-Sixth Division, October 15 1917, to June 17, 1919 *[Blackwell Job Printing Company, 1922].)*

Major Gen. Edwin St. John Greble, commander of Camp Bowie, ca. 1917–1918. General Greble oversaw the division's training at Camp Bowie, but prior to its departure for France the War Department replaced him with Maj. Gen. William R. Smith (Courtesy, Ruth Dearmin Cooke Photograph Album, Special Collections, The University of Texas at Arlington Library, Arlington, Texas.)

Captain Ethan Simpson. Simpson recruited the Donley County company of the 7th Texas Infantry in the summer of 1917 and led his soldiers to France and back. This photo was taken at Camp Bowie, Fort Worth, Texas, 1917–1918 (Photo Courtesy of Pat and Woodene Simpson.)

*Captain Thomas D. Barton. Barton, who made Amarillo his home, had served in militia companies since 1891 and fought in the Spanish-American War. He recruited the Amarillo company and led it to France. During the battle at Saint Etienne, a defensive position near the town earned the nickname "Barton's Hill" during the fighting. Barton later ran unsuccessfully for governor of Texas (*Fort Worth Star Telegram*).*

*Captain Steve A. Lillard. Lillard recruited the Wise County Company and led it through the battles at Saint Etienne and Forest Farm and proved to be a capable and respected officer (*Wise County Messenger, *February 18, 1927).*

*Captain Robert Wagstaff. Wagstaff, who grew up in Abilene, recruited Company I from Taylor County and the surrounding area. Wagstaff remained with the division throughout the war and returned to Abilene where he became a successful lawyer and community leader (*Fort Worth Star Telegram*).*

*Edwin B. Sayles. Sayles helped recruit the Abilene company of the 7th Texas Infantry and remained with the regiment throughout the war, eventually commanding the 37mm cannon platoon during the regiment's time on the Western Front. Sayles was promoted to captain prior to the assault on Forest Farm (*Abilene Daily News*).*

Camp Bowie's 36th Division review parade in downtown Fort Worth, April 11, 1918 (Courtesy, Ruth Dearmin Cooke Photograph Album, Special Collections, The University of Texas at Arlington Library, Arlington, Texas.)

Soldiers training at Camp Bowie, Forth Worth, ca. 1917–1918 (Courtesy, Fort Worth Star-Telegram Collection, Special Collections, The University of Texas at Arlington Library, Arlington, Texas.)

Company E, 142d Infantry at Camp Bowie in 1917. This company included many members of the Choctaw Nation who served as communicators during the battle of Forest Farm, October 27, 1918. Using their native language, the Choctaw soldiers transmitted coded messages that the Germans could not understand (Photo Courtesy of Texas Military Forces Museum).

Corporal Monte Dunaway of Wise County, who was killed during the fighting at Saint Etienne. His uncle penned a eulogy for him in the Wise County Messenger*: "We will miss his cheerful face and quiet way of moving about our homes…" (*Wise County Messenger*, November 22, 1918).*

Camp Bowie's 36th Division memorial stone marks the site of the 36th Division headquarters during World War I, installed at Camp Bowie Blvd. and Thomas Place during the twenty-fifth reunion; l. to r., Dallas Matthews, left, from Austin; Mark McGee, Fort Worth attorney; and R. Wright Armstrong of Fort Worth, October 27–29, 1950. Armstrong, an original member of Cap-

tain Homer Merrill's Lubbock company, went over the top at Saint Etienne on October 8, 1918 (Courtesy, William E. Jary Collection, Special Collections, The University of Texas at Arlington Library, Arlington, Texas.)

Second Lieutenant Oscar Emery, a member of the 142d Infantry Regimental Band (Photo Courtesy of the Texas Military Forces Museum, Austin, Texas).

Medal of Honor recipient Corporal Samuel L. Sampler. Born in Oklahoma, Sampler was an original member of the 7th Texas Infantry, enlisting in Capt. James Wiley's Hardeman County Company D (Photo courtesy of the Texas Military Forces Museum).

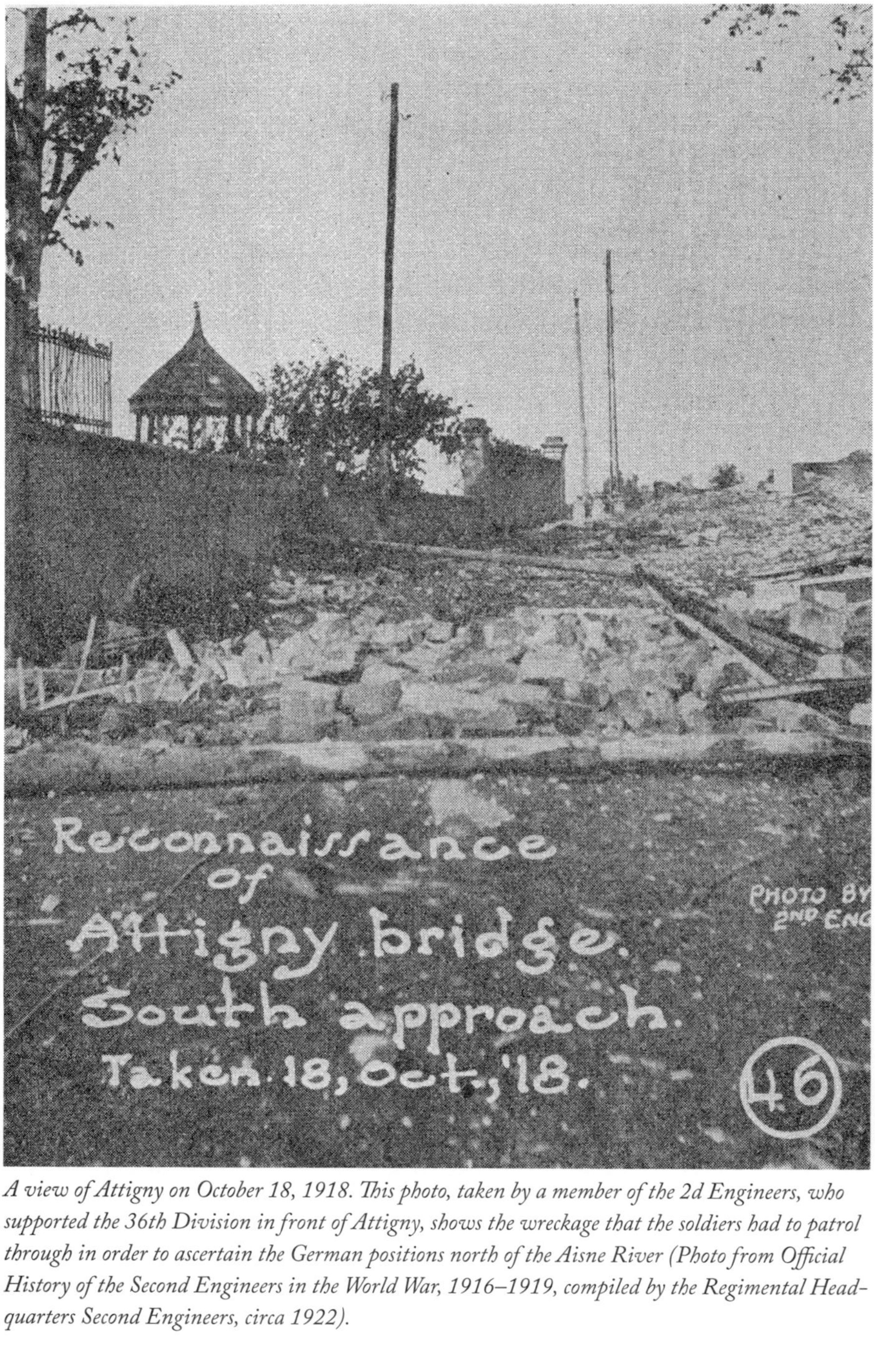

A view of Attigny on October 18, 1918. This photo, taken by a member of the 2d Engineers, who supported the 36th Division in front of Attigny, shows the wreckage that the soldiers had to patrol through in order to ascertain the German positions north of the Aisne River (Photo from Official History of the Second Engineers in the World War, 1916–1919, compiled by the Regimental Headquarters Second Engineers, circa 1922).

Photo taken near Somme-Py by a member of the 2d Engineers illustrates the devastated country that the members of the old 7th Texas marched through on their way to the front. This photo was taken on October 7, 1918, after the majority of the regiment had made it into the lines (Photo from Official History of the Second Engineers in the World War, 1916–1919, compiled by the Regimental Headquarters Second Engineers, circa 1922).

"THE BOYS" ARE COMING HOME JOHNSON COUNTY WILL WELCOME ALL OF THE RETURNING HEROES

"They are coming, Father Abraham, 100,000 strong."

Our soldiers are either at home or coming fast.

Some have been wounded or gassed or have been sent home as casuals of one sort and another.

The Rainbow Division has arrived and been heralded as heroes. Other divisions have come and now the 36th is nearly home. The 90th Division has arrived in part and others are coming. The men who have been away up in the cold and frigid northland of Archangel in Russia have orders to start for the dear old United States. Today this paper has the news of many telegrams recording the safe arrival in New York, Newport News and in other places of men of Johnson county who will be right here now in just a few days. All over this fine county of ours, rejoicing mothers are planning and baking and preparing for many square meals for "their boys" and the fathers are preparing to kill the fatted calf in the shape of dozens of fried chickens and home cured hams which have hung in the smokehouse or cellar against the times when these valiant sons should return to partake of the many good things so long denied them.

Yes, they are coming home, and every one is happy. The earth is fair and smiling and welcome awaits in everyone's heart.

God grant that no further accident will mar their safe homecoming.

A homecoming message from the Cleburne Daily News, *June 8, 1919.*

A typical scene of local residents awaiting the arrival of members of the 36th Division at Camp Bowie, Fort Worth, Texas, in 1919. In this photo, 132d Field Artillery soldiers arrive back at Camp Bowie from the war front, April 7, 1919 (Courtesy, Ruth Dearmin Cooke Photograph Album, Special Collections, The University of Texas at Arlington Library, Arlington, Texas.)

CLEBURNE, TEXAS, SUNDAY, NOV. 9, 1919

"Armistice Day" Proclamation

Whereas, the President of the United States, Woodrow Wilson; and the Governor of our State, William P. Hobby, have issued proclamations declaring Armistice Day a legal holiday, I, as Mayor of the City of Cleburne, do likewise call the attention of the people to this important date in our Nation's history. "Armistice Day" should be properly celebrated, and whether the observance in Cleburne shall take the nature of a public celebration, with a gathering together of the people, or shall be private in character, depends on the will of the people of this city. I declare my solemn and heartfelt sympathy for those whose dear ones lie sleeping on the Fields of Flanders and feel thatthe entire American people shall pause to scatter the flowers of memory on their sacrifices, lives and ambitions; also that we should offer prayers of thankfulness for those who have been spared to return to us. Lastly, but equally important, should we celebrate "Armistice Day," November 11, Tuesday, this good year of 1919, as the day which declared we triumphed in the fight for Freedom and Right and when The Lord of Hosts sustained our might and right on the field of Battle.

(Signed.) MAYOR JOHN H. SHORT.

Attest: MRS. JERRINE HUGHES, Secretary.

*Cleburne mayor John H. Short's 1919 Armistice Day Proclamation (*Cleburne Daily News, *November 9, 1919).*

6

THE WESTERN FRONT, OCTOBER 13–30, 1918

As the 142d Infantry filtered into the lines on the night of October 13, 1918, they were certainly not aware that in several weeks they would have to attack such a strongly fortified position as Forest Farm. Lieutenant Sayles' weapons platoon dug in on the side of a hill and managed to bring up straw from Vaux to line their holes. Several soldiers also found doors to use as roofs over their fox holes, but it turned out they had taken the doors from regimental headquarters and Sayles ordered them to return them. For the most part, the soldiers waited and tried to stay comfortable and warm. Whenever he went to sleep, Sayles wrapped his scarf around his stomach and wrapped his feet in a rain slicker and slept in the same hole as another man so they could keep each other warm. Over the next several days, Sayles's platoon dug a "long gallery" into the side of the hill, covered the floor with straw, used branches to keep the sides from caving in, and created an "arbor" that kept some of the rain out, although the "roof always dripped somewhere, and little rivulets broke out under the deep mat of fallen leaves that covered the ground." The dugout was large enough to hold half of his platoon, who would crowd into the dugout to eat. At the top of the hill, above their "gallery," he placed two 37mm cannon, ready to fire across the river on German positions to the north. Not everyone had it so great, as part of Company I dug into an area that was "so flat it was nearly a lake," and the soldiers lived "in the slush," trying to keep the rain away with half tents stretched over their holes, and covered the bottoms of their holes with blankets and overcoats scrounged from dead Germans. Still, as one man commented, "Everything oozed water."[1]

Sometimes the men ate well. Occasionally, field kitchens got them a hot stew of dried potatoes and carrots mixed with corned beef, and infrequently they received sugar, which they ate on bread and considered a "rare delicacy." As for the bread, Lieutenant Sayles recalled that each loaf had the date stamped on it and that it was so tough it could be stockpiled, covered with a tarpaulin, and last for days. As he recalled, the bread "always tasted good when it could be dried out over a fire," and it was "fine with jam." Besides eating the bread, some soldiers found creative uses for it, such as sticking it on their bayonets when marching, calling it a "practical method for carrying the dishpan sized hunk of fodder," and that "it also would keep rain drops out of" rifles. Other foods the soldiers devoured included condensed milk on bread and "oleomargarine cut in thick slabs which was eaten like cheese." Just as often, the food did not keep warm on its way to the front and the men received cold coffee and stew which congealed into "a solid mass with a hard layer of grease on top."[2]

When the regiment moved into the line south of the Aisne River, the front stabilized and the four regiments of the division dug in. General Smith organized the 36th Division's lines into an outpost zone, a support zone, and a reserve zone. Within each regimental sector, one battalion held the outpost and support zone, and the other two battalions occupied the reserve zone. The battalion in the outpost and support zone pushed forward listening posts and patrols into the outpost zone, which extended five kilometers from the Aisne River and back. Despite the static nature of the front, combat continued. From October 14 through October 26, the 142d stayed in front of the Aisne River, trying to get a feel for the enemy, who posted snipers in Attigny and remained in force north of the river. Cloudy and cold weather prevailed and it rained more often than not. The rain and fog often reduced visibility and made it difficult to detect enemy movements. The regiment's daily operations report frequently described the gloomy weather during the last two weeks of October using terms such as, "very dark and rainy," "raining," and "dark and cloudy, observation poor." Indeed, during this period on the front the regiment reported only two periods of clear weather, October 18 and October 23–25. There were, however, things much more dangerous than the weather.[3]

Artillery fire remained a constant threat. For example, out of thirty-seven operations reports filed during the period October 16 to October 27, twenty-four reported enemy artillery fire somewhere in the regiment's sector. Sometimes reported as light or "desultory" fire without a particular target, such as "occasional shells fell in Attigny between 17:30 and 18:30 o'clock," or "harassing fire on Vaux and advanced positions," at other times the shelling was more purposeful, such as on October 17, when German observers may have spotted American soldiers "attempting to reach a station in church steeple at Attigny," and brought down high explosive shells on the area. By October 25, artillery barrages were so commonplace that the operations report considered 100 high explosive shells falling in the area to be "light," although on October 27, the commander's younger brother and operations officer Captain Bertram Bloor reported that nearly 200 shells fell in the regimental area. Finally, there existed the danger of being shelled by gas. On the afternoon of October 25, the enemy shelled the regiment's support battalion with high explosives and mustard gas. The attack lasted into the evening, and when the shelling ended, regimental personnel estimated 2,000 shells had impacted the area. Still, soldiers seemed to handle the gas situation calmly as Captain Bloor reported that "when these shells land near positions the men move away from it. The general dispersion of gas is not strong and continued wearing of gas masks in not necessary." Nevertheless, the next day 100 rounds of mustard gas fell around the village of Mery during a twenty-four-hour period resulting in thirty-two "inhalation" casualties. While artillery was a constant danger, the regiment also exchanged sniper and machine-gun fire with their adversaries across the river.[4]

On the morning of October 16, a German sniped fired on a regimental patrol, and the next day, Captain Bloor reported "enemy snipers were active this morning, the least exposure of members of our patrol bringing shots. Snipers still located on strip of land between canal and river" referencing a canal that paralleled the Aisne River. On October 24, he again reported that "enemy snipers are very active along front" and reported that "owing to the bright moonlight and clear days action above ground north of Chufilly is practically prohibited. Small parties using cover move at night." Captain Bloor concluded his report with "our snipers returning fire shot for shot." By October 26, Captain Bloor noted that "enemy activity decreased to practically nothing during the night," although American snipers remained active. Lieutenant Sayles and his 37mm cannon also sought targets, at one point firing thirty-two rounds at an enemy strong point which succeeded in reducing the enemy machine-gun fire from that location. Of course, with such threats, it remained very dangerous for soldiers to be seen out in the open, although during this two-week period the regiment could not afford to simply wait and watch. It had to gather intelligence, and did so by sending out patrols.[5]

For example, on October 17, a small patrol of one officer and three men crossed the Aisne River at 8:30 pm, and took two prisoners in a clump of woods to the north. The Germans resisted being captured, so the patrol opened fire, wounding one. Fearing that the firing had disclosed their location, the patrol hustled back across the river with the two prisoners. Later the same evening, the regiment sent out another patrol, although it could not cross the river because of a "lack of facilities to cross." The patrol then came under "heavy artillery fire" and retreated. In another instance, a patrol advanced to the Attigny canal because of reports of moving trucks. When the patrol got close to the river, they realized the truck sounds were coming from the north side of the river but could not determine the purpose of the movement. Other patrols tested the enemy's defenses, such as one that approached the bridges crossing the Aisne River only to report that the "bridge sites remain covered by enemy machine guns and snipers." Such patrols were obviously dangerous and stressful to those who went on them. In one case, Lieutenant Sayles sat in regimental headquarters when a lieutenant returned from a patrol in which he lost three men. The lieutenant came in "wet, muddy, and blubbering," and after explaining what had happened to his patrol, began to cry.[6]

In another instance, on October 14, a patrol moved toward the town but during their approach came under fire. One of the men, Sergeant Ormsby, was wounded by a sniper and could not walk. The patrol leader, Sgt. Charles Lydell, normally in charge of the 1st Battalion intelligence section, placed Ormsby in a protected area and made his way back to Vaux Champagne for help. Lydell managed to convince an ambulance to return to the town with him to get the wounded Ormsby. The ambulance made it part way before the shelling became so intense that the driver turned back to Vaux Champagne. Sergeant Lydell then approached Colonel Bloor and asked him to provide a detail of men to help him get Ormsby out of the town. Because of the artillery fire, Bloor believed he was not justified in endangering a group of men to rescue one wounded soldier, and declined to provide the detail. However, he offered Lydell the use of his motorcycle and sidecar, which the intelligence sergeant accepted. The motorcycle driver, Jesse Morrison, agreed to the mission. Under constant artillery and machine-gun fire, the men dashed into the town on the motorcycle, put the wounded Ormsby in the sidecar, and got him back to Vaux Champagne.[7]

On October 19 and 20, the regiment made efforts to improve its positions, sending out numerous patrols in their sector in order to get a better feel for the ground to strengthen their own positions "for defensive action." On October 21, however, the regiment received word from division headquarters that the enemy "had evacuated the territory to our front." Although Colonel Bloor disagreed, he nevertheless ordered two patrols to "gain contact with the enemy." Neither patrol advanced very far. One made it seventy-five meters beyond the river crossing before it was "fired upon by machine guns and snipers." Two men were wounded, and the patrol sought cover. The second patrol fared even worse, being stopped by enemy fire as soon as it crossed the river. After both of these patrols returned south of the river, a third patrol went out. This patrol, consisting of a corporal and three men, reached the river and attempted to cross a German foot bridge. In the attempt they were fired on and "rushed by about twenty-five or thirty infantrymen." The Germans captured three of the four, and the last escaped by swimming the canal. Finally, two officers, Major Nelson and Captain Barth, took a motorcycle and sidecar in broad daylight and "under direct enemy observation" into the town to verify the enemy remained north of the river and had not withdrawn. Under artillery and machine-gun fire, the two officers moved by foot to the canal, having already accomplished their mission. They were back at the regimental command post in one hour. In the operations report's section titled "general impression of the day," Captain Bloor laconically observed that "enemy is still holding river bank to the north of our sector with a number of machine guns and probably one hundred infantrymen. It is inadvisable to attempt to patrol strip of land between canal and river without considerable artillery support." Indeed, as if to prove that the Germans had not left the area, the next night soldiers spotted a patrol estimated at fifty Germans crossing the river. Later, several flares were shot from the general location of the German patrol but no attack followed.[8]

Patrols also went out to maintain liaison with units to the right and left. The distance between the 141st and the 142d was about 1,200 yards, and only the 142d patrolled the gap to prevent friendly fire accidents. However, Captain Bertram Bloor believed this gap was "far from satisfactory" and worried that Germans could easily infiltrate the area: "They are too far from us," he wrote, referring to the 141st Infantry. The situation along the front remained tense, made worse because of rumors passing back and forth from division to regiments. Soldiers on the front saw and heard unusual things. For example, Lieutenant Sayles awoke one night to the sound of music. At first he believed he was dreaming, but other members of his platoon heard it as well. The last thing he remembered before falling back to sleep was "the sound of the liveliest tunes coming clearly through the cold night air." One night, men at sniper posts reported "a great deal of talking, barking of dogs and noise of motor trucks" across the river, and at one point a fire of unknown origin burned in front of the lines. Finally, a soldier in an observation post saw a "brilliant light" opposite his position, and had no idea what it was. However, intelligence officers believed it might have been a "projector gas attack." Captain Bloor also expressed concern about officers visiting front line positions. Apparently, officers occasionally approached front line positions by "observed routes" which brought enemy shells crashing down. In one day, for example, the regiment lost five men wounded and one man killed after receiving an estimated 2,000 shells, including 100 that fell on an "unimproved road" near Company M's position, perhaps brought on by an unwary officer.[9]

The period from October 14 to October 27 in front of Attigny and the Aisne River passed in a dangerous, wet, and cold haze for many of the regiment's soldiers, and many felt the stress of their position. Lieutenant Sayles often surveyed the area around the village of Voncq to the north. Because of its elevation, the village served as a prime area for German artillery observers. Sayles nervously and constantly watched the area through his binoculars and although he never saw movement, he knew the "Germans were there and no doubt watching us with more powerful glasses, and possessing more information of us than we had of them."[10]

Toward the last week in October, however, things began to change. While senior officers discussed the best ways of attacking across the Aisne River, the French and Americans agreed they needed to take the horseshoe bend area south of the river. French units had earlier attacked Forest Farm twice, only to be repulsed with heavy losses. Now Whitworth's 71st Brigade sat directly across from the bend, and on October 24 word arrived from the French XI Corps, to which the division was now assigned, that the Forest Farm area would again be attacked, this time by General Whitworth's brigade. The men of the old 7th Texas who still remained with the regiment would be among those who found themselves preparing to go "over the top" once more.[11]

On October 24, 1918, General Whitworth submitted his plan for the capture of Forest Farm. In his memorandum, titled "preparation for minor offensive," Whitworth stressed a massive artillery preparation, followed by a frontal assault, in which the "infantry should go over the top in attack formation, using the lanes cut through the wire by the artillery and such other openings as they may be able to make by wire-cutters the night before the attack." Although the experience with tanks had not turned out well at Saint Etienne, General Whitworth suggested that five or six light tanks could crush the barbed wire and aid in "destroying machine gun nests." Also, and perhaps most importantly, General Whitworth pointed out that to take the Forest Farm position, the town of Voncq, situated northeast of the horseshoe bend on a slight hill that commanded the area, had to be taken or else enemy artillery could devastate the attackers. Finally, if they were not careful, German troops in Attigny would be able to fire into the left flank of the attacking soldiers and present significant problems. In other words, the Forest Farm operation required advanced planning and preparation and had the potential to turn into a disaster, such as had occurred with the previous two attacks. To succeed, the 141st and 142d Infantry would have to overcome severe obstacles, and the soldiers were well aware of the failure of the French to capture the position several weeks earlier. Indeed, several of Whitworth's points so concerned General Smith that he wrote a letter to the commanding general of XI Corps, stating several objections to the attack, primarily that the area would be subject to enfilade fire from the north bank of the Attigny and second that the brigade was scheduled for relief immediately after the attack. General Smith believed that could cause problems in evacuating casualties, collecting the dead, and getting the brigade to its assigned area in the rear. Despite the formal protest, the French Corps commander, General Prax, ordered the attack to proceed, and division historian Captain Spence later wrote that "no satisfactory reason for the attack was ever received." General Prax wrote to General Smith: "It will succeed, and will thus give to the brave American troops that I have the honor to have under my command, the occasion of a glorious victory, which will be the crowning of their participation in the great battle of CHAMPAGNE in 1918."[12]

Battle of Forest Farm.

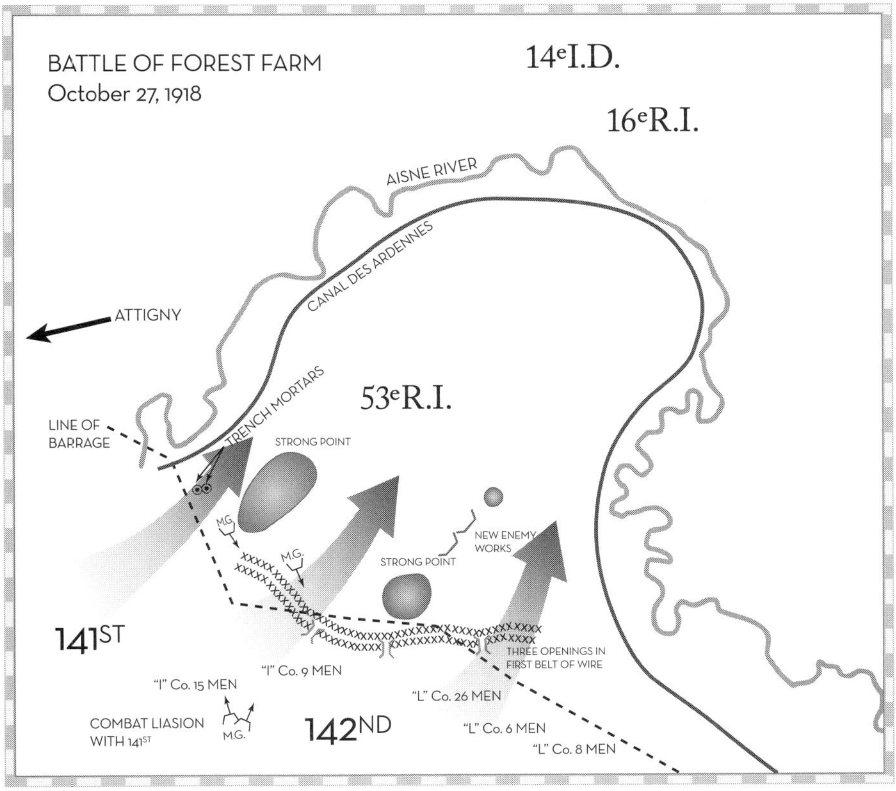

The Battle of Forest Farm, October 27, 1918.

Because of the possibility that the attack could go badly, General Smith wanted to ensure that the preparations for the attack went undetected. Indeed, General Smith and his commanders knew that the Germans tapped into the division's telephone wires and listened to their communications. As Colonel Bloor wrote after the armistice, "There was every reason to believe every decipherable message or word going over our wires also went to the enemy." In fact, at one point the division tested the theory by passing along false coordinates of an imaginary supply dump on the telephone, and in thirty minutes "enemy shells were falling on the point." While it is not clear who thought of the idea, the regiment's officers concluded that they might have a significant advantage over the Germans by using Choctaw Indians from the old 1st Oklahoma Infantry to transmit messages. According to Colonel Bloor, "There was hardly one chance in a million that Fritz would be able to translate these dialects, and the plan to have these Indians transmit telephone messages was adopted." The regiment successfully tested the process on October 26 and then used Choctaw soldiers to relay messages during the assault on October 27.[13]

To lead the attack, Colonel Bloor selected an officer who had been in the thick of the fighting around Saint Etienne and an original member of the 7th Texas, Capt. Steve Lillard. Still with 3rd Battalion, Lillard spent several days in divisional reserve after the fighting around Saint Etienne while the 72d Brigade continued the advance to Attigny. On October 22, Lillard's battalion went into the line near the village of Roche, near the southeastern edge of the Forest Farm horseshoe bend and just across the river from Voncq where the Germans maintained observation of the surrounding countryside. On October 25, Lillard assumed command of the battalion. The battalion was to be relieved after four days in the outpost and supporting zones. The next day, after reporting to Colonel Bloor's command post, he learned of the upcoming attack. According to Captain Spence, Lillard asked permission to lead the assault because his troops were familiar with the enemy positions and the ground they would cover. Bloor granted the request and selected Lillard's battalion to lead the attack on the twenty-seventh.[14]

The final plan called for the 141st and 142d Infantry to assault Forest Farm. In the 142d's zone Lillard's 3rd Battalion led the assault. The battalion included Company I under Lt. Rudolph Fried, Company K under Lt. John Douglas, Company M under Lt. Verne Hillock, while Company L under Lt. Alvin Leubke remained in support. The command arrangements illustrated the regiment's casualties: not one of the assault companies was led by a captain, the normal rank of a company commander. Of the three companies in the assault battalion commanded recently by members of the old 7th Texas, only Lillard was available for the assault. However, there were other 7th Texas officers, including Lt. Nat Perrine, Lieutenant Sayles, who had just found out he had been promoted to captain, and the Stokes mortar platoon commander, Lt. George O. Thompson.[15]

The assault battalion had several days to observe the enemy positions around Forest Farm, and with adequate planning and preparation, Lillard's battalion was ready. As Lillard later wrote, "we had had 24 hours advance notice of this attack, with maps and definite orders. Every man in the organization knew just what he was going to do." Lillard also stressed the cooperation of senior commanders and plenty of artillery support. Such circumstances, he believed, "made it impossible for anything but success." Finally, on October 27, 1918, a day that began clear and sunny, the remaining members of the old 7th Texas waited to go "over the top" across muddy fields and into the teeth of the German main line of resistance blocking the horseshoe bend of the Aisne River.[16]

Lillard's soldiers knew that the enemy barbed wire was thick, the strong points covered by at least three belts of wire that were twelve yards wide, while other areas were blocked by one or two layers of wire. The front itself was approximately two kilometers wide. To overcome those obstacles, Bloor assigned engineers to Lillard's battalion who would advance with the infantry. Lillard's men also knew that the main objective was the trench line cutting across the horseshoe bend. The attack was scheduled to begin with an artillery preparation at 4:00 pm followed by the assault battalions of both regiments moving out at 4:30 pm. As the men waited through the day, the clear skies gave way to clouds and rain. The soldiers ate their usual meal of bread, beans, and coffee several hours before the attack. Somewhere along the line, two soldiers of Company I, Ira Shockley and Sgt. Albert Robinson, talked over the coming battle. Robinson, who had been on duty for the previous four days and four nights, told Shockley that this would be his last battle "for I expect to get killed today." Soon, a lone gun of the 2d Field Artillery Regiment signaled the start of the artillery barrage on the enemy strong points. The Stokes mortars fired on the enemy trenches and tried to cut the belts of barbed wire, a smoke screen was laid, and other artillery units fired barrages against Voncq, Attigny, and north of the Aisne River in an effort to disrupt German observation areas and destroy machine-gun nests which could fire across the river at Lillard's attacking soldiers. Close to the assault battalion, Lieutenant Sayles's 37mm cannons "were firing as fast as they could be loaded." Sayles saw the engineers pass him by with "rifles slung, each man carrying a pair of long-handled wire-cutters."[17]

At 4:30 pm Lillard's battalion moved out and discovered that the artillery preparation had not only cut the barbed wire but succeeded in keeping the enemy in their dugouts. Although the enemy attempted a counter barrage, it did not stop Lillard's men, who moved forward in a "single line of skirmishers" armed with "rifles, Browning Automatic Rifles, pistols, trench knives [and] grenades." Lillard's attackers stayed close behind the rolling barrage, advanced quickly through the wire, and were waiting for the Germans as they began to come out of their dugouts. As the enemy scrambled to man their weapons, Lillard's men either captured or shot them. Lieutenant Sayles recalled the sound of Browning Automatic Rifles firing from the front as he advanced with his cannons, while "machine gun bullets were still cracking overhead" from an American machine gun barrage. Indeed, Sayles believed the sound of the bullets was so close overhead that it "caused many a man to hesitate at first, thinking that he was being fired on by the enemy." The soldiers did not hesitate for long but continued the advance. A shell hit near Sayles, knocking him down and blowing his helmet off. He managed to get back to his feet and continued to direct his platoon. Lt. Nat Perrine, with a platoon of about twenty-eight men, continued to advance and captured a trench. His leadership that day earned him a promotion to captain. Sergeant Albert Robinson, who expected to meet death that day, instead kept his platoon so close to the rolling barrage that they captured a German machine-gun nest before the soldiers could get their guns into action. He survived the day and was recommended for the Distinguished Service Cross.[18]

Less than an hour later, it was over. The attack had gone off almost without a hitch. The only major mistake occurred to Company M, whose men scattered for cover after they ran into their own rolling barrage when it inadvertently fell short of its intended target. Otherwise, the regiment overran the main German line in about forty-five minutes. Lillard's men entered 16 German dugouts and captured 109 prisoners from the 3d Prussian Guard Division, most of whom they captured "as they came out of dug outs and trenches," after the artillery barrage passed. The Germans "seemed to be glad to be taken prisoners and offered no resistance." The attackers also captured German equipment, including twenty-one examples of the Maxim machine gun, known as the "Devil's Paintbrush."[19]

Once Lillard's men captured the German positions, two patrols advanced to the river and rounded up twenty-seven more prisoners. The patrols also reported signs of "enemy confusion" along the north bank. Lillard brought machine guns up for support in case of a counterattack, and mopping up parties "threw grenades into dugouts and trenches, doing excellent work." Captain Lillard wrote that by 6:00 pm, maps had been drawn showing the location of all friendly troops and by 9:00 pm Lieutenant Hillock passed word that "our line would withstand any counter attack of the enemy's, should he dare to make one."[20]

Although the operation went smoothly, it was not without cost to the 141st and 142d regiments. The initial reports estimated that the 142d killed forty Germans in the assault while suffering eight killed and twenty wounded. In total the two regiments lost eleven men killed and thirty-six wounded. Several members of the old 7th Texas lost their lives at Forest Farm, including Pvt. Oscar Fry of Company K, who was knocked down by an artillery shell. Corporal Hart, who was thrown in the air by the same shell, asked Fry if he were hurt and Fry replied that he was not. Hart urged him to keep moving, but Fry "kindly laughed and said that he couldn't go any farther." Hart left him behind and kept on. He later learned that "the shock of the explosion" killed Fry. A sniper shot another Company K veteran, Cpl. Bruce Cobb, in the chest, although one of his fellow soldiers, Pvt. Robert Lynch, saw the sniper's location and shot him in return. Company M lost Pvt. Will C. Curtis at

Forest Farm as well. Curtis was struck in the right temple by a large shell and sank slowly to the ground without uttering a word. While they were perhaps grateful for the minimum number of casualties, the violent deaths that some of their comrades suffered weighed heavily on the survivors' minds.[21]

In the operations report prepared after the battle, Capt. Bertram Bloor wrote that "operations were carried out exactly as planned. The plan was good. The morale of the men was good… The operation was not difficult." At least one officer of the regiment, Capt. Rudolph E. Fried, believed that much of the credit belonged to Captain Lillard. In written observations shortly after the battle, Fried pointed out that when Lillard took command of the 3rd Battalion, all "confusion ceased and from that time on until we were relieved the battalion functioned as smoothly as a well trained organization would at home in peace times." According to Fried, this occurred because Lillard inspired "mutual confidence between battalion and companies," something that arguably only the commander could instill, and Corporal Hart believed that Captain Lillard was as popular in Company K as he was in his own company. Nevertheless, Captain Lillard could not keep the men from hunting for souvenirs as they settled into their new positions that night. Officers engaged in souvenir hunting as well, as Lieutenant Sayles found a heavy cane he believed would help him navigate shell holes as well as a pair of green cloth mittens and a "knitted bellyband" that he wore on his head and over his ears.[22]

On October 28, the Germans began shelling the regiment's position in the horseshoe bend, but it was "without material effect." More importantly for the soldiers, however, they knew that their time in the line was coming to an end. Following a plan developed prior to the attack on Forest Farm, French troops relieved the 1st Battalion, in brigade reserve, and the 2d Battalion, in regimental reserve, on October 28. Both battalions marched south toward Somme-Py, where three weeks earlier they had arrived as inexperienced troops awaiting their first combat experience. However, in accordance with the plan of relief, Lillard's 3rd Battalion remained in position in the horseshoe of the Aisne River for an extra day. This did not sit well with Captain Lillard, who later wrote that "all of our supporting troops, including the artillery were withdrawn and we were left to the mercy of the German artillery with French infantry to support us and with French artillery to give excuses for not firing when we called upon them to do so." The Germans shelled the 3rd Battalion all day on October 28 and into the early morning hours of October 29. While waiting to be relieved, Sayles studied the terrain behind him, trying to memorize it so he would be able to lead his platoon out that night. The stress of waiting for relief increased as each round fell. Every time he heard a shell on its way in, Sayles closed his eyes "so tightly that the sound was partly drowned out." After the shell exploded, he "relaxed until the next one came over."[23]

At approximately 3:30 am on October 29, the French relieved Captain Lillard's 3rd Battalion, including Sayles's 37mm platoon. The battalion marched south to the village of Marchant. Shells continued to fall along their route, and during brief stops, soldiers tried to lighten their packs by dropping some of the souvenirs collected earlier, including Sayles, who dropped a "small automatic pistol and had emptied my pockets of brass belt buckles and red and black decorations." In Marchant, trucks took the 3rd Battalion the rest of the way to the "old artillery camp" just south of Somme-Py, where the remainder of the regiment waited. On their way to Somme-Py, they rode through Saint Etienne. Sayles noticed that the streets had been cleared of "loose stones and timbers," and that several elderly people watched them drive by. As they left Saint Etienne, east of the village they passed the enemy trenches they had fought over several weeks before. Now filled in, a long line of crosses marked the final resting place of many of their comrades killed in the fighting. In fact, as each unit passed through Saint Etienne, they found time to "halt and permit the men to look at various points where comrades had been killed and to clear up hazy impressions that existed about the lay of the land during the fighting." The weather was clear and the daily operations report, for the first time in weeks, made no mention of casualties or enemy machine-gun operations, or the status of patrols. On October 30, the 142d Infantry Regiment marched from the artillery camp to the town of Valmy, arriving in the late afternoon. The weather had become cloudy again, but that probably did not matter much to Colonel Bloor's soldiers. The daily operations report did not take long to write that day, as it contained just four words: "Not in the line."[24]

Although the war continued for almost another two weeks, and the 36th Division received assignment to the American First Army, there would be no more fighting for the 142d Infantry Regiment. At least thirty-five original members of the old 7th Texas had lost their lives in the twenty-three days their regiment spent on the Western Front, and dozens more wounded. Those who survived witnessed the horrors of combat and felt the loss of their comrades keenly. Perhaps for most, their ideas of what war really consisted of had forever changed. Now that they were out of the line, their thoughts would turn to trying to describe and understand what they had experienced. Their thoughts would turn to home.

7

"BAD ENOUGH AT THE BEST"

As they left the line near the end of October 1918 and marched to Valmy, James McCan of Quanah recalled that his comrades were "the worst looking bunch of men you ever saw," and about "half a dozen could barely talk above a whisper as our lungs were full of gas." From Valmy, the division marched southeast toward the American First Army, to which they had been assigned. The division stopped for a rest day near Thiacourt on November 2, but the next day many soldiers could hear artillery at the front more distinctly than at any time since they had left the Aisne River a week earlier, which led to speculation they would soon be back at the front. Soon, the division arrived at Bar-Le-Duc near the southern edge of the Argonne Forest, and began preparations to return to the line. By this point, the 36th Division was short 23 percent of its officers and 34 percent of its soldiers. Replacements poured in, filling each company to nearly 200 soldiers while veterans received new uniforms and fresh equipment. Before returning to the front, however, news came on November 7 that the German high command sought an armistice. While waiting to learn the outcome of the negotiations, the soldiers trained in reducing machine gun positions and "open warfare," and Captain Spence believed the division would return to the front in better shape than when it first entered combat. Four days later, on November 11, many soldiers heard the sound of artillery at the front steadily increasing in volume. That caused more than a few soldiers to believe the Germans had broken off the armistice negotiations, although finally at 11:00 am, "the bombardment ceased and all was quiet" as the armistice took effect. It was none too soon for some members of the regiment, one of whom heard rumors that General Headquarters planned to use them as "shock troops" near Verdun. Once the news hit home that evening the soldiers celebrated and "serious faces that had been drawn for weeks, relaxed and gave vent to smiles and laughter." The nearby village of Loup-le-Petit "woke up" that evening, bedecked with lights and serenaded by music from the 142d Infantry band. One soldier, Wayne Wheeler of Company G, wrote home from the village of Conde that "of course we were not allowed to shoot up the town but we celebrated." Oddly enough, Captain Spence noted a "sneaking sense of disappointment in some quarters that the division was not again to enter the lines and show what it felt itself capable of doing when properly equipped and supplied."[1]

The next day, "the solemn tones of a funeral dirge came floating into Regimental headquarters" causing confusion among several of the officers, who were not sure where the music came from and several went outside to see what was happening. A group of the soldiers had decided to "bury the Kaiser." In a solemn procession of soldiers and townspeople, led by a soldier dressed as a priest and the regimental band, a group carried the remains of the "Kaiser." The procession wended its way to a nearby bridge, and the "remains" were "raised tenderly to the banister and at the proper time were gracefully dropped into the creek." As soon as that occurred, the regimental band "hit up a lively tune and amid cheers" the soldiers "retuned to quarters feeling they had expressed themselves."[2]

Other men quickly wrote home about the armistice. For example, Wayne Wheeler wrote that "the armistice saved us from going back to the front, but we were not so disappointed." Another man wrote honestly to a friend, "I am feeling good since the war is over. I had all I wanted of that front when it closed." Willie Carpenter of the Machine Gun Company wrote of the armistice: "I sure was glad when God looked down on us and said stop. They are whipped and there was a crowd of glad boys and I know that you were too. You should have heard us shooting guns and ringing bells."[3]

Several days after the armistice, the division received orders to proceed to Training Area 16, near Tonnerre. The march began on November 18, although the last units did not arrive until Thanksgiving, in part because of 3,600 additional replacements who joined the division during the march. In an effort to keep the soldiers' minds off of going home and the long march facing them, the regiments competed to see which could reach Tonnerre first. The 142d Infantry won the contest, having the fewest number falling out while remaining "in the van of the movement" and reaching "its billets in the Tonnerre area ahead of all others." Along the way, the regiment passed through Bar-Sur-Aube and some men took the opportunity to hold brief reunions with several of the locals they had known several months earlier.[4]

After arriving at the training area, the regiment spread out across various towns as they had done near Bar-Sur-Aube. Colonel Bloor established regimental headquarters in Flogny with the battalions and support units scattered in nearby towns. One soldier wrote that the town his unit was billeted in once had a population of 1,000 but the war had "cut it down to a small bunch of women and children. They wear wooden shoes and drink red wine, and that is all you can say for them." That village had just one "wine joint" which also sold bread to the entire village and the soldiers. The regiment would stay in Training Area 16 for the next five months while they waited their turn to go home, although conditions were far from ideal on their arrival. But, with "hard work and excellent supervision," the situation improved. Furthermore, large numbers of soldiers had worn out their boots and did not get new ones until January. They dealt with a firewood shortage, and each soldier received just 7.5 ounces of wood per day as the coldest months approached. Captain Sam Owens, who had originally served as a battalion adjutant in the old 7th Texas, wrote that when he left the front he had only his clothes, a watch, a fountain pen, a pocketbook and one American five-dollar bill. He also witnessed the changes in the regiment's personnel, commenting that only 30 of the 232 men in his company were original members. Luckily, Owens had the luxury of living in a house. His bedroom included a white marble fireplace, a tiled floor covered with carpets, and a large mahogany feather bed. Although officers generally had good quarters, the majority of the men lived in stone and brick buildings. Those who did not, lived in barns and other wooden structures. Also during the winter months the worldwide influenza epidemic made its way through the ranks of the AEF, taking a toll on many American divisions in France. Fortunately, the epidemic did not strike the division severely and only 160 cases of the deadly virus and five deaths were reported. The 142d had five cases, although it is not clear if any of those soldiers died.[5]

After the armistice, General Pershing maintained a rigorous training schedule, insisting that his soldiers remain prepared to resume the offensive, and the 142d's chaplain declared that the time they spent in the training area were "not months of leisure by any means." Another soldier, C. M. Harvey, recalled that they spent much of their time holding inspections and reviews, and about five hours per day drilling because of the early winter darkness. Captain Ben Chastaine of the old 1st Oklahoma Infantry wrote that the soldiers would endure just about any hardship to end the war, but once it was over the "work and exercises soon grew uninteresting and irksome." Nevertheless, the regiment participated in many practice assaults and Willie Carpenter of the Machine Gun Company put it in perspective, "I had rather drill than be on the front for that is a busy place."[6]

Of course, organizational changes continued. While Colonel Bloor remained in command, other members of the old 7th Texas took assumed new posts in the division and regiment. For example, division inspector Lieutenant Colonel Culberson took charge of the division's schools. Major Alvin Owsley left to attend a British university through the AEF school program, and Maj. William H. Brownell succeeded him. Captain Wagstaff completed his course at the AEF School of the line and returned to the regiment on December 28, where he commanded Headquarters Company until March 1919 when he became 71st Brigade adjutant. Lieutenant Sayles' promotion to captain came on October 29, 1918, and he moved from the 37mm platoon to command of Company A. After Captain Barton received orders to command a military police battalion in October, he earned a promotion to major and received orders to return to the United States as an instructor. However, when the armistice went into effect, the Army sent him to manage a German prisoner of war camp until his return home late in 1919. Captain Ethan Simpson, wounded on October 8, returned to the regiment on November 4. Although Simpson was "thankful to be alive," he was "intensely grieved" over the deaths of twenty-four men from his company.[7]

The regiment also welcomed back several former prisoners of war, many of whom had been captured on the late afternoon of October 8 outside Saint Etienne. Those soldiers, all from the 142d Infantry, had failed to fall back quickly enough during the fighting that October afternoon and were captured by advancing Germans. After being searched for weapons, the nine soldiers were marched toward Leffincourt, frequently seeking shelter from Allied artillery shells. In Leffincourt, German intelligence officers interrogated them. The soldiers' personal belongings remained untouched, although most had their raincoats confiscated. Several of the soldiers later reported that the German officers questioning them admitted to former residence in the United States and that they were either in Germany when war was declared in 1914 or had "answered the call to the colors" prior to the U.S. entry into the war.[8]

According to the soldiers, no "third degree methods" were used during the interrogation and the German officers kept their questions focused on gathering military information. With the soldiers claiming ignorance, the Germans soon became "disgusted with the process of the examination and said the information was not necessary" and produced maps as well as a book that contained detailed information on the 36th Division. As the report noted, "They had full information that we were Texas and Oklahoma troops, trained at Camp Bowie, date we arrived in France, names of some of our transports in our convoy" and that they had trained in Bar-Sur-Aube. In possession of such information, the officers expressed surprise that an inexperienced division would be placed in "a sector which they considered a hard one and well protected." Several soldiers reported seeing a range of U.S. Army uniforms in the German dugouts, which they assumed the Germans used to gather such accurate information.[9]

On October 10, sixteen men and ten guards continued their march to the rear. While they walked, the soldiers concluded the Germans were in a full retreat: "They were moving everything, artillery, supplies and even household furniture." Indeed, the prisoners were forced to push heavily laden carts and what little food they received consisted of "very thin carrot soup" and two loaves of bread for all sixteen men. Soon joined by more prisoners for a total of thirty-six, the group hiked to the town of Flize, where they spent five days working at "odd jobs." While they were treated well by their captors, the food situation remained poor. However, the prisoners realized their guards received barely more food than they did. Eventually the men marched to Sedan where they boarded a train for Montnedy. They arrived there on October 21 and stayed for five days before proceeding to Rastatt, Germany. While boarding the train for Germany, the men were told that they would be shot if they tried to escape. In response, one of the men quipped, "Hell, Jerry, you have shot at us before and did not hit us." The 142d prisoners arrived in Germany on October 27, the same day their comrades made their attack on Forest Farm on the Aisne River.[10]

The soldiers spent the rest of their time as prisoners of war at Rastatt, in a large camp that contained eleven "blocks," with each block holding approximately 1,000 men. According to the prisoners, the American soldiers occupied four blocks. The Americans remained separate from the rest of the prison population, and when the Germans attempted to house some French prisoners with them, the U.S. prisoners "raised such a howl" that the Germans did not do it. Conditions at Rastatt appeared to be satisfactory, with sufficient bedding and sanitation, although the food did not improve. However, the Red Cross provided enough food and supplies on their own that the American soldiers could get by without eating the German food. While the soldiers praised the Red Cross and the assistance they received from them, some complained about the YMCA, which managed to send the prisoners just one small box of supplies.[11]

Overall, the prisoners believed the German guards respected them and treated them differently than they did French and Italian prisoners in the camp. The Americans were also not shy to take advantage of their status. When a group of prisoners was taken to unload a railcar of coal, the American contingent refused to work and the German guards did not press the issue. Of course, much of this took place after the armistice. Indeed, after the armistice, an American officer of the 101st Infantry was placed in charge of the camp and American soldiers took the place of the German guards. The soldiers left Rastatt on December 9 and 10 and arrived back in France a day later, although it took nearly one month before the men made it back to the 142d Infantry. Interestingly, another man who was captured on October 21, during a patrol into Attigny, recalled being driven thirty-five kilometers behind German lines where he intentionally changed his story every time he was questioned over a four-day period until the Germans simply became exasperated and gave up, placing him in a work party near Sedan. While there, he found out that the corporal of the guard had lived in Galveston. One night the man came to their quarters when drunk and told them that he "had been one of the agitators of the Mexican trouble," presumably meaning problems along the Mexican border between 1914 and 1917.[12]

In sum, those members of the 142d Infantry who were captured by the Germans were treated fairly well. Conditions were, of course, not ideal, and the food was not satisfactory. Still, the soldiers were not beaten or harshly interrogated and with the end of the war approaching there appeared to be little animosity on either side. Furthermore, many of the soldiers seemed intrigued by those Germans who had lived in America, something that was also quite common among American soldiers when dealing with German prisoners. Indeed, the experiences of those prisoners of war highlighted the changing relationship among American soldiers, their French allies, and the German enemy described by historian Jennifer D. Keene, in which many American soldiers came to loathe their French counterparts and developed a respect, of sorts, for German soldiers. While the Germans treated the U.S. prisoners almost cordially for the most part, the Americans' refusal to be billeted with French prisoners illustrated the changing dynamic among American soldiers, their allies, and the enemy that was quite common during and after the war.[13]

Upon their return to the regiment, those soldiers and others realized that the Army's bureaucracy had also caught up with them. One of the more unpleasant activities included investigations into the wounds received by several of the regiment's soldiers at the front and the possibility that they were self-inflicted. Suspicion centered on twelve soldiers, and Colonel Bloor requested detailed information on each case. While it is not clear how each case turned out, the case of Pvt. Lester Whatley of Company K highlighted the complexities of determining motive for actions taken on the front and whether self-inflicted wounds were deliberate or the result of accidents. At the time of the incident, the company occupied the village of Mery, in the Support Zone in front of Attigny on October 26. Several of Whatley's fellow soldiers testified on his behalf and noted that they received orders to prepare to leave the position. Whatley had climbed from his hole to roll his pack and left his rifle, with bayonet fixed, in the foxhole. At that instant several shells landed in the area and Whatley, along with other members of his company, dove for cover. Whatley, unfortunately, landed on his rifle and the bayonet pierced his right leg.

Based on the testimony, Captain Sayles reported to Colonel Bloor that Whatley should not be charged with having a self-inflicted wound. While Whatley's case may have been accidental, there were no doubt some men who resorted to such tactics in order to get out of combat. Indeed, as Colonel Bloor noted in his after action report, the regiment did suffer from some malingering, which should be contrasted with the way Texas soldiers were perceived by their fellow Texans back home.[14]

The remaining members of the old 7th also found themselves spending their second Christmas away from loved ones, although many received gifts from home, such as one man who asked his parents for "a fountain pen and some good stick candy, or most anything will be well pleased" and another who received three pictures of his family. Still, in response to a friend who asked how he spent Christmas, Pvt. Nat Grimes wrote, "You asked me what kind of Christmas I spent, I did not spend any Christmas at all, I did not know when it passed." For most, Christmas at least meant a day of rest. Private Camilla O. Hanks of Abilene described it for his sister: "Christmas is gone. It seemed more like Sunday to me than anything else. I sat around the fire almost all day. We sang songs and ran around most all day and had a pretty good time." The soldiers received all afternoons off between Christmas and New Year.[15]

As winter slowly warmed toward spring the morale of the soldiers remained good and the rigorous training schedule gave way to organized sports. Football again provided an outlet for the division's men as it had back in the early days at Camp Bowie. In France, the 36th Division football team reached the AEF Championship game, held in Paris and attended by the king and queen of Belgium, General Pershing, and other senior AEF officers. Although a close game, the 89th Division defeated the 36th by a score of 14–6.[16]

Local athletic events and theatrical productions helped pass the time as well. Each regiment appointed a "regimental entertainment officer" responsible for scheduling events and keeping up morale. Other sports besides football remained important. For example, one entertainment officer stated that 250 soldiers played 60 volleyball games, five games of baseball, three each of basketball, football, and soccer, as well as boxing and track events in one week. Indeed, according to several platoon sergeants, every man in their platoons boxed at least one two-minute round. Companies also maintained entertainment halls. In a memo to the regimental entertainment officer, officers of companies E and F reported large numbers of men came to their entertainment hall to write letters home, plenty of magazines and books were on hand, and the NCO in charge kept the hall clean and neat. Furthermore, soldiers held "stag dances" almost every night and chaplains hosted religious services on Sunday. As for theatrical shows, a number of impromptu troupes travelled around the divisional area, such as "IK's Worry Chasers" and the "Texas Rustlers." In an April 1919 contest, the prize-winning theatrical troupes included the "Forest Farm Follies" of the 141st Infantry, and the 142d's "Ste. Etienne Warriors." Of those theatrical events, Clifford Bills of the Ambulance Company wrote that "the boys all say that last night's show was the best they've seen or heard since they've been in France, and the beauty of it is, it was held in an old shackly [*sic*] barn with no platform … it was as good as anyone could expect any theater in a large town."[17]

The soldiers also had opportunities to attend various schools, including some of the best universities in England and France as well as more basic schools taught by members of the AEF, through an AEF program. Company I reported thirty-three men interested in some of the AEF courses including Auto Repair, Horseshoeing, Barber, Bookkeeping, Gas Engine, Cobbling, and Telegraph. Besides athletics and educational opportunities, the men took leave and visited Paris or the French Riviera, and the vast majority of those men enjoyed their leave and stayed out of trouble. According to Captain Chastaine, only eighteen members of the division got in trouble while on leave, only one of which was "serious." Others remained close to home to find things of interest. The 71st Brigade's headquarters was near an ancient Roman army camp and members of the 142d Infantry, perhaps including some members of the old 7th Texas, dug up a number of Roman coins and took them as souvenirs.[18]

Also during this five-month period, the division and numbers of individual soldiers received valor awards. In total, four members of the division received the Congressional Medal of Honor, two of whom were from the 142d Infantry. However, only one man, Samuel M. Sampler, from Jackson County, Oklahoma, was an original member of the 7th Texas, having joined Captain Wiley's company in Quanah. Sampler however, did not return to the United States with the regiment, instead volunteering to remain in France for an additional eighteen months. Harold L. Turner from Seminole, Oklahoma, and an original member of the 1st Oklahoma, also received the award as a member of the 142d Infantry.[19]

Although Sampler was the only member of the old 7th Texas to receive the nation's highest award, members of the division received one Distinguished Service Medal and thirty-nine Distinguished Service Crosses, fourteen of which went to former members of the 7th Texas for their actions at Saint Etienne or Forest Farm, including Thomas D. Barton, cited for his actions on Hill 60. Lieutenant Alfred Carrigan, killed while trying to free one of his men from barbed wire, received the award posthumously. Ernest Boggs of Company M received the medal for reorganizing his company during the fighting around Saint Etienne and for refusing to go to the rear after being wounded. Frank Johnston, of Denton's Company M, earned the Distinguished Service Cross for reorganizing his position after they were hit by their own artillery barrage. Will Curtis, also of Company M, posthumously received the award. Lieutenant Stayton Hankins, who was wounded in the leg but who remained with his company until he collapsed from exhaustion, received the award, as did Sgt. William T. Harden of Company L. Company I's Charles Montgomery, of Goodlett, Texas, earned the award after leading a combat group from the support zone to the line during the Forest Farm assault, although he was later caught in an enemy barrage and killed. Private John D. Reese won his DSC for serving as a runner during the Forest Farm fighting despite being sick and refusing to go to the rear, while Lonnie Shoemaker of Cleburne was posthumously awarded the Cross for remaining in the lines after being severely gassed, which later resulted in his death. Clarendon's Bergen X. Waldrop also posthumously received the award, another member of the regiment who refused to go to the rear because of a wound. Two members who joined Captain Underwood's Cleburne company, Sergeants Kelly Nail and Chester Roberts, also received Distinguished Service Crosses and the French Croix De Guerre, Nail for flanking a German position and capturing 112 Germans, and Roberts for leading a seven-man automatic rifle team to within fifty yards of a German position. He then directed the fire of his team with "such skill that the enemy surrendered." He received credit for the capture of 4 officers, 112 men, and 17 machine guns. The *Fort Worth Star Telegram* compared Roberts' actions with those of the more famous Sgt. Alvin York. When Roberts' family learned of their son's decoration, his mother told the local paper, "When the boy comes home I will rest my burdens on his broad shoulders." Other men who received the award included Sgt. Joe Wilson of Quanah, kissed on both cheeks by a French general during the ceremony, an action that caused him to remark that he was more "frightened during the ceremony than he was during the battle." Wilson received three wounds on October 9, but claimed in a letter home that "I am too tough for it to have much effect."[20]

The French government also bestowed seven *Medailles Militares* and approximately 415 *Croix de Guerre* to members of the division. A number of former Texas Guardsmen received that award of valor, including several posthumous awards. Such was the case of Pvt. Orla Shirer, born in Cleburne and killed near Saint Etienne. His medal went to his parents in Johnson County, as did the medal for Pvt. Ben Fuller. Lieutenant Alfred Carrigan also received the French medal posthumously based on Colonel Bloor's recommendation.[21]

Other members of the old 7th Texas who received the French *Croix de Guerre* included Clarence J. Casey, who earned the award for his "courage and zeal in maintaining telegraphic communications between units of the Thirty-Sixth Division," as well as Steve Lillard, Edwin Sayles, James G. Herblin, Bert

Davis, Sneed Staniforth, and Cpl. Roy Green. From Captain Simpson's Clarendon company, Sgt. Matthew Lane and Privates Obe Holland and William H. Hodges received the award, all original members of the 7th Texas. Reporting on the award of the medal to those three men, the *Clarendon News* wrote that the men "covered themselves with glory" and showed "what Texas and Oklahoma could do," and that such actions brought credit upon "the great Panhandle which they call home." Barton also received the Italian *Croix de Guerre*. However, one soldier from Amarillo, Ike Brauney, had the most unique method for earning the award. He served as a color bearer at an awards ceremony and the presenting general, who had several medals left over, gave him one for holding the flag.[22]

As their time to leave France approached, General Pershing reviewed the division on April 9. He presented several awards to men of the division, attached a streamer for the "Meuse-Argonne Champagne Sector" campaign on the division flag, and gave a brief speech. Several days later, General Smith received a letter from the commanding general of the AEF that recapitulated a brief history of the division and noted the 71st Brigade's attack at Saint Etienne and Forest Farm. Pershing wrote that the "bearing of the division, in this, its first experience in battle, showed the mettle of officers and men, and gave promise of what it would become as a veteran."[23]

Although many men received decorations for their actions in the Champagne, and while newspapers would soon begin to describe their actions in larger than life terms, many members of the old 7th Texas began to examine their experiences and put their thoughts on paper in letters to their friends and families back home. Of course, they wrote on a range of topics, but many included glimpses of their experiences at the front and how they were affected by what they saw. For example, Cpl. Clifford Young of Company M penciled a few lines to his parents to let them know he had survived the fighting and had returned from the front where he had spent the last "23 days and you can guess how I felt without washing or pulling off my clothes and no sleep or rest. I went over the top twice, and thank God I never got a scratch." He concluded his letter by telling his parents: "I am a crack shot at these Huns sure is some style of hunting game." Dee McNaney wrote "you can tell the world that being in actual battle is something you will never forget," although he also admitted to a strange attraction when he arrived at the front on October 6: "the fireworks were going on believe me, and it was all new to me, but strange to say, I liked it for some cause."[24]

Clete "Pug" Coleman, a member of the regimental band, wrote in a letter that the regiment's work was "no boys play, for we sure work since crossing the Hindenburg line and there's plenty to do." Even though he served in the band and remained slightly back of the front, he noted that German shells "sing right over us, and when one bursts about fifteen feet from you, it sure makes you think a little." One soldier from Hardeman County who served with the Supply Company wrote home that even though he had seen "many dead Boche," the chief memory that would stay with him was of the artillery, "I will never forget the sounds of those shells. I was never under heavy shellfire, but the shells were passing over me day and night." Another man wrote home relating how he came across a body, examined it to determine how the man had been killed, and identified him only because of a letter lying in the mud next to the corpse. After describing this in a letter home, he wrote, "I couldn't begin to tell you all that I could if I were with you and I will tell you all when I come home." Sergeant W. B. Hardison of Vernon had no qualms writing to his father about the fate of a battalion runner who jumped in the same hole with him. The runner asked Hardison if he might stay in the fox hole with him until the shelling stopped. Hardison wrote: "I told him to get down low, and had no more than gotten the words out of my mouth when a big shell hit a few feet to our rear, caving the ground in on our feet. His brains splashed in my face."[25]

One soldier in Captain Simpson's company, upon hearing from Simpson that they would be on the front lines the next morning, tried to describe his thoughts to his family: "'Look here young fellow, you are about to step into something that you don't know too much about.' I just wondered what it was going to be like." Like W. B. Hardison above, some soldiers wrote about their close calls on the front, which might have only served to increase the worry of parents and relatives. After James McCan left the front with Company H, he wrote that "I learned to pray and do everything else while up there and all who lived did the same, I think. One of those G.I. cans hit almost under my feet. Not a piece hit me, but the explosion was so great that it knocked me senseless for about an hour. Outside of that I never got a scratch." Corporal Wayne Wheeler nonchalantly wrote home that nothing exciting happened on October 7, except for "machine gun bullets whizzing by or a big shell exploding occasionally." He also told his parents that he did not know if he actually killed any Germans although he boasted "I helped take a big bunch of prisoners."[26]

Some soldiers experienced more difficulty writing home. On the one hand, they may not have had enough education to express themselves well, and on the other they may have realized that they simply could not describe what they had been through. One soldier from Abilene, George W. Bolling, tried to express his feelings. On a rainy evening after the armistice, he wrote to his parents that "we have been to the front. I can't write much about it." He mentioned that several friends had been killed and a number wounded and that he "acquired a fondness for holes and dugouts." On the other hand, E. T. Bennett of the Headquarters Company put it simply: "At 8:30 am we went over the top and it was hell from there on out." However, he concluded his letter to a friend by writing, "I will tell you all the war gossip when

I get home. I have seen things that you wouldn't believe." Private Adolph Windel recalled that he "had pulled through several hard shell fires, when the whole earth was trembling, and full of gas, smoke, and shrapnel." One member of the Supply Company, E. P. Taylor, wrote home that although his unit did not lose a man, "You should hear some of the big shells whistle over. Makes you get 'gully low.' You good folks back home, no matter how many descriptions you read, can have no idea of the destruction and slaughter going on and of what an infantry man has to go through." James Kincaid wrote a friend that he was "busy trying to dodge shrapnel and bullets. You tell 'em it was hell."[27]

In another case, C. M. Harvey wrote home about an officer who captured several Germans in broad daylight. However, Harvey realized that in recounting the actions of the officer he might have given the impression that the front might not be too dangerous. Lest his friends or family draw such a conclusion, he added, "Don't think for a minute, however, that those Dutchmen wouldn't or couldn't shoot, for they certainly could." Trying to express his feelings about what he had seen, Arthur Nobles of Decatur wrote that "it was simply hell on the front to see the boys get killed," and Company E's Donald Dealey wrote home that "I have seen and done and endured things that were pretty tough, but I am proud that I am a Doughboy."[28]

Many of the regiment's soldiers took obvious pride in passing through the Hindenburg line, just north of Somme Py. Bryan Autry wrote of it: "that is the one that Germany said could never be broken, but it was and we put the finishing touches on it." James McCan, wrote, "We crossed what used to be the Hindenburg line and such a sight I never saw before or since. There was not a tree or even a bunch of grass living for about four miles across it." The night he first approached the front was one "that I will always remember as if it were last night." Captain Spence described the line as pure desolation and equivalent to a desert. The trenches had been "obliterated" and "the French and German dead who had fallen in the fighting of the week before lay still unburied." Captain Ethan Simpson recalled that as his soldiers approached the front lines they saw "stark, stiff staring things that had once been human beings, now lying cold and stiff or reduced to bits of bloody rags." After hearing artillery for the first time, Simpson wrote: "It certainly made one feel queer and creepy to hear those big shells start miles away and come moaning one's way and not know just where they were going to hit."[29]

Although some bragged, many of the soldiers were not ashamed to express their fears. Corporal J. F. Austin of Company L told his father and sister that "I had some mighty close shaves but what it took to lay close to the ground I happened to have, and a prairie dog hasn't a thing on me when it comes to digging in." Austin told his relatives that he had been gassed and wrote, "Believe me it sure makes you sick. I can still feel the effects of it. Most everybody that is gassed is short-winded afterward." Roscoe Kile of Valley View tried to describe for his brother what it was like to be under artillery fire, writing, "it sure makes you think of everything you ever did. And something you ought to do." In typical Texas fashion, he described the German artillery shells: "He has shot everything at us from a blackland farm to a small town like Fort Worth."[30]

Roscoe Kile wrote one letter that was unique in part because he documented in his letter when enemy shells fell nearby: "Life isn't what it used to be. I used to think if I could get to the front and fight I would be satisfied, but now I think if I could get off, I would like it better." He described the attitude he and his fellow soldiers assumed on the front. When a shell approached, he wrote: "the only thing to do is flatten out on the ground and maybe it will pass over you and maybe it won't, and if it does, why should you worry, and if it doesn't you don't have time to worry." Kile had words of advice for any soldiers who had yet to make it to France: "Well, I'll tell you it is bad enough at the best, and those boys there had better get right with God before they come over here for they might not have time after they get here." He closed this letter to his parents: "Those who get back will have lots to tell and if anyone says war isn't hell you will know he hasn't been here (another damn can. Fritz sure has it in for us, he sent three that time.)"[31]

While many soldiers wrote about their feelings and experiences at the front, at least one member of the old 7th Texas found an outlet through drawing. Although Lt. Edwin Sayles wrote about his experiences, at the time he drew pictures of things he saw during the fighting that were stark, black and white reminders of the devastating effect of war. He drew dozens of pictures, some of which were battlefield scenes or terrain sketches. One of them depicted an American soldier being shot. "Hit" was the caption of the drawing and in the penciled lines the soldier has lost his grip on his rifle and is in the process of raising his other arm and stumbling forward.[32]

Sayles also drew an image of a dead German soldier, with the typical detritus of war lying next to the body, including a helmet and grenade. One can almost imagine Sayles stumbling upon the body near an abandoned machine-gun position and pausing long enough to take in the details. He drew another image of two soldiers resting in a fox hole, only their helmets and long bayoneted rifles sticking out of the top of the hole. The battlefield sketches drawn by Sayles often reflected the confusion of the scene and were obviously drawn during the fighting. Besides drawings of soldiers and the front, Sayles tested his pencil on German prisoners and French refugees. Perhaps the most striking image that Sayles drew was of a fourteen-year-old French boy, who in the drawing looks to have more in common with an eighty-year-old man, including a mustache and a cane. Needless to say, these images impart a different sense than the letters written home. They were most likely done quickly, a reflection of something that caught a soldier's eye on the spur of the moment. Sayles also attempted to capture the sounds of daily life, in one instance jotting down the sounds of a French Village: "Geese … Chickens cackling … Bread wagon horn … Bell at gate … Soldiers cussing … Dog barking … Truck passing on highway … French people talking … Small French kid whistling … Creak of farmer's wagon … Wooden shoes on hard ground … Cattle mooing … Rooster crowing… Chain on well … Wheelbarrow squeaking."[33]

While members of the old 7th Texas described their experiences, they also frequently praised their comrades, and ranged from simple statements of praise to in-depth tributes to men killed and wounded. For example, George W. Bolling wrote that "Of the officers who were with us at Abilene, only Lt. Sayles remains and I expect he will be a captain before long. He has proven to be a brave and excellent officer." Lieutenant Stayton Hankins of Company H recalled that all the officers of his company had been shot by six am on the morning of October 8. Lying in a shell hole with a wound in his left leg, Hankins recalled Capt. Duncan Perkins of the Supply Company doing "for the Quanah boys whatever was humanely possible besides keeping our company supplied."[34]

Captain Lillard's men were "loud in their praise of his work in the front lines" because he "was always in the lead, with words of encouragement for his men, and with aid and sympathy for those who were unfortunate." The *Wise County Messenger* stated that Captain Lillard was "very reticent as to his work in the battle line, always giving credit to his men for the great work done." Lawrence Melton wrote to his parents after the armistice, "At last I am back with Captain Lillard. Mama, I can't express my admiration for him. Anyway, I would gladly die for him if necessary … I can certainly say that he is a brave man." Even though Lillard was modest about his own actions, he wrote in a letter to his parents, "it was the greatest privilege in my life to command, first Company L, composed of the home boys and boys from Cleburne and Childress. There never were braver, truer, nor more loyal fellows than these." During the fighting, he recalled the actions of his first sergeant. He wrote that the man, after being wounded "did not want to go back and leave me to the tender mercy of the Germans without his able assistance." Lillard also took pride in several of his soldiers who advanced with the 144th Infantry and who returned to the 142d after rations became scarce and the men were "kicked out of the mess line a couple of times." Finally, Lillard concluded: "These boys do not think that they can do enough for me, and while I thought a great deal of them before going under fire, there is a closer feeling now than I ever thought ever could be between us." He added, "I think so much of them that I can hardly correct them—and it is a very little correcting that they need, for they are true soldiers and veterans." Lillard also wanted to tell his parents the "little funny things come up to help make you enjoy yourself when you are laying out in a little hole with the enemy sniping at you with six-inch shells." Lillard told his parents to "keep on fattening the fatted calf, for your wandering son is coming home soon. We have fought a good fight and are ready to rest."[35]

The men often expressed personal feelings, particularly when referring to a friend who had been killed. Victor Nobles tried to explain to his mother what it meant to him to see his friend Monte Dunaway killed: "Mother, you said you didn't understand what I meant by losing my pal. Monte Dunaway got killed the first day we went over the top by a machine gun bullet or by a sniper. He was just too brave, but believe me, he did his duty as a soldier. I was in his squad and the only one left the next day."[36]

When Capt. Ethan Simpson learned of the death of First Sergeant Aubyn Clark, he not only praised Clark's actions but offered Clark's family revenge, swearing to them "I will kill in cold blood every Hun I see no matter how quickly he plays the coward and throws up his hands and cries 'kamerad, kamerad.'" The bond between Simpson and Clark was strong enough that Simpson wrote: "I never had a brother and I gave the men of my company who were so loyal to me all the love I would have centered on a brother, through all these years, but as Aubyn was my top sergeant, he and I were closer than any others."[37]

Simpson praised many of his soldiers, calling Harry Warren "brave as a lion" and Cpl. Herman Percival "a real man at all times," and "there was none better" than Sgt. Ira Hanson. Then came Jack Rutherford, who, Simpson wrote, "Fought like a wild man," and George Taylor who "developed into such a cool, capable, brave, clean fellow that I promoted him to sergeant and sent him to school," which also kept Taylor out of combat. Simpson also acknowledged Cpl. Lindsey Taylor, who "coolly rolled a cigarette in front of his squad while under intense shellfire and proceeded to knock down Germans like he was on a rifle range." Finally, Simpson praised three other local Clarendon members of his company, writing that the last he saw of them, "they were fighting like tiger cats." The regiment's chaplain, Charles F. Barnes, wrote: "I am proud to say that I went over the top on two occasions with my boys. They, as you know, are from Oklahoma and Texas—western boys, and as courageous as ever breathed the free air which God supplies."[38]

Corporal Bryan Autry of Company M, an original member of the regiment, praised his entire company, writing his parents that although he joined "this fighting bunch of men" against their wishes, he was glad he had done so and wrote, "Sure am proud that I can say I was one of them." Captain Barton acknowledged the Texas military tradition when he wrote a friend that "I believe our division has done its share in helping win the war and believe that Texas has no right to be ashamed of the part which it has played." Sergeant Edgar O. "Dad" Breeze, a member of the

Headquarters Company, claimed that "in the entire Division there was not a streak of yellow," while one member of Company B wrote that after leaving the front it was strange not to hear "shells bursting and the loud reports of cannon, and the popping of machine guns." Oddly, he claimed that the "boys are as happy there on the front as they are here, especially when we went over the top, every one with a smile."[39]

While clearly the regiment's soldiers did not want to get their hopes up too much about the end of the war and an early return home, they could not help but mention it in their letters. In October 1918, Clifford Young expressed feelings about the approaching end of the war as rumors swirled about a possible armistice in the first weeks of November. Responding to a letter from his relatives that mentioned the possibility of the war's end, Young remained cautiously optimistic: "You spoke of the war being about over, but I can't say for fear it isn't but hope so anyway." Young also told his parents that they "need not worry about me staying over here after the war is over, the old U.S. is too good for me." Willis McMahan of Company K echoed those feelings, writing home that the end of the war could not be very far off, "for the war is going our way in every direction. You know more about it than I do, I suppose, because we hardly ever get any news we can decide upon." Private Adolph Windel, a recent transfer to the regiment although originally from Texas, wrote home that "the hopes [*sic*] of being at home soon makes me extremely happy." Interestingly, Windel could not write to his parents in their native German because no officer in his company could "read or censor the letter." By October 24, Captain Duncan Perkins optimistically wrote his wife that "the Kaiser's days were numbered as the Allies armies were advancing all along the line." One of Captain Perkins's men, E. P. Taylor of the Supply Company, wrote "I shall be glad when we get back to civilization and sanity," and C. M. Harvey, a late addition to Company M, hoped to return to more favorable weather. Complaining of the fall and winter rains, he wrote: "Talk of sunny France, but give me sunny Texas all the time."[40]

Besides rumors about the war's end, rumors also swirled about when the soldiers might return home. Of course, most were ready to leave immediately and many were prepared to leave France without a second thought, having seen enough of the country. Again, C. M. Harvey, like many soldiers, heard nothing but rumors as to when they would go home, writing "It is hard to even express an opinion. I suppose somebody knows when but I am not sure many [do]." He also wrote that his captain said they would be lucky if they made it home by April. Because of the uncertainly, Harvey resigned himself to not knowing: "Just be patient and remember there are two million of us and each wants to go home as bad as the rest and we all can't go at once." Similarly, Captain Barton wrote to a friend that they had moved to a training area and spent much of their time "speculating on when we will be sent to God's country, but this you know as much about as we do." Barton also heard rumors that the division would join the American Third Army on occupation duty. Oscar Horton of the Machine Gun Company plaintively wrote that there was "very little sickness, except for homesickness" in his camp. Writing in April of 1919, he believed the division would not sail for home for at least another three months, too long to suit him: "I will not be a bit sorry when we leave this God-forsaken country. You have heard of 'Sunny France' but it is all a mistake." Horton also let his impatience with the French get the better of him and called them "the filthiest people on earth." In his last letter home before he was killed, Sgt. Aubyn Clark had written to his sister: "I wouldn't take a million dollars for the experience but I wouldn't give five cents to see any more of the country." In a letter to a girl from home, James Kincaid wrote, "I wish you were over here to see this beautiful country. It is a Dinger—rains here all the time, mud is about knee deep. But that don't worry me a little bit. Nothing don't bother me [*sic*], only having to stay over here." Indeed, Kincaid concluded his letter by telling a friend that if she harbored any grudges against anybody in Texas, then "Send them to France. That will be punishment enough for them. Makes no difference how bad you hate them."[41]

William T. Phillips wrote his mother that "I have had some tough experiences over here, but it is worth ten years of my life." Nevertheless, he expressed readiness to come home, "Believe me, it is good to think about getting back home and among friends, for the people here are strange to me, and when I get back to the states I will take myself to Rosston faster than the Germans took themselves back to Hun-land when once they started." Corporal Austin wrote to his father that "this trip over here had made a home stayer out of me and most all the rest of them, so you might just figure on my staying close around when I get back." Carl Appling of Company H also looked forward to coming home, hoped to find a job around harvest time, and longed to be paid in "biscuit and pie."[42]

Finally, on April 10, 1919, "out of a clear blue sky," the 36th Division headquarters received a message from the First Army Chief of Staff announcing that General Smith's division had been relieved of duty with the Eighth Corps of the American Expeditionary Forces. The Texans and Oklahomans were finally going home five months after the armistice. The message transferred the 36th Division to the AEF Services of Supply for the trip home. First Army tasked the division with proceeding by rail from the Sixteenth Training Area to an embarkation center on the coast. Smith's order stated that he was to begin moving his division by April 27, 1919, and to appoint baggage and billeting officers to handle the work of moving the division to its port of embarkation. Just over two years since the United States declared war on Germany, the soldiers of the 142d Infantry received their orders to return home. The regiment's soldiers spent the five months since the armistice of November 11, 1918, impatiently training, playing sports, attending schools and taking leave. Many of them received decorations and awards for their actions in combat and the press lauded their combat record. They discovered old friends whom they thought had been killed in combat, and perhaps most importantly, they talked and wrote about their experiences to each other and their families. At the same time, the communities of Northwest Texas from which the soldiers of the old 7th Texas left so long ago, struggled to gather information about their loved ones while the excitement of the soldiers' impending return generated enthusiasm, praise, pride, and celebration. Like hundreds of thousands of other soldiers throughout the AEF, in a few short weeks they would be home and all of their experiences would become memories.[43]

8

COMING HOME AND THE WAR'S LEGACY

While the soldiers of the old 7th Texas and their comrades in the 142d Infantry and the 36th Division reflected on their experiences and tried to put into words what they had seen and felt, the press and other observers quickly picked up on the division's exploits. For example, Gen. Stanislas Naulin, commander of the French XXI Corps, under whom the 36th Division served for a time, wrote to General Smith while the regiment was still at the front. Naulin wrote that Smith's "young soldiers … rivaling, in push and tenacity with the older and valiant regiments of General Lejeune, accomplished their mission fully. All can be proud of the work done." Naulin also expressed "appreciation, gratitude, and best wishes for future successes. The past is an assurance of the future." This was followed shortly after the armistice by the governors of Texas and Oklahoma, who sent telegrams to General Smith. Governor Hobby wrote that "all Texas is proud of her brave sons and rejoices over their wonderful achievements." From his perspective, the soldiers of the old 7th Texas had carved their own place in Texas military history.[1]

The press soon published Naulin's remarks and quite a few newspapers picked up the story. In fact, accounts of the division's actions began appearing even before it had made its successful assault against Forest Farm. Of course, much of this praise found outlets in Texas, where newspapers across the state quickly picked up on the division's activities, and even the *New York Times* carried the story of the division under the title "Texans heroic in first battle."[2]

The *Wichita Daily Times* printed the Associated Press story that focused on the exploits of both the 2d and 36th Divisions and considered their contributions to the fighting in the Champagne region as "the most glorious contribution of American military history in this war." While overstating the importance of the role of those two divisions, it is clear that the communities back in Texas began to perceive the division's actions as a monumental effort to be written into the lore of Texas and U.S. military history. The Associated Press report also specifically praised the 36th as it was "new to fighting and without ever having heard shell fire before, the division withstood the most bitter German counterattacks without flinching," a theme which only served to add luster to the division's actions in the minds of many Texans. Other Texas papers soon echoed the Associated Press article. The *Dallas Morning News* wrote the division's exploits were being celebrated across Texas because "Texans and Oklahomans knew all the time that the 36th Division would at once begin the winning of the war when they got into action." In Quanah, the *Tribune-Chief* headline blared: "Panhandle Kids Swept Prussian Veterans before them."[3]

All such articles, although not completely accurate, served to shape the way that Texans perceived "their soldier boys" as they prepared to return home. This magnification of the division, while understandable, and propagated to a certain extent by the soldiers themselves, resulted in some of the soldiers referring to themselves as that "famous outfit of Texas Rangers and Oklahoma ranchers and oil men" whose "smartness and snap" in saluting made them "famous all through the AEF." One soldier of the 133rd Machine Gun Battalion cited praise from the Marines that they fought with at Saint Etienne. As that soldier put it, although the Marines fought on "five different fronts … we had the men with the 'guts.' Nothing can stop them, and when the Marines give it to a bunch of National Guardsmen, you may rest assured that they are the real thing."[4]

Later, when General Smith returned to the United States, Fort Worth officials held a dinner in his honor, and he too contributed to the magnified view of the division when he spoke of his soldiers' "fighting character." Smith considered the division's officers "too brave" and the soldiers too "eager to follow their leaders, regardless of the danger." Smith also highlighted his own longstanding "interest in Texas" because his grandfather was a cousin of Sam Houston. General Smith remarked on the "marvelous physique of the Texans and Oklahomans" and was impressed by "the spirit of the men." Replacements received by the division looked like "weaklings" compared to the Texans and Oklahomans. According to General Smith, "the world has known no greater soldiers," and concluded his speech, "we knew that men like the Texans and Oklahomans could whip the stuffing out of the Huns but we had no idea that they'd be as fearless as they were." Former Division Commander General Greble expressed his feelings as well, writing a friend in Fort Worth that he was not surprised that the division would not be stopped once in combat. Just a week before the armistice, he wrote that "it was a great satisfaction" for them to have been in combat and he "would like to pat them on the back." In fact, the amount of press coverage received by the 36th Division caused some hard feelings among soldiers of the 90th Division, the Texas and Oklahoma draft division. That division suffered far more casualties and served in France longer than the 36th. As one member of the 90th Division's 359th Infantry Regiment quipped, "the people of Texas have forgotten about the fact that the Ninetieth Division is a Texas Division and it has made much bigger name and done about ten times as much as the Thirty-Sixth Division."[5]

While many families back in Texas read the press reports and waited for news of their soldier boys, some received news that all dreaded. Because of the confusing nature of the fighting in France and of the number of letters written home with conflicting information about who had been killed or wounded, a writer for the *Clarendon News* cautioned local residents not to generalize about what they read. The reporter pointed out that many of the reports they received from soldiers were "more or less exaggerated after they have passed the mouths of a few folks." Nevertheless, the reporter asked Donley County residents to "nerve ourselves up for what may come." Occasionally, families learned of the deaths of their relatives through letters from other soldiers, such as Cleburne soldier Art Miller, who had been killed in France and whose body was not recovered until well after the fighting. Another Cleburne soldier, taking a walk while presumably on leave, described discovering the body to his parents: "He was covered with brush and had lost his right arm and the side of his head was blown off."[6]

Sometimes the papers printed in-depth tributes that expressed the anguish people experienced with the loss of their loved one. In some cases, leading citizens of the communities penned such eulogies. Thus, much as they had led the recruiting drives of 1917 with rhetoric and patriotic speeches, after the armistice when the news filtered in of soldiers killed in action, leading citizens frequently considered it to be their duty to comment on the deaths of those soldiers. For example, Harwood Beville, a member of the Donley County Exemption Board and father of 7th Texas veteran Arthur Beville, eulogized Sgt. Aubyn Clark: "I turned away with tears coming to my eyes when I heard it for he was my friend." Beville wrote that Clark had made the "supreme sacrifice" and that he "went to his death" proving that "American and Texas soldiers are not to be sneered at." Beville also laid claim to the soldiers of Captain Simpson's Donley County company, "loving them as my own." He concluded by saying "they are the bravest of the brave, and better fellows never breathed … Clarendon and Donley County is honored in honoring these brave men."[7]

Monte Dunaway's uncle eulogized his nephew, killed near Saint Etienne. In the *Wise County Messenger* his uncle wrote simply: "We will miss his cheerful face and quiet way of moving about our homes. As we walk life's path, we will cherish the memory of our nephew." A friend eulogized Sgt. Loyd W. Smith, who had joined Captain Lillard's Decatur company on June 15, 1917. His friend stated that "when last seen in action he was splendidly upholding the American reputation as a fighter and those who knew him here know that he gave his country his best service."[8]

Finally, the *Abilene Reporter* carried a eulogy of Pvt. Ben Fuller in the fall of 1918. Fuller enlisted in Captain Wagstaff's company, and secured a "minor's release" in order to join, which his father signed after accompanying his son to the recruiting office, where the older man realized his son was "determined to enlist and serve his country in her need." The news of Fuller's death came in a letter from a close friend of his, Billy Hughes. Because the news was not official, it left a sliver of hope for Fuller's parents that perhaps a mistake had been made, even though they "placed much credence" in Hughes's letter "because of the personal friendship existing between Ben and Billy Hughes and particularly because the latter is known to be thoroughly reliable." Nevertheless, the lack of official news and the snippets of information that relatives received in letters from others must have made it difficult for them to resign themselves to a relative's fate when they first learned of it.[9]

Of course, officers also felt duty-bound to explain to family members how a soldier met his death. In one case, Lt. Joe Kell, who commanded Company K after the armistice, received a letter from Vernon, Texas, by the wife of Amos R. Childress, an original member of the regiment. Kell told her the full story and spared no detail. He explained to her what happened by quoting a soldier who witnessed the event: "I was near Corporal Childress when he was shot in the left side and closely followed by a shot in the head, which caused his death to be instantly and he made no remarks at all." However, Kell could not furnish Corporal Childress' wife with the exact location of her husband's grave.[10]

While much painful news of soldiers who had been killed arrived in the communities of Northwest Texas, opportunities for celebration also occurred. The news that the armistice had taken effect caused wild celebrations throughout North and Northwest Texas. In Fort Worth, the news arrived late in evening of the tenth, and at 1:57 a.m. the *Star-Telegram* rolled its first Extra Edition. Next door, the Central Fire Station rang its bell, and soon all of the city's fire stations rang their bells for nearly twenty minutes. As the local paper observed, "Like an electric charge, the news spread throughout the city and to the army camps. Lights flashed on in almost every home in Fort Worth." While the celebration got started early in Fort Worth, caution prevailed in Donley County to the northwest. Word of the armistice reached Clarendon over the "railroad wire" from Fort Worth, but the *Clarendon News* reported that "our people were cautious at receiving such momentous news and refused to accept it" until the *Fort Worth Star Telegram* confirmed the armistice had gone into effect. When confirmed, the "wild-cat siren broke the news to the surrounding community and from that moment the lid was off and a general jollification ensued." Indeed, in Clarendon, the local paper believed the "jollification," which lasted until midnight, was "the most gigantic celebration in the history of Donley County."[11]

The party in Clarendon went into full swing as residents sang patriotic songs, trucks were "put in place for the speakers and singers" to stand on, and locals even placed a piano on a truck to provide accompaniment. As the celebration grew in intensity, the *Clarendon News* reported that 1,500 men and women "did a snake dance from one end of the business district to the other, following the Stars and Stripes." Much like the members of the 142d Regiment and their procession to bury the Kaiser, Fort Worth residents burned "Ex-Kaiser Bill" at the corner of Seventh and Main, while in Clarendon residents held a "super sad event" to bury the Hohenzollern leader. Children tossed firecrackers as the procession wended its way through Clarendon and eventually approached a stand "erected for the orator whose sad duty it was to deliver the enthusiastic address over the low-lying body of the departed, who was low-lying in death as he was in life." Once the orator finished the "funeral oration," the "body" was thrown into a bonfire. As the *Clarendon News* facetiously reported, "a paroxcism [*sic*] of sorrow seized those 'round about the funeral pyre and no other method of expression could be thought of except the aboriginal dance around the cremation."[12]

In Wichita Falls and surrounding counties, the celebration followed similar lines. The county presented a "gala scene" as the news of the armistice took hold. Before the sun rose on November 11, the citizens of Wichita Falls celebrated the armistice with "a fusillade of shots in true western style," about the same time as the *Wichita Daily Times* "rolled" its first extra edition of the day. The city's population "went mad, wildly gloriously and enthusiastically mad." This "patriotic fervor" brought the local residents of Wichita Falls onto the streets "long before the accustomed rising time" and lasted throughout the day without regard to "business, meals, or any other consideration." The only thought on people's minds, reported the *Wichita Daily Times,* was "victory and the end of the war." Impromptu parades formed that drew thousands of people. Additionally, the soldiers at Call Field, the aviation field on the edge of the city, joined in the celebrations. Continuing in true "western style," a man pulled out a "six-shooter" and shot up several Western Union telegraph wires. Needless to say, the paper reported that the celebration was of the kind "the likes of which has never before been seen on the streets of Wichita Falls." By the evening of

November 11, city officials held, "as a fitting climax," a "mass meeting of jubilee and thanksgiving" at a local theater. The *Wichita Daily Times* urged all the citizens of the town and county to attend, and for those who could not find seats in the theater, organizers arranged an "overflow" meeting. By the time the day ended, the *Wichita Daily Times* had printed three editions.[13]

There was a similar outpouring in Abilene, where the *Abilene Reporter* headline read: "Stores close at noon and the people give themselves up to rejoicing!" The paper claimed the day "would go down in history as a great holiday upon which most nations will celebrate." Schools and businesses closed, children paraded in the streets, and in an open area "there was a gathering such as was never witnessed in this city," estimated at seven to ten thousand people. Congressman Thomas Blanton wired news of the armistice to the city: "Terms of armistice are unconditional surrender. No American need be ashamed of armistice terms. All draft calls are cancelled. Our brave soldiers will be streaming home shortly." While an energetic missive to his constituents, the German surrender was not unconditional. In Cleburne, the *Enterprise* advertised a "public celebration" to be held on the courthouse square, which would be "swept and roped off for the purpose." The Santa Fe Railroad Band played and the paper urged citizens to "come out and put Cleburne on the map for a genuine old-time rejoicing. Music—pep—big crowd—'n everything!" Such armistice celebrations occurred with their own local feel across the United States, although many displayed similar characteristics to those held in the communities of the old 7th Texas. For example, in Mobile, Alabama, residents rang church bells and blew factory whistles, shops closed, and an impromptu parade led to celebrations lasting far into the evening.[14]

After nearly six months in France since the armistice, on May 2, 1919, the 142d Infantry Regiment finally moved to its port of embarkation, Brest. The regiment underwent several rigorous inspections in the Le Mans area. According to the regimental chaplain, the commander of the Le Mans area "informed Colonel Bloor that of over 500,000 troops to pass through his area, the 142d Infantry had passed the best inspection." On May 18, the regiment arrived at Brest, and twenty-four hours later, the majority of the soldiers boarded the *USS Pueblo*. The 3rd Battalion, with many Texas troops, boarded a separate transport for the journey. On May 19, 1919, the 36th Division and the 142d Infantry began the journey back to the United States.[15]

On the trip home, the division's soldiers wore new patches signifying their status as members of the 36th Division. Prior to the armistice, General Pershing directed that each AEF division design a unique divisional patch to be worn on the shoulder. The final design approved for the 36th Division was a khaki "T" superimposed on a blue arrowhead. The "T" represented Texas while the arrowhead signified Oklahoma. The division had nicknamed itself the "Lone Star" Division in September of 1918 after Texas and Oklahoma National Guard officers decided that the division's current nickname at the time, the "Panther" division, "was in no way appropriate." The original emblem consisted of a five-pointed star with "36" superimposed over it. Although officially named the "Lone Star" division, some Texas soldiers continued to refer to themselves as the Panther Division, the name by which "they are mentioned in fondest affection in the southwest." While boarding their transports for the trip home, port inspectors on the docks noted that most of the men already wore the new patch.[16]

The trip home was not without cost, however. On the second day at sea, the transports moved into an area of "heavy, deep swells," that became "quite rough" as the day passed. Unexpectedly, the ship "nosed into a wave much larger than any" experienced earlier, and "a wall of water swept over the bow," injuring several men and washing two soldiers overboard. One of the men swept overboard was an original member of the 7th Texas, Pvt. Joseph C. Strong of Clarendon. The sailors recovered the body of Cpl. Harry S. Hovey of Company E, but failed to recover Strong's. Cleburne soldier Osborne Banks received a serious injury in the mishap and was only saved from being swept overboard by a soldier standing near him. Although Banks escaped with his life, he lost an eye and was "unconscious for several days." The next day, sailors covered the hatchways of the transport and officers kept their men below decks until May 25.[17]

On May 31, 1919, the *Pueblo* arrived in New York and the division moved to Camp Merritt, New Jersey, where the soldiers remained for about one week before beginning the journey to Camp Bowie for demobilization. Officers arranged for the 142d Infantry to travel through Oklahoma on its way to Texas. Five trains, each carrying 10 officers and 885 men, finally left New York for Oklahoma and Texas, but not before Colonel Bloor sent a telegram to Fort Worth mayor W. D. Davis advising him of their travel plans to Fort Worth. After a mostly uneventful trip, the regiment arrived in Oklahoma and paraded through Enid, El Reno, and Chickasha before finally wending its way to Camp Bowie. Not all of the soldiers, however, went to Texas. For example, Company I's officers reported that the unit's 226 men would be sent to 15 different camps closest to their homes for demobilization. Of that number, 156 were destined for Camp Bowie, most of whom were probably from the old 7th Texas.[18]

While the regiment made its way back to Texas and Oklahoma, thousands of miles away in Texas confusion among the population reigned as to exactly when the Texas soldiers would arrive. Some soldiers passed along bits of information in letters and telegrams, but for the most part, news of the division's movements remained difficult to come by. For example, the War Department did not release the news of the 36th Division's convoy assignment until May 18, 1919, the day before the division departed France. While local newspapers estimated the division's arrival back in the United States, reports were not accurate until early June, about the time the division arrived in the United States. On June 2, the *Cleburne Enterprise* could finally proclaim: "Company L arrives in New York." Besides Company L, the contingent that landed in New York contained medical troops, 3rd Battalion headquarters, and Companies I, K, and M, all of which contained large numbers of the old 7th Texas. Even though the company's personnel had changed significantly over two years, that did not matter to the *Cleburne Enterprise*, which stated, "Cleburne claims Company L as its own, as this city formed the company not only in the present war, but in the Spanish-American conflict, and so feels that Company L is peculiarly its own organization."[19]

In preparation for the homecoming, many local communities flew flags and those with family members in the military placed "service" flags on their homes, churches, schools, businesses and public buildings, while anticipation continued to build through the first few weeks of June. In Fort Worth, an editorial remonstrated with residents, "Let's not have a grouch in the whole town—not a single one—while the boys are coming home." In Gainesville, excited residents found out that a troop train carrying some members of the 142d Infantry would be passing through the city on its way to Camp Bowie. The next day, four more troop trains passed through Gainesville, carrying the division's 111th Engineer Regiment. Although only two men on the train were from the local area, a "large crowd assembled at the station to greet the returning heroes," who switched trains in the city prior to completing their trip. Unfortunately, Gainesville residents could not determine if the local machine gun company was aboard any of the trains or whether or not they had arrived at Fort Worth. Two days later, The *Gainesville Daily Register* received word that the local machine gun company would pass through Whitesboro, several miles east of Gainesville. Nine car loads of Gainesville residents drove to that town to "greet the home boys" during the company's brief stop there. Those who made the trip to Whitesboro returned with news that the soldiers "were looking fine" and were glad to be back in the state. There were a few brief reunions as well. For example, the wife of Gainesville soldier Nick Fairless held up their infant son for him to see for the first time. Furthermore, the *Gainesville Daily Register* added to the reputation of the 36th Division by writing, "No men in all the great American armies did more valiant work than these Cooke County boys of the Thirty-Sixth Division…."[20]

Once residents of North and Northwest Texas realized that 142d Infantry and other units were arriving at Camp Bowie, many gathered in Fort Worth to greet them. In one case, when the expected troop trains failed to arrive by midnight, Camp Bowie guards forced the large crowd to disperse and go home for the night. However, the crowd was back in force before 5:30 am the next morning and as the troop trains pulled in, the crowd gave the soldiers a "demonstrative welcome." On other occasions, every time a train arrived, "the throng would surge toward each individual eagerly looking for his or her soldier. Disappoint did not daunt, hope was uppermost." In spite of that particular welcome home effort, some of the 142d's soldiers believed their reception in Fort Worth was "cool." As historian Lonnie White pointed out, however, residents of the city had witnessed the arrival of thousands of troops in a very short time and arriving troop trains soon became a common occurrence. Nevertheless, for some members of the old 7th Texas, family members and fellow soldiers who had come home early waited to greet them at Camp Bowie, including Roy Ormsby, who had lost an arm at Saint Etienne. Abilene sent a welcoming committee that included the wife of Capt. Ed Sayles. However, most of the reunions at Camp Bowie did not last long as the soldiers required physicals and a number of administrative tasks to complete before discharge, and many soldiers had not slept for several nights. Still, some of the returning men held brief exchanges with their friends and families, although as the local paper observed, "the homecoming was not without sorrow" as people heard details of those who had been killed or who still remained in France. One young woman, after learning that her "sweetheart" had volunteered to remain in France for an additional eighteen months, sat down on the side of the road and cried.[21]

Although the soldiers expected to be discharged as quickly as possible, they paraded through the city one final time. Colonel Bloor led the march, followed by the regimental band and the soldiers. Although the men were glad to be home, the strain of the trip home was apparent. The soldiers seemed tired and officers stopped them frequently so they could change their guns to the opposite shoulder. Although no longer used to the Texas heat, the Fort Worth *Star Telegram* gushed, "Their bronzed faces, weather-worn and the stolid swing of their stride proved that they had become accustomed to hardships." After that, the regiment began its demobilization process, which neared completion by June 17, 1919. Once a man received his discharge paperwork, officers provided him with a train ticket and a sixty-dollar bonus. While working through the discharge process, quite a few of the soldiers visited the "old regimental site" where they had trained the year before, and recalled the memories of their arrival at Camp Bowie and what they had gone through since. Despite those more thoughtful moments, the city held dances and band concerts as well as receptions for the division's former general officers, including one which included Brig. Gen. Pegram Whitworth of the 71st Brigade, now assigned to Camp Dix, New Jersey, and the man he replaced, Brig. Gen. Henry Hutchings.[22]

While the demobilization continued at Camp Bowie, the communities that had helped raise the regiment's companies buzzed in anticipation of the arrival of their local soldiers. The *Cleburne Enterprise* reported "Our men now nearly home; messages come hourly from them—some received today." In some cases, this anticipation was heightened when a wounded soldier returned early from France. For example, Sgt. Henry Warren of Captain Simpson's Company H received a severe chest wound early in the fighting on October 8, 1918, which doctors did not believe he could survive. However, after several months in a Paris hospital and a transfer to Camp Bowie, he finally received a furlough to visit his parents. As the local newspaper phrased it, Warren survived because "a good physique, a will to live and superb treatment brought him through and made it possible for him to again walk the streets of Clarendon to the unspeakable delight of his parents … and his hundreds of friends in this city." In Quanah, the *Tribune Chief* reported on the increasing numbers of returned servicemen, and stated "with fine crops and prosperity before them why shouldn't our people be happy over all these good things coming to them this year?" Along similar lines, when the mother of Distinguished Service Cross recipient Chester Roberts of Cleburne found out her son was on his way home, she compared the just-ended 1918 with the possibilities of 1919: "Isn't this a perfect world now? Only last year there was no rain, the whole earth was burning up, the war on and our boys going away to what seemed certain death. This year everything is abundant, the flowers blooming everywhere, the grain is high … the earth seems to smile and our boys are nearly home."[23]

Farther west in Abilene the County Judge appealed to Taylor County citizens and pointed out that every resident represented a "welcoming committee" for returning soldiers who should receive the "welcome of their lives." When word arrived that the Headquarters Company's train would arrive the next day, the news spread quickly and the paper exclaimed: "Let us make this the grand reception in the history of Abilene." Plans called for residents to pin bouquets on the returning "veterans of the Champagne" and pelt "them with flowers." Following a custom common throughout the nation, the *Abilene Reporter* printed a full picture of the 142d Infantry on its arrival in New Jersey, and printed pieces by Captain Wagstaff and Captain Sayles describing their experiences. Portraits of both officers appeared prominently on the front page.[24]

The same situation prevailed in Amarillo, where the *Daily News* kept watch for the arrival of local soldiers, reporting on June 18 that "members of Captain Barton's old company of the 142d infantry, who did valiant service in France," would arrive that day. The paper reported that although no "formal celebration" was scheduled, "every man, woman, and child in the city is expected to be at the depot when the train pulls in and cheer the return of Amarillo's boys." Again adding to the regiment's luster, the paper stated "Captain Barton's Company distinguished themselves in action, advancing in the face of terrible machine gun fire many times the distance they had been ordered to cover," and belonged to the "organization which 'put the Hun on the run.'" Again not entirely accurate, such comments nevertheless illustrated how the regiment's actions began to be translated from reality to memory mere months after the end of the fighting.[25]

As the soldiers made their way home from Camp Bowie, they often arrived in groups rather than as complete units. Regardless, local residents made sure all received a welcome. Several days after the Gainesville Machine Gun Company arrived in Fort Worth, word spread in Gainesville that the local soldiers of the Machine Gun Company had been discharged and would arrive in Gainesville late on the evening of June 20, 1919. When the train pulled into the station late that evening, a crowd estimated at 1,000 people waited to meet "the returning heroes." As a reporter wrote, "Probably no train has ever brought so much joy and sunshine into the hearts of Gainesville and Cooke County people as that which brought home this bunch of our soldier boys."[26]

For those who lived north of Camp Bowie, such as those from Denton, Wise, and Cooke counties, the trip home was short and many received their discharges in the morning and arrived home the same evening. Unfortunately, a train derailment caused delays for some of those soldiers, but that did not stop a group of Company M veterans from renting a private car to drive them to Denton. Once they arrived at the courthouse square, they met one of their comrades, Ernest Boggs, who had returned home early because of injuries. In a simple ceremony on the south side of the square, they read Boggs' citation for the Croix de Guerre and pinned the medal to his chest. For those Denton County soldiers, they had finally come home.[27]

In Wise County, soldiers from the 36th and 90th Divisions began to trickle into Decatur and the surrounding communities by the middle of June. Whenever a soldier arrived, the *Wise County Messenger* reported that "when a boy hits the square it takes him an hour to get around the square, for everybody has to shake his hand and tell him 'glad to have you home!'" In a published welcome home message to Texas soldiers, the *Wise County Messenger* exclaimed: "We welcome the Wise County heroes home. We hope the future holds for each of you enough of happiness to repay you for the great sacrifice you have made." Of course, with all the arriving soldiers, officers and enlisted, the local paper could not help but quip: "The country will soon be in the condition prevailing after the civil war, when you couldn't throw a brick in any direction without hitting a colonel or major or at least a captain!"[28]

In Clarendon, local residents awaiting the arrival of local soldiers displayed "faces eager, faces intent, faces longing, and all expectant." While overstated and stylized, the local paper believed it was a blessing to "see a mother clasp her son as he stepped from the train with the sturdy tread of the conqueror," or to see "some father's eyes grow filmy as he embraced his son." Such descriptions contributed to the perception of the returning soldiers as "conquering heroes." Like other papers in these communities, the *Clarendon News* also described the soldiers in an outsized manner: "One who saw those boys did not have long to ask why we were able to whip Germany. Everyone showed that he had been developed until, from the mere physical side, he was a giant. This plus his character and his ability to do for himself spelled certain defeat for Imperial Germany."[29]

Captain Ethan Simpson returned to Clarendon several days after his company, joined on the trip from Camp Bowie by his wife. According to the paper, Simpson looked his best and "is in fine spirits" but was more "than glad to be at home once more." The *Clarendon News* printed his citation for the French Croix de Guerre, but refrained from additional praise: "Any words of praise that we might attempt are useless—he has been cited by those who saw him fighting."[30]

While most of the Northwest Texas soldiers arrived home before July 4, Maj. Thomas D. Barton did not return to Amarillo until November. After his arrival, a number of his fellow citizens honored him with a dinner, one of whom described Barton as "one of the best known men in the Panhandle that had ever worn the American uniform." A number of speakers offered praise on his behalf, including Clarendon's Ethan Simpson. His friends gave Barton a gold watch, and the well-wishers included Col. Ernest Thompson and Maj. William Brownell, both veterans of the division. Offering short remarks, Barton suggested the most fitting memorial to the soldiers of Company G was a memorial in Amarillo.[31]

Perhaps the *Cleburne Enterprise* best expressed the generally optimistic feeling that descended over North and Northwest Texas as the soldiers returned home. "Our soldiers are either at home or coming fast," the paper exclaimed. "All over this fine county of ours, rejoicing mothers are planning and baking ... Yes, they are coming home, and everyone is happy. The earth is fair and smiling and welcome awaits in everyone's heart." Likewise, the Lubbock *Avalanche* also proclaimed optimism: "The rains have come and the country is rapidly recovering from the serious drouth [*sic*] stroke, the people are returning, the soldiers are coming home, and there is every reason for us to feel exceedingly good." For many across the region, the last week in June represented the conclusion of a long journey begun in the summer of 1917.[32]

In addition to welcoming the soldiers home, many communities across the state and nation sought to recognize the hardships the soldiers experienced during the war and North and Northwest Texas was no different. Residents in dozens of Northwest Texas communities concluded that the Fourth of July provided a ready-made occasion to celebrate their servicemen. The patriotic nature of the holiday, combined with the desire to thank newly returned veterans, served to foster major celebrations. Often large, boisterous affairs, the planning for many such celebrations began long before the soldiers had set foot on U.S. soil. In Wise County, planners began work shortly after the armistice declaration. Even Texas Governor William Hobby connected the Fourth of July with the soldiers' homecoming, and declared it a "special day of welcome" for all veterans. He asked recently returned soldiers to wear their uniforms and become "familiar" with the American Legion, the newly established veteran's organization.[33]

On occasion, tempers flared during the celebrations. In several instances, the perception existed that local residents were not doing enough for the soldiers. For example, in Cleburne the *Enterprise* editorialized that "Cleburne has certainly signally failed to show any sort of appreciation for what these men have done." According to the article writer, local soldiers returned home and "what are doing for them? Absolutely nothing. What is the matter with Cleburne? Do we lack patriotism? Do we lack appreciation of our own men?" The writer urged the city to appoint "a leader" to organize some type of celebration "for all the boys of all divisions as soon as they all get home." By June 12, the Cleburne Chamber of Commerce had taken up the task of organizing the Johnson County celebration, and the *Cleburne Enterprise* credited its own editorials for drawing "hundreds of requests" for an official homecoming celebration. An editorial in the *Fort Worth Star-Telegram* described returning soldiers of the 36th as "men who 'just went in and licked the German' and thus saved civilization." The writer then asked: "How is it possible for us to welcome them adequately and in keeping with what they have done?"[34]

By July 2, the Cleburne paper cautiously asked: "Are we all ready for the soldiers Fourth of July? If anything has been left undone committees want to know." The paper admonished residents: "don't let a single soldier go hungry or uncared for!" Such worries turned out to be unfounded as "the good people of Johnson County came together as a unit to make pleasure for our soldiers." Indeed, the "tables groaned with good things to eat" and those in attendance listened to speeches, watched "broncho [*sic*] busting," track and field events, a boxing match, and a baseball game between soldiers and sailors. In this instance, the speeches failed to draw an obvious connection to Texas military history, and instead compared the "soldier boys" with George Washington, Ulysses S. Grant, and Robert E. Lee. Residents considered the homecoming celebration a success and an example of "good old Texas hospitality," and the local paper estimated that between fifteen and twenty thousand people welcomed home Johnson County's soldiers and sailors of Johnson County.[35]

Amarillo, Abilene, Lubbock, Denton, Fort Worth, and Clarendon followed suit with their own celebrations, while Crowell and Vernon combined theirs, all scheduled around July 4. In Abilene, residents planned to have a real "home cooked dinner," although organizers cancelled an open air dance. Much like Cleburne, residents established a committee to plan the event in Amarillo, while in Clarendon the celebration continued a thirty-two-year trend. Nevertheless, the 1919 celebration was to be "turned into a gala day for 'the boys.'" In Lubbock, organizers scheduled two airplanes to fly over the city during its celebration. Gainesville residents promised "an old time basket picnic" for the combined holiday and homecoming, and offered free refreshments for everyone. The local paper stated, "It is up to Gainesville and Cooke County to give a royal welcome to all her brave boys who served in any capacity during the war," although some citizens expressed concerns similar to those in Cleburne. The *Gainesville Daily Register* asked, "Will Gainesville fail the soldiers?" The Chamber of Commerce reported that few people had volunteered to furnish food for the proposed picnic. The newspaper lambasted local citizens, writing "we can't believe that the good people of Gainesville will refuse to render this small service for the men who placed their all upon the altar of our freedom and safety." The paper urged citizens to remember that the soldiers "went hungry days and days in the trenches in order that we might continue to live in peace and plenty...." Although some residents feared that Gainesville might fail the returning soldiers, the city of Valley View in southern Cooke County did not: three hundred people attended the town's dinner and celebration. The soldiers from Valley View "marched in formation to the banquet yard," although a heavy rain delayed the feast for several hours. Rain also hampered the celebration in Fort Worth, although that did not stop about 1,000 soldiers from enjoying the picnic under trees with local young women.[36]

The Gainesville celebration finally got on track after enough local residents stepped forward to provide food. Organizers asked soldiers to attend the picnic in their uniforms so that "the various committees may show them special favors and that the people generally may recognize easily the guests of honor." At least one resident of the county, Lillian Gunter, chairwoman of the Cooke County Historical Committee, urged each soldier to stop at a "historical booth" set up on the fairgrounds and fill out a brief questionnaire documenting their military service. In the local paper, Gunter wrote that although such records "may not seem important right now, the time will soon come when they will be of great historical and perhaps of personal value." Finally, in order to keep the theme of an old fashioned picnic, the *Gainesville Daily Register* reported there would be no "steam swing, no snake charmers, no forty-nine camp, no wheel of fortune, no doll racks, no knife table, no shell games, nor other skin games, classed as 'amusements.'"[37]

The celebration in Amarillo started with a parade led by 36th Division veteran Col. Ernest O. Thompson, older brother of 7th Texas veteran Lt. George

O. Thompson. The parade drew an estimated fifteen thousand people, and at its conclusion the crowd watched a baseball game, ate a picnic lunch, and held a street dance. Soldiers played baseball in Gainesville as well, although that contest pitted 36th Division soldiers against 90th Division veterans. The 36th Division team included Lt. Bert Davis of the old 7th Texas among others. After an "interesting game of ball," the 36th Division Panthers won the seven-inning contest nine to four.[38]

Although Abilene held a celebration as well, residents expressed conflicting views about the planning for the event, including some who opposed holding a dance. The deeper problem, however, might have been with the soldiers, many of whom were tired and more interested in spending time with loved ones. Homecoming Committee Chairman Deter Hardwicke pleaded with local soldiers to wear their uniforms on the Fourth of July for local townspeople: "I hope we will not let the very unpleasant condition that has arisen as to the street dance keep us from doing what has been asked by the people who have us at heart." Then he got to the crux of the matter: "There has been some talk like this: 'Let's not wear our uniform or take any part in this celebration.' Fellers, don't do this, just remember this: 99 percent of the people in this county have not seen soldiers parade or drill, they will appreciate this, so on the Fourth let's do this for those people." The soldiers finally consented, although they refused to wear their "blouses" because of the hot weather and insisted that captains Wagstaff and Sayles lead the march to the fairgrounds.[39]

The Abilene parade turned out well and included a ribbon studded group of "grizzled" Confederate veterans and small boys who struggled to keep step with the soldiers. The parade included approximately 500 men not only of the 36th Division, but the 90th, the 42d, and "practically of every division of the United States Army." As the soldiers lined up in preparation for the parade, the paper reported that "formalities were nil when the officers and men met on the side walk. They shook hands and slapped each other on the back. Funny what a little time will do." Finally, the men got into the spirit of the celebration and the paper described them as "a good natured lot of boys, despite the heat and glaring sun. They took pride in showing people they took pride in the uniform that they wore." Captain Wagstaff's father, Judge R. W. Wagstaff, gave the keynote address, and added to the image of Texas soldiers in the war: "427 years ago Columbus discovered America; 143 years ago England discovered America; and a little less than two years ago, Germany discovered America; and a little less than a year ago at Chateau Thierry, Germany discovered Texas and discovered Abilene and Merkel and the other towns represented by the boys who went from Taylor County." Indeed, the *Abilene Reporter* believed that Wagstaff's speech "portrayed to the crowd perhaps better than they ever read in any books just what grand old Texas did in the great war …." After the celebration, the *Abilene Reporter* wrote, "Abilene feels proud. Taylor County feels proud."[40]

In Clarendon, the County Fair Association extended the homecoming celebration into a three-day affair, July 3–5, with a "great free barbecue dinner" on July 3. As the *Clarendon News* illustrated, these homecoming celebrations did not always aim to please just the soldiers. Although the soldiers remained the center of attention, other motives were sometimes involved: "During the stress of war our people have gotten together very little and this great gathering of the citizenship of this and adjoining counties will do much to wipe out the bitterness of war's sacrifices and bring about more good fellowship." The paper concluded: "Tell all your friends and neighbors that Clarendon will celebrate the Fourth of July as it never has been celebrated before." In Clarendon, a baseball game pitted two African-American teams from Clarendon and Amarillo, one of the few instances in which minority groups participated in the mostly all-white celebrations. While U.S. Congressman Tom Connally spoke at the Clarendon celebration, the major address of the day was a speech given by Capt. Ethan Simpson, who planned to present a "narrative" of the combat service of the 142nd Infantry. The *Clarendon News* expected Simpson's speech to be "remembered as one of the platform gems of this generation" and "worth going a hundred miles to hear." As the Fourth of July drew closer, the *Clarendon News* issued a warning to those who might not want to participate in the celebration: Anyone who attended the celebration and left hungry or "who isn't hoarse from wild applause when the day is over is not fitted for citizenship in this grand and glorious republic and ought to be deported on the same ship with the Bolshevists, IWWs, Pro-Germans, etc…." Underneath the patriotic rhetoric and the homecoming celebrations, an undercurrent of fear still existed. Those who did not fit in were not wanted.[41]

Of course, such celebrations across the state held in honor of the returning soldiers followed a typical pattern across the nation. Parades, picnics, and general celebrations occurred in most major cities and communities, such as the all-day celebration held in May 1919 in Montgomery, Alabama, for returning National Guardsmen and other service members. Likewise, Chicago held a massive celebration for the returning 370th Infantry. The 15th New York Infantry, which had been excluded from parading through New York City in 1917, paraded by itself on its return home in February 1919. That regiment marched through Manhattan to Harlem in French Army formation "amid cheers and shouts of greeting from family, friends, and neighbors and proud citizens of the black community." And, like the soldiers of the 142d, the predominantly Tennessean 117th Infantry Regiment's soldiers faced a grueling, tiresome parade through the summer heat of Memphis. However, in South Carolina, historian R. Jackson Marshall III wrote that many soldiers did not march in parades but simply received their discharges and went home to a welcome by their families.[42]

Echoing another common postwar theme, most North and Northwest Texas communities looked into developing permanent monuments to the service and memory of the soldiers who came from a particular county or city. Of course, in most cases these monuments were not strictly for the local National Guard companies, but included all servicemen, regardless of their service. As early as November 14, 1918, Donley County broached the idea of a soldiers monument that residents hoped would succeed in "emblazoning their names high on the tablets of fame which time in its furthermost recesses cannot efface." While citizens made plans and discussed what the monument might look like, the *Clarendon News* suggested that "the unveiling of the monument be reserved until the return of Company H, 142d Inf., upon which day the county will be host to the company at this place, with a ceremony even surpassing that vouchsafed for kings." Although the *Clarendon News* reported that a monument might be had for $5,000, some residents expected the final price to be closer to $10,000, and hoped that "no one is likely to be found miserly enough to begrudge this voluntary, public, democratic way of showing our pride and love for OUR BOYS!"[43]

Cleburne residents also followed suit with an early suggestion for a monument as the cornerstone of a new park system. According to the local paper, a park would "serve a practical purpose," but would also "notify all who visit of the patriotic nobility of our sons." Such a park would memorialize the soldiers and sailors of the county, those who "gave their whole hopes, their prospects, their future, their comfort, their sound, young bodies, their lives, that we might be safe and peaceful at home." It could also serve a practical purpose: "no city is complete without an adequate park system and if Cleburne is ever to secure a park, now is the time to begin to lay the foundation." Much as in Clarendon and Donley County, the issue rested on the will and ability of the citizens of the community "to acknowledge our everlasting debt of gratitude to these boys in some way."[44]

The push for monuments in Wise and Potter counties came quickly as well. In Decatur, the suggestion originated with a local schoolteacher. The teacher's design "would be a source of pride, not only to the boys who will return, but to the relatives and friends of those who have died; also to every citizen in the county." In Potter County, local Red Cross representatives suggested a massive monument to the soldiers and sailors of the county which included a "great auditorium, with a natatorium, reading-room, library, gymnasium and ballroom." According to the Red Cross representatives, the memorial would be a "comfort house and trophy room for all visitors from across the Panhandle sector." In Gainesville, Congressman Lucian W. Parrish pushed to have a captured German cannon delivered to the county seat as a monument to the soldiers of the 36th and 90th Divisions. If they succeeded in getting the cannon to Gainesville, the paper crowed that "our citizens may be able to look upon one of those grim monsters fashioned to subjugate the world but which failed in that design."[45]

In Abilene, prominent resident Judge J. M. Wagstaff pushed the idea for a monument to soldiers of the war, a popular idea since the armistice. In response, the city appointed individuals from each precinct to raise money. The committee, which Wagstaff chaired, studied options including a building, a statue, or a "club room." Another member of the local elite, John W. Woods, stated the city should "erect a monument that time will not efface," because "no county in Texas, population considered, gave more boys to this great cause than Taylor County." While many counties wished for a unique and timeless design, at least four of the counties, Foard, Wilbarger, Tarrant, and Wichita, eventually opted for purchasing copies of E. M. Viquesney's popular statue *Spirit of the American Doughboy*. The residents of Foard County also purchased a copy of Viquesney's *Spirit of the American Navy*. Also in Crowell, a former member of the 36th Division, Claude Adams, managed to smuggle a German 77mm artillery piece back from France. The artillery piece was dedicated in 1929, while the statues were "unveiled" in 1932.[46]

Although not specifically dedicated to the men of the 7th Texas or the 142d Infantry, in 1920 citizens of Fort Worth, in conjunction with the local American Legion post, dedicated a park at the site of Camp Bowie, which had already been dismantled. Eight years later, a temporary monument of seventeen stones was placed at the future site of a divisional memorial, planned by the 36th Division Association. The seventeen stones represented the men killed and wounded by the Stokes Trench Mortar accident in May 1918, that took the life of Lt. Alan McDavid of Abilene and ten others, and wounded six "while the rest of the division's 30,000 officers and men were looking on." A permanent granite marker was not put in place until 1950. While many local communities planned monuments, the United States government did not build a monument reflecting the service of the American units that fought in the Champagne until 1937. The monument, fittingly placed atop Blanc Mont, included a description of the 36th Division's participation in the fighting around Saint Etienne.[47]

Of course, communities across the nation planned memorials to commemorate the service of their soldiers. Still, in cities and towns, groups struggled to find appropriate ways to memorialize their soldiers and secure funding for their projects. In Mobile, Alabama, the Mothers Army and Navy League started memorial planning and fund-raising two weeks after the 1918 armistice, as did Chicago's African-American community, which sought a monument for the 370th Infantry Regiment. As historian Mark A. Snell wrote, such monuments around the nation consisted of "statues, bronze plaques, parks, bridges, and buildings … named after individuals who had made the supreme sacrifice or had been locally recruited and fought overseas." However, like some Texas communities, they would not unveil their memorial until years later. Indeed, Alabama, not Texas, first passed legislation to establish a statewide memorial. Likewise, the idea of establishing a monument such as a building or a park was not unique to places like Wichita Falls and Cleburne as other communities considered such concepts.[48]

Historian G. Kurt Piehler saw in the creation of such monuments and memorials an effort to "camouflage the divisions caused by the war." As he observed, at the national level leaders attempted to use the war to supplant "class, ethnic, and sectional loyalties" by portraying the war as a struggle "for liberty and democracy waged by a united people." Furthermore, local communities, including several of the 7th Texas' communities, often selected monuments like that of the *Spirit of the American Doughboy*. Piehler argued that the "popularity of the Doughboy statue suggests the eagerness among many community leaders and veterans to remember the First World War as a national cause," while the placement of Doughboy monuments next to Civil War memorials served as a form of reconciliation between the North and South. Besides using the war to foster reconciliation, as mentioned, Texans used the war to draw comparisons between modern soldiers and their earlier ancestors. For example, even before the war had ended, the Fort Worth *Star-Telegram* printed an article titled "Civil War Soldiers Pleased with Record of Texans in France" which proclaimed that "Texans on the battlefields of Europe are keeping up the fighting record established by their grandfathers in the Civil War." Indeed, the paper reported that Civil War veterans were "strong in their commendation of the advance of Texans in the world war."[49]

By the end of summer, the celebrations had ended, many communities planned to build monuments, and the soldiers returned to their lives, the two-year "adventure" at an end. All that they had done and experienced, all that they had seen belonged to the past, and time would begin to dim their memories of Saint Etienne and Forest Farm. So too would time takes its toll on their local communities and the state which took so much pride in celebrating the return of its "conquering heroes" and "soldier boys."

In the immediate years after the war, residents continued to celebrate the war's end, and President Wilson issued an Armistice Day proclamation in 1919, which was echoed by proclamations from many governors, including Governor Hobby. In turn, many local officials in North and Northwest Texas issued their own statements, such as that by Cleburne Mayor John H. Short, who called "the attention of the people to this important date in our Nation's history." Short wrote that for many residents, the question remained whether or not the celebration should be public or "private in character." Regardless, the mayor believed that the "entire American people shall pause to scatter the flowers of memory on their sacrifices, lives and ambitions" of those "whose dear ones lie sleeping on the Fields of Flanders." While many residents of Cleburne doubtlessly echoed such sentiments, a few people did object to closing the business district for the day, and the school board declined to close the Cleburne schools because "no set program had been prepared" for Armistice Day. Expressing its disappointment, the *Cleburne Daily Enterprise* pointed out that November 11 was a "legal holiday" because of Governor Hobby's proclamation, and asked its readers: "Have we forgotten so soon? How have we remembered those heroes? How have we commemorated that historic day when shells ceased to shriek and shrapnel burst no more? Have we forgotten in one short year the flood of ecstasy that filled our hearts...?"[50]

Ten years later, in 1928, Armistice Day had become a well-recognized holiday across the nation. Most of those who had thrilled with excitement at the end of the war were still alive, and many Texas communities, including those of the old 7th Texas, acknowledged the holiday, mainly with church services and parades. In Amarillo, workers completed the "Dough Boy memorial," which was dedicated and "presented to the World War veterans of the Panhandle." Oddly enough, an advertisement taken out by an Amarillo department store seemed to carry the sense of the war and its place in American history: "The rancors of the struggle have vanished long ago. With our generation will die the distant recollections of undersea destroyers, Liberty Loan parades and ghostly troopships fading down the misty reaches of New York Bay. But the memory of the lad who marched into the east on those long ago mornings shall ever remain sacred in our hearts and those of our children and our children's children." Of course, at that point, World War II was still years in the future.[51]

In Decatur, while businesses participated in a "general" closing of stores, no special celebrations or parades were planned. In Donley County, the local American Legion post sponsored a program. Local churches urged their congregations to attend a combined church service, followed by patriotic music performed by a local band and the "school glee clubs." In Gainesville, the city held an armistice parade that "traversed the principal business sections" in the morning followed by a memorial service by an out of town speaker. After the "solemn" services, the locals spent the rest of the day in "various forms of amusement," including a rodeo and a turkey shoot. While most businesses closed for the anniversary, the Gainesville schools remained open, although teachers scheduled "patriotic programs."[52]

By 1938, however, some Armistice Day celebrations took on a slightly different cast, in part because observers stressed the political and human costs of the war rather than the sacrifices of those who were involved through somber reflection, the typical approach in earlier years. For example, in Dallas, the theme of the 1938 parade was "reconciliation" between the "Peace" and "Preparedness" groups while in Fort Worth, organizers denied a peace group's float a place in the city's parade. The *Dallas Morning News* aptly titled its story on the 1938 Armistice Day celebration, "Ghostly Hosts of Nov. 11, 1918 to March Again …," and opened the article with the words: "Dead men with bayonets will rule Dallas …."[53]

However, in Abilene, at least 9,000 people attended the twenty-year anniversary of the armistice. The day included a high school football game followed by a "sham battle" and fireworks, which simulated "actual artillery, rifle, machine gun, and bomb barrages." Organizers kicked off the event with a parade of World War I veterans. Despite the more martial atmosphere, one of the speakers during the celebration sounded a controversial tone, arguing that the last twenty years of peace was on the verge of failing. Beyond the parades and reminiscences of the war, a writer for the *Abilene Reporter* pointed out that not all was well with many veterans and that for some, "their bodies were wrecked by the ravages of armed strife, even their souls scarred. Thousands and thousands have died prematurely because of that war; others are skeletons of their former selves."[54]

By 1948, armistice remembrances were much less personal, instead focusing on the war itself rather than its effect on individuals and local communities. Obviously, that change occurred because of the nation's participation in World War II. The *Dallas Morning News* expressed how that war changed the way people remembered the earlier world war. The editorialist sarcastically questioned whether or not, at the conclusion of World War II, France had regained possession of the railway car where the 1918 armistice had been signed and where Germany later accepted France's surrender in 1940. But, as the writer claimed, it no longer mattered whether or not France had the railway car back again because "the events of November 11, 1918, matter no longer, either." Furthermore, the writer pointed out, "We go on celebrating the day. Americans behind the lines the world over in 1942–45 observed it as a holiday of sorts, for there was not much of any kind of holidaying with a war going on. And our troops abroad had too many dead of their own to think back on the men who fell in 1917–18."[55]

In 1954, President Dwight D. Eisenhower changed Armistice Day to Veterans Day as a way to commemorate all war veterans, not just those of World War I. Indeed, by 1958, the armistice's fortieth anniversary, far fewer World War I veterans remained and were now vastly outnumbered by World War II and Korean War veterans. The *Dallas Morning News* reported that few people paused to remember the armistice on November 11, 1958, because "another world war, a violent 'police action' in Korea, and a never-ending, ever-grinding cold war, filled with the horror of nuclear bombs which people just won't discuss … apparently took the glory away from the armistice of the war to end all wars." At a small celebration for veterans at Dallas' Adolphus Hotel, the *Dallas Morning News* reported that when the speaker, Army Adjutant General Major General Robert V. Lee asked the assembled veterans, "Where were you 40 years ago today?" many "had to try to recall."[56]

By 1968, the armistice remembrances shifted again, this time in the midst of the Vietnam War. While the bitter memories of 1948 and 1958 might have resulted in disparagement of the holiday, the tragedy of Vietnam combined with the fiftieth anniversary of the armistice shifted the focus away from the armistice's failures and instead focused on surviving "doughboys." The *Dallas Morning News* reported that 7,100 veterans of World War I still lived in Dallas County, while another story focused on one veteran's memories of the war. Additionally, the Council of Veterans Organizations of Greater Dallas held two memorial celebrations in 1968, one at the Memorial Auditorium and the second at a local veteran's hospital, another indicator of the effects of the passage of time on the World War I veterans. In Abilene, the American Legion hosted a veteran's celebration in which sixteen veterans of the war received a "fifty-year pin" from legion officials. The *Abilene Reporter* printed an overview of the war but made no mention of the contributions of Texas soldiers. Indeed, the fiftieth anniversary of the armistice did not merit front page attention in the *Abilene Reporter*. Instead, the newspaper focused on a local soldier who had just been killed in Vietnam and pointed out that American forces were fighting three different battles in that country. Thus, fifty years later, although the focus had returned to the veterans of the war, the local impact and consequences of the war took on the sepia tones of an old photograph as compared to the all too real and bloody television footage of the Vietnam War.[57]

While the reminders of what North and Northwest Texas experienced during the war decreased as time passed, in the immediate years after World War I, the consequences of the war remained vivid as soldiers who had died in France were returned to Texas for burial. In one case, the government transported Mess Sergeant Arthur McNitzky's body, of Denton's Company M, back to Texas where he was buried in the local International Order of Odd Fellows (IOOF) cemetery, and the local American Legion Post carried his name for years. The remains of Lt. Arthur Stuart Brown, a doctor who was not a member of the regiment, but who had performed physical inspections of many of the men, was returned to Abilene for burial in 1921, while the remains of Sgt. Aubyn Clark and Pvt. Nelse Nelson, both original members of the 7th Texas, were returned to Clarendon. Also in 1921, the *Dallas Morning News* reported that an army transport ship, the *Wheaton*, arrived in New York with the remains of 5,212 American soldiers, forty-two of whom had served with the 36th Division, and ninety-nine with the 90th Division. The War Department initially planned to send the *Wheaton* on one round trip to France every six weeks until all of the war dead had been returned. Of course, many soldiers of World War I remained in European cemeteries.[58]

The passage of time also wrought changes to the 36th Division. After the war, the division and its infantry regiments reverted to the control of the Texas National Guard and became a purely Texas organization at that point, no longer combined with Oklahomans. However, the old 7th Texas Infantry was gone forever. In 1924, Brig. Gen. John Hulen, who led the 72d Brigade during the war, commanded the division with headquarters in Houston. Also in 1924, Col. Robert D. Field, a wartime member, commanded the 142d, then headquartered in Gainesville. Headquarters Company was in Amarillo, commanded by Capt. George O. Thompson, while the Service Company, commanded by Capt. Robert Wright Armstrong, was stationed at Brownwood. Major Robert Wagstaff commanded the 1st Battalion at Abilene, which included companies at Brownwood, Bangs, Ballinger, and Stephenville. Major Ethan Simpson commanded the 2d Battalion in Claude, Texas, with companies in Hereford, Canyon, and Clarendon. Finally, Maj. Claude Adams, also a veteran of the division, commanded the 3rd Battalion, headquartered at Crowell, with companies at Crowell, Stanford, Vernon, and Chillicothe. Thus, within a few short years, only a handful of officers from the original 7th Texas remained with the National Guard, and several of the communities that had raised companies in 1917 no longer had a connection with the Guard seven years later.[59]

More changes followed by 1930. Most of the officers who served in the war and remained in the Guard had retired. However, Maj. Nat Perrine, who had helped raise the Donley County company with Ethan Simpson and who earned a promotion to captain during the attack on Forest Farm, still served on the regiment's headquarters staff. Years later, a World War II veteran of the 36th Division recalled serving under Perrine during the annual two-week training camp at Camp Hulen near Palacios, Texas, in the 1930s. The man remembered that Perrine had "close cut hair" and frequently woke them at 3:00 am to go on fifteen-mile hikes. Evidently Perrine, who endured the constant training marches at Camp Bowie and marched hundreds of miles in France during the war, preferred not to let the next generation of National Guard soldiers off easily. Finally, the Army ensured that the soldiers from North and Northwest Texas would be remembered by approving a special designation for the Army National Guard's modern 142d Infantry Regiment, giving the regiment the special designation, "Seventh Texas," which the unit retains to this day.[60]

Although the 36th Division remained an active unit of the Texas National Guard and saw extensive combat in World War II, veterans held reunions as early as 1919. The first veteran's meeting was held on October 10, 1919, the first anniversary of the day when both brigades of the division were active on the battlefield near

Saint Etienne. The date also marked the creation of the 36th Division Association. Colonel Bloor presided over the first session and delivered the opening address. According to the *Dallas Morning News*, his speech focused on current National Guard legislation in Congress, particularly the Wadsworth-Kahn bill on compulsory military training. In addition to other speakers, the association held a memorial service for the division's dead. Furthermore, the *News* reported that the day would be "devoted to renewing old friendships and to living over the days when the division was 'Over There.'" Although the Adolphus Hotel served as the association's headquarters, former members who could not find or afford accommodations could "procure a cot, mattress, pillow, two sheets and two blankets at the temporary camp" while attending the celebration.[61]

The association continued to meet through the 1920s, holding reunions around the state. In 1922, the association held a major reunion in conjunction with the State Fair of Texas. Commemorating the four-year anniversary of the division's time in combat, organizers invited former division commander Gen. William R. Smith to speak. In his speech, Smith recalled "when the immortal Thirty-Sixth began a drive that stopped only after they had pushed back the crack troops of the German army to a point beyond the Aisne River." He also commemorated the "memory of those matchless soldiers of the Thirty-Sixth Division, who lie out there on the chalky hills of France." A local paper considered Smith's speech one of "exceptional brilliance." In truth, Smith followed the trend of expanding the actions of the division and at one point placed the division's feats above those of the Civil War: "I would not detract from the heroism of the Confederate troops who faced what was then an insurmountable artillery fire—I do want to say though that those battles were nothing as compared with the obstacles the Texas and Oklahoma boys faced and conquered." Smith summed up by claiming the "men from Texas and Oklahoma showed the Germans a brand of fighting they had never dreamed was in existence."[62]

Prior to World War II, the last major reunions for the World War I veterans occurred in Fort Worth in 1931, 1932, and 1934, in which at least 50,000 invitations were sent to former members of the division and guests including General Pershing, former French Army Commander General Henri Philippe Petain, and U.S. Secretary of War Patrick Hurley. The list of distinguished invitees also included Texas Governor Ross Sterling, Oklahoma Governor William H. Murray, and New Mexico Governor Arthur Seligman. General William R. Smith, now superintendent of West Point, also returned for the reunion. Although nowhere near the 50,000 mark in attendance, many considered the 1931 reunion the largest held at the time. Like the one in 1922, organizers held the 1931 reunion in conjunction with the Texas State Fair, which designated October 18 as "Thirty-Sixth Division Day." Veteran's events included a parade through Dallas, a dinner honoring the distinguished guests, and finally a "grand ball" at the Adolphus Hotel. Several members of the old 7th Texas remained active in the association and served on various committees, including Thomas D. Barton, Robert W. Armstrong, Henry Hutchings, and Ethan Simpson, while Alvin M. Owsley greeted General Smith upon the latter's arrival at the Dallas train station.[63]

Fort Worth hosted the 1934 reunion, where the veterans "piled back into town Saturday, staged a colorful parade and made merry with their old buddies." For some, the highlight was a dance held by a woman who had welcomed Camp Bowie soldiers to her home back in 1917 and 1918. By 1938, the division association held a small reunion in Dallas in which only sixty veterans "answered the roll call." Although a larger reunion occurred in Fort Worth, the veterans spent much of their time watching current National Guardsmen "use new combat equipment to maneuver over the same terrain" where the Camp Bowie trench system once existed. After World War II, the 36th Division Association began changing with the influx of thousands of World War II veterans. Indeed, although the 1950 convention witnessed the unveiling of the permanent monument to the World War I 36th Division, a press release for the event failed to spell the names of World War I campaigns correctly: "Former members of the 36th who fought at St. Meihl [*sic*], the Muese [*sic*] Argonne in 1918 will join with veterans of Salerno, Anzio, Cassino, Southern France and the battle for Germany…"[64]

While the 36th Division Association represented thousands of veterans, some former members of the old 7th Texas formed the Company G Association of Amarillo. As late as 1967, this association included eighty-nine members of the regiment, including John K. Boyce, Homer T. Merrill, Sam H. Owens, and Gordon R. Porter. The association also listed eighty-five deceased members of the association, including Robert W. Armstrong, Alfred W. Bloor, Thomas Barton, Duncan M. Perkins, Ethan Simpson, and George O. Thompson.[65]

While veterans held reunions and formed associations of old combat buddies, and the combat actions of the division and the bravery of the soldiers increased in luster, the Army had already begun studying the lessons of the Great War. In 1920, members of the Army's General Staff authored a study of the 2d and 36th Divisions at Blanc Mont and Saint Etienne. The study's authors characterized the 71st Brigade's attack on Saint Etienne as a "failure," noting that "haste seems to have characterized this whole attack." A number of years later, an officer of the Infantry School at Fort Benning, Georgia, Lt. Col. George C. Marshall, also turned a critical eye on the action around Saint Etienne. Marshall published his study, *Infantry in Battle,* in 1934 in the hope that the work would validate "the ideas acquired from peacetime instruction against the experience of battle." In it, Marshall examined how infantry tactics might be improved, and he studied dozens of examples from the Great War. One of the lessons he sought to impart covered "the importance of timely orders," and he used the 71st Brigade's attack near Saint Etienne on October 8 to demonstrate the importance of this. Marshall highlighted the failure of higher headquarters to provide timely orders to subordinate units, commenting that "no matter how perfect an order may be, it fails in its purpose if it does not arrive in time." Thus, for at least a few Army officers, and particularly for one who would later become Chief of Staff and lead the Army during World War II, the actions of the Texans and Oklahomans received a critical examination and led to the conclusion of the importance of time and adequate preparation on the battlefield, something the soldiers themselves understood when they compared their actions at Saint Etienne and Forest Farm. Indeed, perhaps a second lesson might be observed in that the regiment learned from its experience at Saint Etienne and successfully applied what it learned about timeliness, planning, and preparation at Forest Farm. Finally, the innovative use of Native Americans to transmit messages appeared not to have been closely studied by the Army after the war.[66]

What became of the men who joined the 7th Texas in the summer of 1917? Many of the officers and men of the old 7th Texas returned and lived out full lives in Texas. Thomas D. Barton remained in the Texas National Guard and Governor Pat Neff appointed him adjutant general in 1921, although the appointment spurred some political opposition. Neff supposedly selected Barton because he wanted an "actual soldier" in the position instead of a "desk warrior" or "theoretical soldier." Barton served successfully as adjutant general, and received praise for increasing the strength of the Texas National Guard so that it moved from forty-seventh to fourth largest in the nation. By 1924, rumors swirled that Barton would run for governor, although he initially claimed "he was too busy with official duties to discuss politics." However, he did not dispel the rumors. Barton described himself as a "straight Democrat" but claimed to be content to watch rather than participate in politics. Also reportedly in the mix for the governor's office was Alvin M. Owsley of Denton, another original member of the 7th Texas, and a friend of Barton's. In fact, Owsley's name had been discussed for Congress as early as November 1918. However, observers believed that Barton, because of his "brilliant war record," could control as much as 80 percent of the veteran vote. The 1924 Texas Democratic Primary had nine candidates, including Felix Robertson (a world war veteran) and Miriam "Ma" Ferguson. Barton finished fifth in the balloting, securing just 29,217 votes and did not make the general election ballot.[67]

Steve Lillard, who had raised the Decatur Company and fought at both Saint Etienne and Forest Farm, returned to Texas and became vice president of the Ranger State Bank. In December 1926, Lillard and a friend were involved in an automobile accident while returning from a hunting trip. Lillard's friend was killed and he suffered serious injuries. Lillard returned home but complications forced him to enter a Dallas hospital. Several days later, the *Wise County Messenger* reported that Lillard was "making a losing fight against an enemy more dangerous and overpowering than those he had met on the battlefields of France," but was "cheerful and faced the issue with that bravery and fortitude that characterized his conduct on the fire swept ground." He died on February 17, 1927, and was buried in Decatur.[68]

Upon his return to Clarendon, the *Clarendon News* reported that Capt. Ethan Simpson would resume his law practice, which he did for a short time in Clarendon before moving his family to Amarillo. In 1921 he returned to Clarendon and in 1926 moved permanently back to Amarillo. While living in Clarendon, Simpson provided room and board for a former member of his company, a Native American named George Smith. Also in Clarendon, the Simpsons' home burned. After returning to Amarillo, Simpson retired as a colonel from the Texas National Guard, and belatedly received the Distinguished Service Cross in 1930. Simpson wanted the ceremony held in Clarendon, however. As he put it, because "any honors coming to him accrued through the heroism and loyalty of the Donley County boys, it was his wish that the ceremony be held in Clarendon." Simpson held the ceremony at the Aubyn Clark Post of the American Legion, named in honor of Simpson's First Sergeant, and with whom Simpson had crouched in the trenches and talked of home and family on the night of October 7, 1918. Simpson's son, Everett Selden Simpson, not only joined his father's law firm, but followed his father into the Texas National Guard, serving with the 142d Infantry Regiment in World War II. Everett also received the Distinguished Service Cross and finished his career commanding the 36th Division from 1961–1969.[69]

Captain Robert Wagstaff returned to Abilene where he enjoyed a long career in law and politics, serving in the Texas legislature from 1929–1932 and running unsuccessfully twice for Congress. He later helped establish the World War II training base Camp Barkeley and later Dyess Air Force Base. He also secured a historical marker describing Company I, 7th Texas Infantry, and their 1917 temporary camp in Abilene's Fair Park. However, political opponents criticized him for his attendance at the AEF School of the Line when his regiment entered the front lines, the implication being that he secured a school assignment to stay out of combat. In an effort to dispel such criticism, Wagstaff sought and received an endorsement from Colonel Bloor in 1920. As Bloor pointed out regarding Wagstaff's attendance at the school and its timing, "You did not ask to be sent to this school, but, like the excellent officer which you are, you obeyed the order detailing you to the school." Bloor summed up Wagstaff's service in the following manner: "Your company was always among the best in my regiment, and I attribute its excellence to your good management and soldierly attributes." Indeed, Wagstaff was a key figure of the old 7th Texas, staying with the organization from the beginning to the end. After the war, Alvin M. Owsley, who had served as one of the original battalion commanders of the 7th Texas, remained overseas, attending a university in England and then receiving an assignment as a military envoy to Great Britain. In 1921 he became National Commander of the American Legion, and later served as the United States Ambassador to Romania, Ireland, and Denmark, before leaving the service of the United States government.[70]

At least one former officer of the old 7th Texas had a successful, if notorious, postwar career. Captain Noah Roark, who had raised the Denton County Company, did not go overseas with the unit after failing a physical. Roark accepted a discharge and returned to Dallas, where he became a prosperous and well-known attorney. He dabbled in local politics, and considered running for Dallas Police and Fire Commissioner in 1920. Roark also participated in several high profile trials in Dallas County. His notoriety reached its peak in February of 1933 when Roark argued with two men in a Dallas building, pulled out a revolver, and shot both men. Roark was charged with two counts of assault to murder, but after one of the men died, prosecutors elevated the charge to murder. After two trials, Roark, who pleaded insanity and whose own wife testified that he was "failing mentally," was found guilty of murder and received a forty-year prison sentence.[71]

In 1936, Roark tried to secure a six-month furlough but Governor James V. Allred denied the request. Roark finally received a furlough in 1941 and in 1942 received a full pardon from Governor Coke Stevenson, who also restored his citizenship. Roark was sixty-two years old at the time of his pardon. In 1952, at age seventy-three, Roark died at a Dallas Hospital. His obituary described him as a "fiery tempered man," but only briefly mentioned his role in organizing Company M of the 7th Texas.[72]

Two men in the regiment wrote of their experiences. Ed Sayles, who helped raise Abilene's Company I and who led the 37mm gun platoon, worked for a mining company after the war in Globe, Arizona. There, he penned a memoir about his experiences in a manuscript titled, "To Sommepy and Back." Sayles attempted to have his story published by the *Dallas Morning News* and *Fort Worth Star Telegram* in the 1930s, but neither paper committed to printing it in serial form. Sayles eventually tucked it away and it was largely forgotten until discovered in his personal papers at Texas Tech University. Sayles went on to study archaeology, co-founded the Texas Archeological Society, and wrote several books. Corporal Archibald S. Hart of Wichita Falls succeeded in publishing his memoirs, titled *Company K of Yesterday,* in 1969.[73]

Shortly after the armistice went into effect, Col. Alfred Bloor received high praise from divisional commander General Smith, who wrote that Bloor was the "only regimental commander of the division who brought his regiment to France and took it back to the United States," a feat in itself, considering the not always congenial relationship between Regular Army and National Guard officers. Smith complimented Bloor's ability as an officer, and believed that he demonstrated "sound judgment, force, energy, and initiative." Smith praised Bloor's leadership of the 142d, stating that he was "extremely fortunate to have had the services of so able an officer as yourself in command of a regiment in this, the world's greatest war."[74]

After the 142d returned to Texas in 1919, members of the Texas Senate invited Bloor to speak during the senate's second session. Bloor gave a brief history of the regiment from its formation through combat, praised the enlisted men of the regiment and singled out the actions of Lt. Alfred Carrigan of Wichita Falls, killed outside of Saint Etienne. Finally, Bloor argued that when National Guard soldiers were properly trained, they were the "equal of any troops." The *Dallas Morning News* also published his after action report of the regiment's time in combat, which ran in several installments starting on March 29, and he had two special maps of the combat actions of the regiment made which he presented to the governments of Texas and Oklahoma. As mentioned, Bloor presided over the first meeting of the 36th Division Association, and on September 1, 1919, Governor Hobby appointed him commander of the 2d Texas Cavalry of the Texas National Guard.[75]

In 1920, Bloor served as Provost Marshal in Galveston after the violent Longshoremen's strike that spring and summer. In the fall, he attended the School of the Line at Fort Leavenworth, Kansas, and earned distinction as a "distinguished graduate" in the summer of 1921 although at the reduced rank of major, a common occurrence in the postwar drawdown. Bloor obviously impressed his superiors at the school for he remained at Leavenworth and completed the General Staff School in the summer of 1922. At its conclusion, he received notice that the Army considered him eligible for service on the General Staff and that he would be eligible to attend the Army War College at a future date.[76]

Bloor continued his service in the Army, and like many others belatedly received decorations for World War I service. In Bloor's case, he received a French Croix de Guerre in 1924. In 1925, Bloor travelled overseas and served as a military attaché in Guatemala, Honduras, Salvador, Nicaragua, Panama, and Costa Rica, also earning membership in the Order of Neptunus, an unofficial Navy award given to those who cross the equator for the first time. In 1928, Bloor returned to Texas where he served as Provost Marshal of Fort Sam Houston for two years. In 1930, he received a four-year assignment to Washington as a member of the War Department General Staff, and served briefly as Chief of the Legislative and

Liaison Division. Bloor retired from the Army in 1940 and returned to Austin and resumed law practice. Prior to his death at the age of seventy-eight, he and his wife planned a trip to Europe, in part to walk over the ground where the regiment had fought in 1918. Also in Austin, Bloor's younger brother Bertram, the operations officer of the 142d Infantry, joined him as an attorney, and died a year after his older brother and former commander.[77]

Unfortunately, it is not as easy to track the nearly 2,000 enlisted men of the old 7th Texas Infantry to see how they fared in later life and how the war affected them. The evidence suggests that in most cases, the soldiers returned home and picked up their lives. Twenty-five years after the war, the *Abilene Reporter News* tracked down and listed the occupations of many of the soldiers who had joined Captain Wagstaff's Company I in 1917 and listed their occupations. Some returned to farming, such as the oldest man in the company, Edgar O. Breeze, nicknamed "Dad." Others worked in the drug, automobile, or retail businesses, a few were bankers, and at least two worked for the Taylor County Sheriff's Department. One man, Joe Clemons, became the superintendent of a New York City hospital.[78]

While anecdotal evidence of the regiment's soldiers after the war is scarce, research in the 1930 Federal Census revealed data on 502 former members of the regiment. Data from the census illustrates how many of those veterans of Saint Etienne and Forest Farm established successful lives for themselves and their families after their return from France. For example, 431 soldiers (86 percent) had married since the end of the war, and 343 (69 percent) fathered children. While 175 (40 percent) of the former soldiers owned their own homes, even more rented their homes (60 percent). Overall, just thirty-six former members of the regiment never married and still lived with their parents, 75 percent of the forty-eight former members who lived at home in 1930. Most of the soldiers still lived in the same region they did in 1917. For example, 195 veterans (39 percent) still lived in the same county from which they had joined the Texas National Guard in 1917, while just 32 (6 percent) no longer lived in the state. Still, 273 former soldiers (54 percent) lived in other parts of Texas, although 169 of that number lived in counties adjacent or near the one they lived in back in 1917. Thus, 73 percent of the sample of 502 members of the 7th Texas still called North and Northwest Texas home.[79]

Finally, how had those veterans faired economically at the close of the 1920s and prior to the onset of the Great Depression? The census data showed that they had done well, although there were some differences in occupations when compared with 1917. While in 1917 the majority of the regiment either farmed or worked as unskilled labor (63 percent), by 1930 a different story unfolded in which only 97 veterans of the sample farmed (20 percent) while 94 worked in occupations considered unskilled (19 percent), and combined for just 39 percent of the 1930 sample. On the other hand, veterans working in a professional or business (176) capacity or as skilled workers (119) increased, representing 36 and 24 percent of the veterans, or 60 percent of the sample. Likewise, 262 of the veterans switched occupational classes since 1917. However, the 1930 census offered another way to look at economic self-sufficiency by classifying an individual's occupation as either "Employer," "Wage earner," or "On their own account." Using those criteria, 57 members (12 percent) of the sample were classified as "Employers," meaning they owned their own business and employed their own workforce. Likewise, 324 former veterans (67 percent) considered themselves to be "wage earners," meaning somebody paid their salary, while 105 former veterans (21 percent) earned money "on their own account," meaning they farmed or were self-employed. Finally, unemployment remained low among the veterans, with just 32 (7 percent) within the sample reporting no occupation on census day. By 1930, then, many of the veterans had settled back into their lives and established themselves. Many had married and raised families, more rented homes than owned them, and most had moved into more lucrative economic pursuits and left behind farming and unskilled work.[80]

And what of the regiment's combat experience? How can their participation in two battles be understood within the larger context of the American military experience in World War I? The experiences of the soldiers of the 142d and the old 7th Texas might be examined through a comparison with historian Mark Ethan Grotelueschen's thesis that adaptation and innovation in the AEF occurred from the lowest levels and moved upward rather than being dictated from headquarters down. For example, at Saint Etienne, the untested 142d had gone into combat with 58 officers and 1,715 men, suffered 8 officers and 117 men killed and 566 wounded. It is clear that the 142d Infantry's attack suffered from time pressure and a lack of preparation, an experience common among AEF units in their first combat. The regiment had little time to become acclimated to the front before their first attack and preparations were slowed because of the delays getting into the line, numerous meetings between brigade and division, and the issuance of verbal orders rather than written orders, which, in all likelihood, changed when passed from one individual to another. The ad hoc way in which the attack was planned would not have boded well for any group of soldiers, no matter how experienced. In sum, the regiment had a limited idea of what to do. They did not rely on massive firepower to attack a limited objective, and no innovative tactics were developed during that battle. Although individuals performed well and two of the regiment's soldiers received the Medal of Honor for their actions that day, the attack was not successful.[81]

However, just three short weeks later, the regiment participated in the battle of Forest Farm. As noted, the 142d received the unenviable task of attacking a fortified position that other forces had twice failed to capture. The plan of attack took shape on October 24 and was carried out on October 27. It envisioned a rolling artillery barrage followed by a machine gun barrage, while the two regiments advanced directly toward the German positions. The attack took place as scheduled, and within one hour had overrun the German position, while suffering only eleven men killed and thirty-six wounded, significantly less than at Saint Etienne. How did they manage to do this?[82]

Obviously, much like other combat units in the AEF, the 142d learned the difference between warfare that relied on the rifle and maneuver and warfare that employed massive firepower to achieve limited objectives. At Saint Etienne, the regiment followed the general doctrine of the AEF, and soldiers who advanced without support quickly bogged down. At Forest Farm, they learned their lesson and adapted to conditions, using both rolling barrages and machine-gun barrages, tactics that had yet to receive full endorsement from AEF Headquarters. Furthermore, the regiment's officers had more time to prepare and the soldiers executed those tactics with a degree of expertise not seen at Saint Etienne. First, execution of a proper rolling barrage appeared to have the greatest effect, as many of the regiment's soldiers noted that they reached the German positions before the enemy could get out of their dugouts and man their weapons after the barrage had passed. Second, the regiment had time to study the terrain around Forest Farm. Captain Lillard, the battalion commander who led the assault, wrote after the fact, "we had had 24 hours advance notice of this attack, with maps and definite orders. Every man in the organization knew just what he was going to do."[83]

While the regiment demonstrated the efficacy of Grotelueschen's argument, the regiment also proved to be innovative in its use of Choctaw Indians to pass messages the Germans could not decipher. As Colonel Bloor noted in a later report, the regiment's Native Americans spoke twenty-six different languages or dialects, only a few of which had ever been written down. After testing the process, the regiment used the Choctaw code-talkers "repeatedly on the 27th in preparation for the assault on Forest Farm." Colonel Bloor believed that "the enemy's complete surprise is evidence that he could not decipher the messages."[84]

The regiment's officers realized the importance of this innovation. Three days after the battle of Forest Farm, the 36th Division was pulled from the line in preparation for assignment to the American First Army. While they waited to go back into the line, the regiment held a training course to prepare more of their Native American soldiers to transmit messages. In order to handle the military terminology, they substituted Choctaw words for "big gun" in reference to artillery, "little gun shoot fast," for machine guns, and the battalions were "indicated by one, two, or three grains of corn." Colonel Bloor observed that after the short training period, he was confident that if his regiment had gone back into the line, "fine results would have been obtained," by using the Choctaw soldiers to transmit messages. Furthermore, he acknowledged the relationship between innovation and technology: "We were confident the possibilities of the telephone had been obtained without its hazards."[85]

Reviewing the combat history of one AEF regiment and its combat experience endorses Groteleuschen's point that adaptation and innovation occurred from the ground up. The 142d Infantry Regiment benefited from time and preparation, they adapted their tactics to fit the situation, and they increased their chances of success by using innovative communications techniques to give themselves every possible advantage. It seems clear that the soldiers of the 142d Infantry learned to adapt in a very short period of time. They learned to innovate, and because of that many more of them came home than might have been the case had they remained tied to the idea of the rifle and the bayonet. The experiences of those soldiers can provide additional insight into the way the U.S. Army fought in the early twentieth century, and how tactics and innovation influenced the outcome on the battlefield.

In the end, what is to be made of the actions of the 7th Texas Infantry Regiment and its participation in World War I? Did those soldiers have a unique Texas military experience? Based on their experiences, it appears that those soldiers did not experience the war from a unique perspective because they were from Texas. However, while the soldiers had an experience shared by hundreds of thousands of other members of the AEF, Texans at home drew heavily on the concept of a unique Texas military experience and viewed the participation of Texas soldiers in the war from that not altogether accurate perception. There are several salient points: Studying those soldiers at the local or county level provides a closer look at certain aspects of Texas society in the early twentieth century, as well as provides a more personal glimpse of the nature of combat in World War I. The men who made up the regiment were young, averaging just twenty-three years of age. The majority consisted of farmers or unskilled laborers, although a large minority of professional and skilled workers also joined the ranks, including the officers. Most of the original members hailed from Texas, and most of those who did not came from other southern states. An overwhelming number were not married although more than might be expected claimed dependents, particularly a mother or father. Most of these men had no prior experience in the military and most had no reason to seek exemption from military service.

Second, while not unique to Texas, the importance of the relationship between the regiment's soldiers and their communities should not be understated. From the very beginning of the war, the attitude throughout much of North and Northwest Texas was one of patriotic fervor and support. Residents held a surge of patriotic rallies and speeches and parades, all designed to generate support for the policies of the federal government. These rallies, speeches and parades also helped convince some of the young men of these communities to serve their country. The more prominent members of those communities frequently took it upon themselves to assume a leadership role in generating support for the draft and in recruiting for the Army, Navy, and National Guard. Young men faced pressure to enlist, and an undercurrent of fear and anger against foreign-born citizens, minorities and those who did not wish to serve prevailed. This sense of community, with its both good and bad aspects, is an important factor to note in the recruitment and development of the regiment. That sense of community remained strong and could be seen at several levels: the county, Camp Bowie, and the state. Indeed, this sense of community provided a means for the soldiers and citizens of the state to place the 7th Texas within the Texas military experience.

Observers continually drew connections between those North and Northwest Texas soldiers and the experiences of Texans in the Revolution and the Civil War. Many residents expected the 7th Texas to live up to the examples of early Texas military figures not because of training and experience, but simply because they were from Texas and it was expected of them. Texans closely identified with units established across their state. This was true with regard to the 36th Division, which began its service as a predominantly Texas and Oklahoma organization. Although it had changed significantly by the time it went into combat because of draftees and replacements, residents of the state and others continued to identify with the division and the Army gave it the nickname the "Lone Star" Division. The same was true of the 7th Texas, which started out almost completely composed of Texas men but by the time it went into action in October 1918, as the 142d Infantry could only count a little more than 600 original members remaining. And yet it too, retained its Texas identity. Finally, after the war, several observers, including Gen. William Smith, recalled the almost foolhardy courage of the Texans, something that could also be compared to the service of Civil War Texas soldiers. Overall then, while the soldiers of the 7th Texas did not experience war uniquely, the fact that Texans believed they did appeared to be all that mattered, and that led to the addition of their own chapter to the Texas military experience albeit with one unique difference. As historian Roger Beaumont pointed out, throughout Texas military history, the relationship between Texans and Native Americans remained nearly constantly adversarial. In the case of the 142d Infantry, however, the regiment relied heavily on the abilities of Choctaw Indians in order to successfully attack the German position at Forest Farm. In that sense, then, the 142d Infantry sharply diverged from the Texas military experience and created something new.[86]

Another point related to the Texas military experience was the development of a "myth" altogether fitting within Texas military history. In World War I, and as demonstrated by the 142d Infantry, the "myth" story might be described as this: that Texas soldiers, in spite of incomplete training, inadequate equipment, and inexperience in combat, nevertheless fought well above expectation. Although the 36th ranked in the middle of the AEF divisions in combat in terms of miles advanced, prisoners taken, and equipment captured, the reactions of the media and of those at home magnified the combat service of the unit until many Texans came to believe that the 36th Division ended the war on its own. The magnification of the division's actions was directly related to the fact that many of the soldiers were from Texas and Oklahoma, which led many observers to believe that they would easily defeat the enemy. This was also supported by the frequent comments on the physical size of the Texas soldiers, as if they were larger than life. This myth of the combat record of the division added to the legend of Texas military prowess. While such a perception existed amongst Texans, it was not altogether a common picture among the soldiers themselves.

Prior to arriving in France, a number of soldiers believed their own rhetoric that they would help quickly end the war. After engaging in combat, many of the soldiers of the old 7th Texas gained a new and altogether more sobering assessment of war and the destruction it caused. Many expressed a desire to get away from the front, and few seemed to exaggerate or glorify war. The soldiers frequently praised the actions of their comrades, and marveled at their feats of bravery or their calm demeanor under fire. For many, the bond between them grew stronger during their time in combat, and in many cases officers and men evinced continued respect and friendship for each other. When combat severed those relationships, such as that between Ethan Simpson and Aubyn Clark, the pain, anger, and sorrow were deeply felt.

In essence, the soldiers of the 7th Texas Infantry were not different from thousands of other soldiers in the Army of the United States during World War I. For various reasons, they left their farms and jobs and careers across Northwest Texas, volunteered to serve in the National Guard, trained for war and found themselves in combat for the first time on October 8, 1918, outside of an obscure French village near the Hindenburg Line. There, they fought, advanced, and fought again before being relieved from the line. When the armistice came, they waited their turn to come home, where residents treated them as heroes. The government established a national holiday to celebrate the end of the war. Throughout the states, local communities built monuments to honor the soldiers of 1917–1918, and memorialize those who lost their lives. Indeed, in all fourteen counties that raised companies for the 7th Texas Infantry some type of monument remains. Some, such as in Crowell in Foard County, are old and isolated. Others, such as in Lubbock, have been enlarged to include veterans of other wars.

Over time, however, because the combat of 1917–1918 was eclipsed by World War II, the Korean War, Vietnam, and more recent conflicts, the experiences of World War I soldiers have often been overlooked. As the soldiers returned home, most were able to merge back into society and carry on meaningful and successful lives, although many were also doubtless changed by their experience of war. In 1919, the soldiers of the old 7th Texas Infantry laid down their weapons and celebrated their homecoming on the Fourth of July, the most patriotic of holidays. The war was over, and the rest of their lives awaited them. Perhaps many thousands of Texans echoed the sentiments of the *Clarendon News* when it wrote about members of Captain Simpson's company on their return home: "Success to them all—they heard their country's call in the hour of need, and responded—they have done their work well—success to all of them."[87]

NOTES TO INTRODUCTION

[1] D. W. Meinig, *Imperial Texas: An Interpretive Essay in Cultural Geography* (Austin: University of Texas Press, 1969), 66; Jo Hitt, Cynthia Myers, Jim Rich, and Faye Statser, *Foard County and World War I* (No publisher, 2007), 4–5.

[2] Joseph G. Dawson, ed., *The Texas Military Experience: From the Texas Revolution through World War II* (College Station: Texas A&M University Press, 1995); Ralph A. Wooster, *Texas and Texans in the Great War* (Buffalo Gap, TX: State House Press, 2009); Jose A. Ramirez, *To the Line of Fire! Mexican Texans in World War I* (College Station: Texas A&M University Press, 2009). Other works that contain material on World War I and Texas include: James Storey and Mary E. Kelley, *Twentieth-Century Texas: A Social and Cultural History* (Denton: University of North Texas Press, 2008); Lewis L. Gould, *Progressives and Prohibitionists: Texas Democrats in the Wilson Era* (Austin: Texas State Historical Association, 1992), 224; Walter E. Buenger, "World War I and Northeast Texas," *Locus* 8:2 (Spring, 1996); Benjamin Paul Hegi, "Old Time Good Germans: German-Americans in Cooke County, Texas, during World War I," *The Southwestern Historical Quarterly* 109 (Oct. 2005); Richard W. Bricker, *Wooden Ships from Texas: A World War I Saga* (College Station: Texas A&M University Press, 1998).

[3] Lonnie J. White, *The 90th Division in World War I: The Texas-Oklahoma Draft Division in the Great War* (Manhattan, KS: The Sunflower Press, 1996); Lonnie J. White, *Panthers to Arrowheads: The 36th (Texas-Oklahoma) Division in World War I* (Austin: Presidial Press, 1984), v. Other works that touch on the military aspects of Texas in World War I include: Bruce Brager, *The Texas 36th Division: A History* (Austin: Eakin Press, 2002), 18; Charles Spurlin, "The Victoria Sammies," *Texana* 7 (1969): 56–76; Garna L. Christian, *Black Soldiers in Jim Crow Texas, 1899–1917* (College Station: Texas A&M University Press, 1995); Bernice Blanche Miller Maxfield and William E. Jary Jr., *Camp Bowie, Forth Worth, 1917–1918: An Illustrated History of the 36th Division in the First World War* (Fort Worth: B. B. Maxfield Foundation, 1975); Jimmy M. Skaggs, "Lieutenant General Hulen," *Texas Military History* 18 (1970); Lonnie J. White, "Chief of the Arrowheads: Major General William R. Smith and the 36th Division in France, 1918–1919," *Military History of Texas and the Southwest* 16 (1982); Lonnie J. White, "Major General Edwin St. John Greble," *Military History of Texas and the Southwest* 14 (1976); Heath Twitchell, *Allen: The Biography of an Army Officer* (New Brunswick: Rutgers University Press, 1974). For works on the 36th Division in World War II, see Robert L. Wagner, *The Texas Army: A History of the 36th Division in the Italian Campaign* (Austin: State House Press, 1991); Bruce Brager, *The Texas 36th Division: A History* (Austin: Eakin Press, 2002); and Kelly Crager, *Hell Under the Rising Sun: Texas POWs and the Building of the Burma-Thailand Death Railway* (College Station: Texas A&M University Press, 2008); Martin Blumenson, *Bloody River: The Real Tragedy of the Rapido River* (College Station: Texas A&M University Press, 1998); Duane Schultz, *Crossing the Rapido: A Tragedy of World War II* (New York: Westholme, 2010).

[4] For an in-depth discussion of the Texas military experience see Dawson, *The Texas Military Experience*, 3–13, 184–92.

[5] Randolph B. Campbell, *Gone to Texas: A History of the Lone Star State* (New York: Oxford, 2004), 325.

[6] Campbell, *Gone to Texas,* 325, 328; University of Virginia Library Historical Census Browser, general population, Texas, 1910 and 1920, http://fisher.lib.virginia.edu/collections/stats/histcensus/ (accessed 30 November 2009).

[7] For the story of the rise of the Republican Party in Texas, see Roger M. Olien, *From Token to Triumph: The Texas Republicans Since 1920* (Dallas: SMU Press, 1982).

[8] Meinig. *Imperial Texas*; *Texas Almanac and State Industrial Guide, 1914* (Dallas: A. H. Belo &

Company, 1914); University of Virginia Library Historical Census Browser, general population, Texas, 1910, http://fisher.lib.virginia.edu/collections/stats/histcensus/ (accessed 1 March 2012.

NOTES TO CHAPTER 1

Richard F. Hamilton and Holger H. Herwig, *Decisions for War, 1914–1917* (New York: Cambridge University Press, 2004), 221–22. The Zimmerman Telegram was a diplomatic dispatch sent from the German foreign minister to the German Ambassador to the United States. The telegram broached the idea of returning Texas and other parts of the United States to Mexico if that country would enter the war on the side of Germany; see Friedrich Katz, *Secret War in Mexico: Europe, the United States and the Mexican Revolution* (Chicago: University of Chicago Press, 1981).

[2] John Whiteclay Chambers, *To Raise an Army: The Draft Comes to Modern America* (New York: Free Press, 1987) 130, 133; Campbell, *Gone to Texas*, 353.

[3] Wooster, *Texas and Texans in the Great War*, 166, 170.

[4] *Dallas Morning News*, June 3, 10, 1917. The Dallas Recruiting District, which included many of the counties under study, reported total enlistments in the Army, Navy, and Marine Corps for 1917 as 10,672 men, *Dallas Morning News*, January 1, 1918.

[5] *Dallas Morning News*, September 10, 1917, October 19, 1917, March 10, 1918. For more on the FLPA, see Jeannette Keith, *Rich Man's War, Poor Man's Fight* (Chapel Hill: UNC Press, 2004), 87–101.

[6] *Wichita Daily Times*, June 28, 1917.

[7] White, *Panthers to Arrowheads*, 1–2, 5; *Report of the Chief of the Militia Bureau, 1917* (Washington, DC: Government Printing Office, 1917), 71. For an overview of National Guard reform, see Jerry Cooper, *The Rise of the National Guard: The Evolution of the American Militia, 1865–1920* (Lincoln: University of Nebraska Press, 1997), 108–27.

[8] White, *Panthers to Arrowheads*, 6–8. However, the *Fort Worth Record* indicated that the 4th Texas Infantry was also recruiting out of Fort Worth, and a recruiting station was opened for it by late May 1917. See *Fort Worth Record*, May 26, 1917; Chaplain C. H. Barnes, *History of the 142nd Infantry of the Thirty-Sixth Division, October 15, 1917, to June 17, 1919* (No City: Blackwell Job Printing Company, 1922); Alexander White Spence, "Services of the 36th Division with the American Expeditionary Forces, July 1918–May 1919," 1919, National Archives and Records Administration (NARA), Record Group 120, Records of the American Expeditionary Force, 36th Division, 142nd Regiment, p 1–5, hereafter cited as Spence, "36th Division." Spence claimed that recruiting the units in various parts of the state "met with such obstacles that they were finally raised without regard to geographical apportionment," Spence, "36th Division," 3.

[9] Barnes, *History of the 142nd*, 59; *Texas Almanac*, 1914; Spence, "36th Division," 8; Henry C. Dethloff and John A. Adams Jr., *Texas Aggies Go to War: In Service of Their Country* (College Station: Texas A&M University Press, 2004), 27; *Fort Worth Record*, July 3, 1917. Some dates come from Alfred S. Bloor's and Alfred W. Bloor's memorial marker in the Oakwood Cemetery Annex in Austin, Texas; *Tenth Census of United States* (Washington, DC: Government Printing Office, 1880), population, Travis County, Texas, precinct 2, Alfred S. Bloor; *Twelfth Census of the United States* (Washington, DC: Government Printing Office, 1900), schedule 1, population, Alleghany County, Pittsburgh, Pennsylvania, Martha W. Bloor; *Thirteenth Census of the United States* (Washington, DC: Government Printing Office, 1910), schedule 1, population, Travis County, Texas, precinct 3, Alfred W. Bloor; *Texas Almanac and State Industrial Guide, 1914* (Dallas: A. H. Belo and Company, 1914), 22; *Forth Worth Record*, July 3, 1917; White, *Panthers to Arrowheads*, 39.

[10] *Wichita Daily Times*, June 4, 1917; *Dallas Morning News*, June 26, 1917.

[11] 36th Division Association Papers, Hulen Correspondence, 1916–1917, "Instructions for the use of those designated as officers of proposed organizations of the National Guard of Texas," no date, Texas State Library and Archives, Austin, Texas; Hulen Correspondence, 1916–1917, "Instructions."

[12] *Gainesville Daily Register*, June 26, 1917.

[13] United States Federal Census, 1910, Population, Potter County, 1910; *Abilene Reporter*, June 18, 1917, and July 20, 1917; *Wichita Daily Times*, June 17, 1917; *Wise County Messenger*, October 12, 1917; *Amarillo Daily News*, July 25, 1923.

[14] *Denton Record Chronicle*, June 18, 22, 1917. Unfortunately, little is known of Lt. James B. Stiff. However, he did not remain with the company all the way through the war. In fact, a James B. Stiff from Denton County, aged twenty-one, filled out a draft registration card on June 5, 1918. Thus, Lieutenant Stiff, for whatever reason, must have been discharged from the National Guard.

[15] *Wichita Daily Times*, April 15, and June 13, 15, 17, 21, 29, 1917; Archibald S. Hart, *Company K of Yesterday* (New York: Vantage, 1969), 36.

[16] *Foard County News*, June 15, 1917; *Cleburne Daily Enterprise*, June 17, 1917; *Quanah Tribune Chief*, June 14, 1917; Memorandum, War Department Bureau of Insular Affairs, February 28, 1912, Memorandum from Brig. Gen. Herman Hall, Headquarters Philippine Constabulary, March 28, 1916, Memorandum from New Mexico Military Institute, to General John A. Lejeune, April 18, 1917, Homer T. Merrill Papers, 1899–1964, Folder: Correspondence, 1912–1927, Southwest Collection, Texas Tech University, Lubbock, Texas; *The History of Donley County, Texas, 1879–1990, Presented by the Families of Donley County, Texas, Both Past and Present* (Dallas: Curtis Media Corp, 1990), 385.

[17] *Gainesville Daily Register*, June 24, 1917; *Quanah Tribune Chief*, June 21, 1917; General Orders No. 2, June 15, 1917, 36th Division Association Papers: Hulen Correspondence, 1916–1917, Texas State Library and Archives, Austin, Texas.

[18] *Gainesville Daily Register*, June 13, 15, 1917; Hulen Correspondence, 1916–1917, "Instructions."

[19] Hulen Correspondence, 1916–1917, "Instructions"; *Gainesville Daily Register*, June 14, 1917; *Foard County News*, June 15, 1917; *Quanah Tribune Chief*, June 14, 1917; *Amarillo Daily News*, June 16, 17, 1917; *Cleburne Daily Enterprise*, June 15, 17, 19, 1917. Barton's recruiting office was evidently "maintained at personal expense" although residents donated money to keep his expenses from getting out of control; see *Amarillo Daily News*, July 3, 1917.

[20] *Gainesville Daily Register*, June 14, 15, 1917; *Abilene Reporter*, June 21, 22, 1917.

[21] *Foard County News*, June 22, 1917; *Quanah Tribune Chief*, June 14, 1917.

[22] *Denton Record Chronicle*, June 30, and July 2, 5, 7, 23, 1917; *Wichita Daily Times*, June 21, 1917.

[23] *Fort Worth Record*, May 26, and June 13, 21, 29, 30, 1917; Fancher D. Reagan claimed in October of 1917 that he enlisted because Captain McGrath had promised to make him a sergeant, which never happened. Instead, he and McGrath agreed that he should attend the officers training course at Leon Springs, which would give him better opportunities for advancement. However, Reagan did not make it through the course and was returned to his regiment at Camp Bowie in October of 1917, NARA RG391, HQ Corr. And Doc File 10–499, Memorandum from Noah Roark, to A. W. Bloor, subject: Investigation of Civil Life of Private F. D. Reagan, November 8, 1917.

[24] *Gainesville Daily Register*, June 19, 1917; *Quanah Tribune Chief*, June 21, 1917.

[25] *Gainesville Daily Register*, June 24, 1917; *Amarillo Daily News*, July 11, 1917; *Cleburne Daily Enterprise*, July 4, 8, 1917; *Wichita Daily Times*, June 27, 1917.

[26] *Wise County Messenger*, June 22, 29, and July 13, 1917; *Wichita Daily Times*, June 15, 1917; *Gainesville Daily Register*, June 24, 1917.

[27] *Fort Worth Record*, June 28, 1917.

[28] *Gainesville Daily Register*, June 24, 25, 26, and July 11, 1917.

[29] *Cleburne Daily Enterprise*, June 29, 1917; *Wise County Messenger*, July 27, and August 10, 1917; *Wichita Daily Times*, July 15, August 2, 12, 1917.

[30] Barnes, *History of the 142nd*, 214–17; *Foard County News*, June 15, 1917; *Abilene Reporter*, July 6, 1917. The Owsley brothers were the sons of A. C. Owsley, a prominent Texan and member of the state Council of Defense.

[31] *Gainesville Daily Register*, July 5, 1917; *Wichita Daily Times*, June 21, 1917. Although recruiting week was scheduled to end on July 11, General Hulen requested on July 9, that July 12 be designated as "banner recruiting day," and called on the press to get the word out that "each volunteer enlist another volunteer"; *Gainesville Daily Register*, July 9, 1917.

[32] *Gainesville Daily Register*, June 19, 22, and July 2, 1917.

[33] *Fort Worth Record*, July 3, 6, 1917; *Dallas Morning News*, July 22, 1917.

[34] *Gainesville Daily Register*, July 11, 1917; *Amarillo Daily News*, July 5, 14, 1917; *Denton Record Chronicle*, July 16, 23, 1917.

[35] *Dallas Morning News*, July 7, 9, 1917; *Cleburne Daily Enterprise*, July 11, 12, 1917.

[36] *Abilene Reporter*, June 29, and July 1, 1917.

[37] *Wichita Daily Times*, July 1, 5, 8, 1917.

[38] *Gainesville Daily Register*, June 29, 1917; *Amarillo Daily News*, July 5, 1917; *Abilene Reporter*, July 3, 1917; *Wise County Messenger*, July 27, 1917; *Cleburne Daily Enterprise*, July 19, 1917; *Wichita Daily Times*, July 15, 1917; *Quanah Tribune Chief*, July 5, 1917; Barnes, *History of the 142nd*, 214–17.

[39] *Abilene Reporter*, July 8, 1917.

[40] *Cleburne Daily Enterprise*, July 9, 1917; *Fort Worth Record*, June 29, 1917; *Amarillo Daily News*, June 29, 1917; *Wichita Daily Times*, June 25, 1917.

[41] *Cleburne Daily Enterprise*, July 17, 1917; *Wichita Daily Times*, July 19, 1917; *Gainesville Daily Register*, July 12, 1917; *Abilene Reporter*, July 10, and August 9, 1917; *Clarendon News*, July 26, 1917; *Quanah Tribune Chief*, July 5, 1917.

[42] *Cleburne Daily Enterprise*, July 11, 19, 1917.

[43] *Abilene Reporter*, July 12, 16, 20, 1917; *Cleburne Daily Enterprise*, 17 July 1917; *Wichita Daily Times*, July 11, 17, 22, 1917; *Dallas Morning News*, July 17, 1917; *Clarendon News*, July 19, 1917. Although Lieutenant Brown was not part of the 7th Texas, he would meet his fate in France, being killed in action during the war. See *Abilene Reporter*, November 24, 1918.

[44] *Foard County News*, July 13, 1917; *Gainesville Daily Register*, July 15, 1917; *Abilene Reporter*, July 16, 1917; *Cleburne Daily Enterprise*, July 18, 1917.

[45] *Abilene Reporter*, July 20, 23, 1917; *Gainesville Daily Register*, July 17, 1917; *Cleburne Daily Enterprise*, July 24, 1917.

[46] *Clarendon News*, July 26, 1917; *Gainesville Daily Register*, August 8, 1917; *Wichita Daily Times*, August 14, 1917; *Foard County News*, August 3, 1917.

[47] *Wichita Daily Times*, July 16, 1917; Barnes, *History of the 142nd*, 18; Spence, "36th Division," 14.

[48] Robert Saunders Jr., "World War I: Catalyst for Social Change in Alabama," in *The Great War in the Heart of Dixie: Alabama During World War I*, ed. Martin T. Olliff (Tuscaloosa: University of Alabama Press, 2008), 185–200; Jennifer D. Keene, *Doughboys, the Great War, and the Remaking of America* (Baltimore: Johns Hopkins University Press, 2001), 26.

[49] It should be stated that this was not quite the same thing as being drafted under the selective service system. The National Guard could be brought onto active duty for the duration of the conflict.

[50] *Report of the Acting Chief of the Militia Bureau*, 1918, 6; *Cleburne Daily Enterprise*, July 29, 1917; *Wichita Daily Times*, August 7, 1917; *Abilene Reporter*, July 16, 26, 1917.

[51] *Cleburne Daily Enterprise*, August 6, 1917; *Gainesville Daily Register*, August 8, 1917.

[52] *Foard County News*, July 13, 1917; *Quanah Tribune Chief*, July 5, 13, 1917; *Clarendon News*, August 9, 1917; *Wise County Messenger*, August 24, 1917; *Amarillo Daily News*, August 15, 1917; *Denton Record Chronicle*, July 23, 24, 25, and August 6, 10, 1917.

[53] *Wichita Daily Times*, July 5, and August 5, 6, 12, 23, 26, 1917; *Gainesville Daily Register*, August 6, and September 2, 1917; *Cleburne Daily Enterprise*, August 12, 28, 1917; *Amarillo Daily News*, August 15, 1917; Hart, *Company K of Yesterday*, 10.

[54] *Wichita Daily Times*, July 2, and August 22, 23, 26, 1917; *Dallas Morning News*, July 8, 1917. In Quanah, Captain Wiley spent $175 of his own money on his company, and Lieutenant Murphy spent $80. See *Quanah Tribune Chief*, July 5, 1917.

[55] Ruth Smith Truss, "Military Participation at Home and Abroad, 1917–1918," in Olliff, *The Great War in the Heart of Dixie*, 24–40; Frank E. Roberts, *The American Foreign Legion: Black Soldiers of the 93d in World War I* (Annapolis: Naval Institute Press, 2004), 8–10, 36–37.

[56] *Cleburne Daily Enterprise*, August 6, 1917; *Denton Record Chronicle*, August 6, 16, 1917; *Quanah Tribune Chief*, July 13, 1917; *Gainesville Daily Register*, July 23, 1917; *Wichita Daily Times*, August 12, 14, 1917.

[57] Oral History #1214, Hazen Armstrong, March 29, 1986, University of North Texas Oral History Collection, Denton Texas, 17–18; *Cleburne Daily Enterprise*, August 6, 30, 31, 1917; *Denton Record Chronicle*, August 2, 4, 6, 1917; *Abilene Reporter*, August 20, 21, 1917.

[58] *Amarillo Daily News*, August 17, 1917; *Gainesville Daily Register*, September 2, 1917; *Denton Record Chronicle*, August 16, 1917; *Cleburne Daily Enterprise*, August 12, 28, 1917.

[59] *Wichita Daily Times*, August 3, 12, 14, 1917.

[60] *Clarendon News*, August 30, 1917; *Gainesville Daily Register*, August 31, 1917; *Wichita Daily Times*, July 5, 1917; *Amarillo Daily News*, August 14, 1917.

[61] *Cleburne Daily Enterprise*, August 14, 15, 1917.

[62] *Foard County News*, August 24, 1917.

[63] After Captain Simpson's company departed for France in 1918, his wife Marybelle received a visit from their local Southern Baptist minister who "admonished" her for dancing. Eventually, she was forced to move from the Clarendon Southern Baptist Church to the Episcopal Church. *The History of Donley County, Texas, 1879–1990, Presented by the Families of Donley County, Texas Both Past and Present* (Dallas: Curtis Media Corp, 1990), 385.

[64] *Clarendon News*, August 9, 16, 1917; *Gainesville Daily Register*, July 23, and August 6, 12, 19, 1917; *Wise County Messenger*, August 24, 1917. The Gainesville Machine Gun Company attended services at a local African-American Church, where they cheered the pastor when he told them there were "twelve million Negroes who would stand loyally by Old Glory…," and who were "anxiously watching every move that the American soldiers make." *Gainesville Daily Register*, August 22, 1917.

[65] *Wichita Daily Times*, August 23, 26, 1917.

[66] *Gainesville Daily Register*, August 14, 19, 23, 1917; *Abilene Reporter*, August 15, 1917.

[67] *Gainesville Daily Register*, August 31, and September 12, 16, 18, 1917; *Abilene Reporter*, August 16, 1917.

[68] *Cleburne Daily Enterprise*, August 6, 9, 1917; *Gainesville Daily Register*, September 2, 1917; *Wichita Daily Times*, August 12, 1917.

[69] *Wise County Messenger*, August 24, 1917.

[70] *Wise County Messenger*, August 10, 1917; *Gainesville Daily Register*, August 10, and September 7, 1917.

[71] *Amarillo Daily News*, August 21, 1917; *Gainesville Daily Register*, August 19, 1917; William D. Hornaday, Volume 5, p. 70, William Deming Hornaday Transcripts of World War I Letters and Personal Accounts, Archives and Information Services, Texas State Library and Archives Commission, Austin, Texas.

[72] *Amarillo Daily News*, August 25, 30, 1917; *Gainesville Daily Register*, September 4, 1917.

[73] *Cleburne Daily Enterprise*, September 9, 10, 1917; *Denton Record Chronicle*, September 3, 7, 1917.

[74] *Foard County News*, September 7, 1917.

[75] *Quanah Tribune Chief*, September 6, 1917.

[76] *Clarendon News*, August 30, 1917; *Amarillo Daily News*, August 21, 1917; *Wichita Daily Times*, September 4, 6, 7, 1917. Although the plan to march the Wichita Falls soldiers to Camp Bowie did not occur, there was an attempt to have the soldiers driven to Camp Bowie in automobiles. Although Brig. Gen. James Parker, Commander of the Southern Department initially approved of the plan, it eventually fell through and the men went by train; *Wichita Daily Times*, August 8, 9, 13, 19, 26, 31, 1917.

[77] David Alsobrook, "A Call to Arms for African Americans during the Age of Jim Crow: Black Alabamians' Response to the U.S. Declaration of War, 1917," in Olliff, *The Great War in the Heart of Dixie*, 81–100; Roberts, *The American Foreign Legion,* 10–11; Keene, *Doughboys, the Great War, and the Remaking of America*, 107; see also R. Jackson Marshall III, *Memories of World War I: North Carolina Doughboys on the Western Front* (Raleigh: North Carolina Division of Archives and History, 1998), 11; White, *90th*

Division in World War I, 1–25.

[78] *Clarendon News*, September 6, 1917.

[79] Barnes, *History of the 142nd*, 18.

NOTES TO CHAPTER 2

[1] All of the information gathered on the regiment's soldiers came from the Selective Service Registration Cards for World War I, M1509, Texas microfilm, available at the National Archives and Records Administration Southwest Branch, Fort Worth, Texas. The complete, original collection of all twenty-four million draft registration cards is maintained by the National Archives regional branch in Atlanta. The draft registration cards are also available through the military records collection of www.ancestry.com, which provides a searchable database of the entire set of the draft registration cards.

[2] Draft Registration Cards, M1509, Texas Microfilm, NARA Southwest Branch.

[3] Ibid.

[4] Ibid.

[5] Ibid.

[6] Ibid.

[7] Ibid.; Meinig, *Imperial Texas*, 106–7.

[8] Draft Registration Cards, M1509, Texas Microfilm, NARA Southwest Branch.

[9] Ibid.

[10] Ibid.

[11] Ibid.

[12] Ibid.

[13] Ibid.

[14] Ibid.

[15] Ibid.

[16] Ibid.

[17] Ibid.

[18] Ibid.

[19] Richard Lowe, *Walker's Texas Division, C.S.A.: Greyhounds of the Trans-Mississippi* (Baton Rouge: LSU Press, 2004), 19–25; Joseph T. Glatthaar, *General Lee's Army: From Victory to Collapse* (New York: Free Press, 2008), 18–23.

[20] Gerald E. Shenk, *"Work or Fight!" Race, Gender, and the Draft in World War I* (New York: Palgrave,

2005), 1–8.

[21] Draft Registration Cards, M1509, Texas Microfilm, NARA Southwest Branch.

[22] Ibid.

[23] Ibid.

[24] Ibid.

[25] Ibid.

[26] Ibid.

[27] Although 136 men listed reasons for exemption from the draft, some men simply wrote "yes," in answer to the question without giving a reason, while other answers were not readable because of the handwriting.

[28] Draft Registration Cards, M1509, Texas Microfilm, NARA Southwest Branch.

[29] Gary Mead, *The Doughboys: America and the First World War* (New York: Overlook Press, 2000), 73.

NOTES TO CHAPTER 3

[1] *Wichita Daily Times*, September 6, 1917; *Abilene Reporter*, September 4, 1917; *Report of the Acting Chief of the Militia Bureau* (Washington, DC: Government Printing Office, 1918), 151.

[2] By August 31, 1917, the 7th Texas had increased slightly to 56 officers and 2,009 men; *Report of the Acting Chief of the Militia Bureau*, 1918, 120, 122–23, 152.

[3] White, *Panthers to Arrowheads*, 15–16.

[4] White, *Panthers to Arrowheads*, 16–17; Spence, "36th Division," 6.

[5] White, *Panthers to Arrowheads*, 17–18.

[6] White, *Panthers to Arrowheads*, 18–19; Spence, "36th Division," 6.

[7] *Dallas Morning News*, August 26, 1917; Spence, "36th Division," 5.

[8] *Gainesville Daily Register*, September 12, 1917; *Abilene Reporter*, September 9, 1917. The rain was fairly heavy at the time, as a member of the Abilene company reported that cars were stuck in the mud all around the camp and that it had rained for the past two days. *Abilene Reporter*, September 9, 1917, and the *Dallas Morning News* reported a rain so heavy that some men of the Camp were sent to Fort Worth to spend the night because their tents were blown down in the storm; *Dallas Morning News*, September 27, 1917.

[9] Spence, "36th Division," 15; *Dallas Morning News*, October 4, 1917; *Abilene Reporter*, September 9, 1917; *Gainesville Daily Register*, September 10, 18, 1917. The *Dallas Morning News* reported that supplies and equipment had begun arriving at Camp Bowie as early as August 15, 1917; see *Dallas Morning News*, August 15, 1917.

[10] *Wichita Daily Times*, September 11, 1917.

[11] *Clarendon News*, September 20, and October 5, 1917; David G. Clark, *Aubyn's War and Tales from Mr. Billy's Family* (Colorado: Bingham Hill Press, 2009), 66.

[12] *Gainesville Daily Register*, September 16, 18, 1917; *Wise County Messenger*, September 28, 1917; *Clarendon News*, September 20, 1917.

[13] *Gainesville Daily Register*, September 12, 1917; *Wichita Daily Times*, October 8, 1917; *Wise County Messenger*, October 5, 1917; *Dallas Morning News*, October 4, 1917; *Fort Worth Star Telegram*, December 24, 26, 1917; Spence, "36th Division," 15, 18–19; see White, *90th Division in World War I*, 30, for shortages of rifles in the 90th Texas-Oklahoma Draft Division.

[14] *Wise County Messenger*, October 12, 1917.

[15] *Report of the Acting Chief of the Militia Bureau*, 1918, 10–12; Edward Coffman, *The War to End All Wars: The American Military Experience in World War I* (1968; repr., Lexington: University Press of Kentucky, 1998), 61; John B. Wilson, *Maneuver and Firepower: The Evolution of Divisions and Separate Brigades* (Washington, DC: US Army Center of Military History, 1998), 47–57.

[16] *Wichita Daily Times*, December 26, 1917. About general officers visiting France so Pershing could get a look at them, see Timothy K. Nenninger, "Unsystematic as a Mode of Command: Commanders and the Process of Command in the American Expeditionary Forces, 1917–1918," *The Journal of Military History* 64 (July 2000): 739–68.

[17] *Report of the Acting Chief of the Militia Bureau*, 1918, 10; *Congressional Record*, Volume 55, part 6, 6199.

[18] White, *Panthers to Arrowheads*, 31–33; Barnes, *History of the 142nd*, 19; *Dallas Morning News*, September 27, 1917; Spence, "36th Division," 7.

[19] White, *Panthers to Arrowheads*, 34; Barnes, *History of the 142nd*, 19; *Report of the Acting Chief of the Militia Bureau*, 1918, 11.

[20] *Wichita Daily Times*, September 21, 23, 1917.

[21] *Dallas Morning News*, September 25, 30, and October 3, 1917.

[22] White, *Panthers to Arrowheads*, 34.

[23] White, *Panthers to Arrowheads*, 35; NARA, RG391, Box 2378, Doc File 10-499, 2nd Indorsement, Hq. 142nd Infantry to the Commanding General 71st Infantry Brigade, Oct 29, 1917; Barnes, *History of the 142nd*, 21–22; *Fort Worth Star-Telegram*, December 15, 1917; White, *90th Division in World War I*, 24.

[24] *Wichita Daily Times*, October 8, 1917; Spence, "36th Division," 7–8; *Report of the Acting Chief of the Militia Bureau*, 1918, 11; *Clarendon News*, September 19, 1917. This prejudice against National Guard officers was evident when Captain H. B. Gilstrap, an Oklahoma Guardsman and Company B commander, requested that 2d Lt. Charles T. Forrester be reassigned from Company B because he displayed a "prejudice against the National Guard" and originally "declined assignment to the National Guard." Captain Gilstrap stated that Forrester's "permanent value to the company is limited." RG391, WWI-Organizational Records, 142nd Infantry, HDQRS Miscellaneous Correspondence, Box 2388, Memorandum From CO, Co. B, 142nd Infantry, to C.O., 142nd Infantry, subject: assignment of new officers, December 14, 1917.

[25] *Dallas Morning News*, September 13, 1917; Barnes, *History of the 142nd*, 186, 244, 246–247.

[26] In one case, prior to the merger of the 7th Texas and the 1st Oklahoma, several Oklahoma officers talked to Captain Tyler and Colonel Bloor about transferring the bugler of the Machine Gun Company, "Skeeter Herblin," to the Oklahoma regiment. Apparently they were turned down; *Gainesville Daily Register*, September 16, 1917.

[27] Barnes, *History of the 142nd*, 245–47; White, *90th Division in World War I*, 30.

[28] Barnes, *History of the 142nd*, 214–17; White, *Panthers to Arrowheads*, 32; *Dallas Morning News*, April 21, 1918; Spence, "36th Division," 11.

[29] White, *Panthers to Arrowheads*, 40, 42–43; RG391, WWI-Organizational Records, 142nd Infantry, HDQRS Miscellaneous Correspondence, Box 2388, Drafted Men assigned to 142nd Infantry, no date; Spence, "36th Division," 11, 13, 24.

[30] RG391, 142nd Infantry, Box 2388, Miscellaneous Correspondence, Letter, Governor A. L. Williams, to Col. L. W. Bloor [*sic*], December 20, 1917, and letter, Colonel A. W. Bloor, to His Excellency A. L. Williams, December 23, 1917.

[31] *Dallas Morning News*, September 3, and October3, 7, 1917; *Gainesville Daily Register*, September 4, 1917; Spence, "36th Division," 20.

[32] *Gainesville Daily Register*, September 5, 1917; NARA, RG391, Box2378 HQ Corr: Books and Doc File, Memo from: C.O. Sanitary Detachment, To: C.O. 142nd Infantry, Subject: Assignment of medical officer, Oct 17, 1917; Spence, "36th Division," 19.

[33] *Dallas Morning News*, September 25, 1917; NARA, RG391, Box 2378, Doc File 10-499, Memorandum from Commanding Officer, 142nd Infantry, to Commanding General 36th Division, subject: Text Books for Non-commissioned officers school, October 27, 1917; NARA, RG391, Box 2378, Doc File 10-499, Memorandum from C.O. Co. D, 142nd Infantry, to Commanding Officer 142nd Infantry, subject: Purchase of Text Books, October 27, 1917.

[34] White, *Panthers to Arrowheads*, 66; Spence, "36th Division," 21; RG 120, World War I Organizational Records, Records of the 36th Division, Box 12, 71st Brigade, 1st Indorsement, Headquarters, 71st Infantry Brigade, Camp Bowie, Texas, 23 Feb. 1918, to Commanding General, 36th Division, Camp Bowie, TX, "List of officers who have attended Infantry School of Arms."

[35] Spence, "36th Division," 26; White, *Panthers to Arrowheads*, 64; *Abilene Reporter*, May 9, 10, 1918; *Dallas Morning News*, May 10, 1918; *Fort Worth Star Telegram*, December 14, 1917; Hart, *Company K of Yesterday*, 36; *New York Times*, May 9, 1918.

[36] *Abilene Reporter*, May 9, 10, 1918.

[37] *Abilene Reporter*, May 10, 1918.

[38] *Abilene Reporter*, May 10, 1918.

[39] Rumors swirled that the training at Camp Bowie was easier than the training at other bases in Texas, such as Camp Travis in San Antonio and Camp MacArthur in Waco. Regular Army officers complained that the training at Camp Bowie was "a huge joke," and that soldiers at the Fort Worth Camp were "their own instructors and come and go at will"; *Wise County Messenger*, March 1, 1918.

[40] NARA, RG391, Box 2378, Doc File 10-499, Memorandum from R. M. Wagstaff to Commanding General 36th Division, subject: Leave of Absence, November 2, 1917; NARA, RG391, Box 2378, HQ Corr and Doc File 10-499, Memorandum from Second Lieutenant Bertram H. Bloor to Commanding General, 36th Division, subject: Leave, November 19, 1917.

[41] NARA, RG391, Box 2378, Doc File 10-499, Memorandum from Private Ellis A. Richardson, to Commanding General 36th Division, subject: Application for discharge, November 1, 1917.

[42] NARA, RG391, Box 2378, Doc File 10-499, Memorandum from Private Henry A. Montgomery, to Commanding General 36th Division, subject: request for discharge, November 1, 1917.

[43] NARA, RG391, Box 2378, HQ Corr: Books and Doc File, Memorandum from Private Paul K. Fancher to Commanding General, 36th Division, Requesting Transfer, Oct 28, 1917; NARA, RG391, Box 2378, Hq Corr and Doc File, 10-499, Memorandum from Pvt Jesse Alexander, to Commanding Officer, 142nd Infantry, subject: Request for Transfer, November 21, 1917; Memorandum from H. T. Merrill, to Commanding General 36th Division, subject: Assignment to Aviation Corps, November 9, 1917, and 4th Indorsement, from Hq. 142nd Infantry to Commanding General 36th Division, November 19, 1917. Captain Merrill's name appears on a number of charge sheets with a signature line as "Captain, 142nd Infantry, Summary Court," throughout December 1917–February, 1918, RG391, WWI-Organizational Records, 142nd Infantry, Box 2387, Charge Sheets; Memorandum, City of San Antonio, From Mayor O. B. Black to Homer T. Merrill, June 30, 1921, Homer T. Merrill Papers, 1899–1964, Folder: Correspondence, 1912–1927, Southwest Collection, Texas Tech University, Lubbock, Texas.

[44] NARA, RG391, HQ Corr: Books and Doc File, Box 2378, Fourth Endorsement, from Company B, 142nd Infantry to C.O. 142nd Infantry, October 29, 1917.

[45] NARA, RG391, Doc File, 10-499, 2nd Indorsement, from Company B, 142nd Infantry to Commanding General 36th Division (Through Commanding Officer, 142nd Infantry), no date.

[46] NARA, RG391, Headquarters Correspondence: Books and Doc file, Box 2378, Memorandum From: Camp Ordnance Officer, To: Commanding Officer, 142nd Infantry, Subject: Failure of enlisted men to report for duty with Ordnance Detachment, Oct 26, 1917; Clark, *Aubyn's War*, 98.

[47] *Wichita Daily Times*, September 13, 1917; *Wise County Messenger*, February 15, 1918.

[48] NARA, RG391, Box 2378, HQ Corr and Doc File, 10-499, Memorandum from Company G, 142nd Infantry, to Commanding Officer, 142nd Infantry, subject: Private Merton B. Foreman, November 27, 1917.

[49] NARA, RG 391, Box 2378, Doc File 10-499, Special Order No. 50, October 22, 1917; NARA, RG391, Box 2378 HQ Corr: Books and Doc File, Letter from J. B. Self to Colonel A. W. Bloor, September 29, 1917, and Memorandum from A. W. Bloor to J. B. Self, Subject: Payment of Reward for apprehension of Deserters, October 22, 1917; NARA, RG391, Box 2378, Doc File 10-499, 2nd Indorsement, Hq. 142d Infantry to the Commanding General 71st Infantry Brigade, Oct 29, 1917.

[50] RG391, HQ Doc File 500-1150, Memorandum from Captain Clifford Childers to Commanding Officer, 142nd Infantry, subject: Statement to accompany charges, November 19, 1917; Barnes, *History of the 142nd*, 344–47.

[51] NARA, RG391, Box 2394, Machine Gun Company, Correspondence, Doc. File, and Sick Reports, Strength Returns for the Week of January 28, 1918–Februay 2, 1918; White, *90th Division in World War I*, 72; Keene, *Doughboys, the Great War, and the Remaking of America*, 69–71.

[52] NARA, RG391, Box 2378, From Hq., 142nd Infantry to Commanding General 36th Division, October 29, 1917; RG391, Box 2392, Miscellaneous Reports, "Captain T.D. Barton, After Being Duly Sworn, Testifies as Follows," no date.

[53] NARA, RG391, Box 2378, Doc File 10-499, Memorandum from Noah Roark to Brigadier General Henry Hutchings, subject: report of Tour of Duty, November 9, 1917.

[54] NARA, RG391, Box 2378, Memorandum from Commanding General, 71st Infantry Brigade to Commanding Officer, 142nd Infantry, November 9, 1917.

[55] NARA, RG391, Box 2378, 1st Indorsement, from Hq. 142nd Infantry, to Commanding General 71st Infantry Brigade, November 9, 1917; Hart, *Company K of Yesterday*, 19.

[56] *Gainesville Daily Register*, September 12, 16, 1917; *Abilene Reporter*, September 24, 1917; Clark, *Aubyn's War*, 115.

[57] *Clarendon News*, October 5, 1917.

[58] *Abilene Reporter*, August 21, 1917; White, *Panthers to Arrowheads*, 75, 77; *Dallas Morning News*, September 1, 1917.

[59] *Gainesville Daily Register*, September 12, 16, 18, 1917; *Abilene Reporter*, September 25, 1917; RG391, Box 2378, Doc File 10-499, 2nd Indorsement, Hq. 142nd Infantry to the Commanding General 71st Infantry Brigade, October 29, 1917.

[60] White, *Panthers to Arrowheads*, 71; NARA, RG391, Doc File 10-499, 1st Indorsement, Hq. 142nd Infantry to the Commanding General 36th Division, October 29, 1917; 3rd Indorsement, Hq. 142nd Infantry to the Comdg. Gen'l 36th Division, November 10, 1917, doc 364; Clark, *Aubyn's War*, 111.

[61] White, *Panthers to Arrowheads*, 72–74; *Dallas Morning News*, February 16, 1918; Richard F. Selcer, *Hell's Half Acre* (Fort Worth: TCU Press, 1991).

[62] White, *Panthers to Arrowheads*, 58–59; *Dallas Morning News*, December 3, 4, 5, 6, 30, 1917; Spence, "36th Division," 17.

[63] Lonnie White pointed out that about 1,000 soldiers went AWOL for Christmas. Unfortunately, it is not clear how many of these men were from the 142d Infantry, or the old 7th Texas. Lonnie White, *Panthers to Arrowheads*, 60–61; *Dallas Morning News*, December 16, 26, 1917; *Fort Worth Star-Telegram*, December 15, 18, 19, 26, 1917; Spence, "36th Division," 18. Greble's order for 50 percent furloughs met some resistance from the War Department, which considered a furlough for just 5 percent of the men. See *Fort Worth Star-Telegram*, December 19, 1917.

[64] *Dallas Morning News*, January 22, 1918.

[65] *Dallas Morning News*, January 30, February 1, 1918; Hart, *Company K of Yesterday*, 38; Clark, *Aubyn's War*, 125.

[66] *Dallas Morning News*, February 2, 1918; Hart, *Company K of Yesterday*, 38.

[67] *Wise County Messenger*, June 7, 27, 1918; Clark, *Aubyn's War*, 167; White, *90th Division in World War I*, 73.

[68] White, *Panthers to Arrowheads*, 82; *Dallas Morning News*, November 22, 1917.

[69] It was reported that Governor Hobby was persuaded to take a few shots at the rifle range and scored a "bull's eye" from 1,000 yards, *Dallas Morning News*, November 22, 1917; White, *Panthers to Arrowheads*, 82–83; Spence, "36th Division," 25.

[70] White, *Panthers to Arrowheads*, 83, 89; Clark, *Aubyn's War*, 154–55.

[71] *Wichita Daily Times*, July 8, 1918; White, *90th Division in World War I*, 41; White, "Chief of the Arrowheads," 149–76; Spence, "36th Division."

[72] NARA, RG 391, World War I-Organizational Records, 142nd Infantry, Box 2394, Machine Gun Company, 1–100, Memorandum from Commanding Officer, MG Co., 142nd Infantry, to Commanding Officer, 142nd Infantry, subject: List of men recommend for SCD and Transfer, June 23, 1918; 65th Congress, 2nd Session, Document No. 271, National Guard Officers Discharged and Dismissed, Letter from the Secretary of War (Washington: Government Printing Office, 1918), 27–28.

[73] RG 391, Box 2394, Machine Gun Company, Correspondence Book, Doc. File, and Sick Reports, letter from Mrs. Jesse B. Scott to Captain Whitney, June 22, 1918; RG391, Box 2395, Supply Company, Memorandum from Pvt Robert H. Trimble, 142d Infantry, to The General commanding the 36th Division, Subject: Discharge from the military service of private Robert H. Trimble, Supply Company, 142d Infantry, Camp Bowie, Texas," ca. April 1918.

[74] RG 391, WWI Organizational Records, Machine Gun Company, Memorandum, subject: Report on Memo, June 27, 1918, June 28, 1918; RG 391 WWI Organizational Records, Machine Gun Company, Memorandum, June 28, 1918; RG 391, WWI Organizational Records, Machine Gun Company, Memorandum, June 29, 1918; RG 391, WWI Organizational Records, Machine Gun Company, Memorandum: Report of Indebtedness, July 7, 1918; RG 391, WWI Organizational Records, Machine Gun Company, Memorandum: Absences, July 16, 1918; RG 391, WWI Organizational Records, Machine Gun Company, Memorandum: Appointment of Non-Commissioned Officers, July 18, 1918; RG391, WWI Organizational Records, Machine Gun Company, Memorandum: Recommendation for reduction and appointment of non-commissioned officers, August 1, 1918; Clark, *Aubyn's War*, 183.

[75] Spence, "36th Division," 29; White, *Panthers to Arrowheads*, 91; Hornaday Collection, Volume 4, 241; Hart, *Company K of Yesterday*, 40–41; Daniel O. Blackmon Collection, Southwest Collection, Texas Tech University, Lubbock, Texas.

[76] Hart, *Company K of Yesterday*, 43–44; Hornaday Collection, Volume 4, 241.

[77] *Clarendon News*, August 1, 1918.

[78] Hart, *Company K of Yesterday*, 44; RG120, Records of the 36th Division, Box 14, 142nd Infantry Regiment, Station Lists. While in New York, Colonel Jules Muchert, a Texas Guardsman and commander of the 143d Infantry, was allegedly relieved of duty simply because he was born in Germany, had served in that country's army, and spoke with a German accent. See Spence, "36th Division," 30.

[79] RG 120, Records of the 36th Division, Box 2, "Annal of Mobilization," circa July 1918.

[80] Hornaday Collection, Volume 12, 88, Volume 4, 241, Volume 7, 129, Volume 10, 65, Volume 12, 243; Hart, *Company K of Yesterday*, 46–47.

[81] Hart, *Company K of Yesterday*, 48; RG 120, 36th Division, Box 14, 142nd Infantry Regiment, Station Lists; Letter from Lt. Shine, *Houston Post*, date unknown.

[82] *Wise County Messenger*, September 20, 1918, August 23, 1918; *Cleburne Enterprise*, August 27, 1918; *Wichita Daily Times*, August 2, 1918.

[83] *Cleburne Enterprise*, August 26, 1918; Letter from Lt. Shine, *Houston Post*, date unknown.

NOTES TO CHAPTER 4

[1] David F. Trask, *The AEF and Coalition Warmaking, 1917–1918* (Lawrence: University of Kansas Press, 1993), 84.

[2] Coffman, *The War to End All Wars*, 262–63.

[3] Spence, "36th Division," 31; John. J. Pershing, *My Experiences in the First World War, Volume II* (1931; repr., New York: Da Capo, 1995), 201; *Wichita Daily Times*, October 14, 1918; Ben H. Chastaine, *Story of the Thirty-Sixth: The Experiences of the Thirty-Sixth Division in the World War* (Oklahoma City: Harlow, 1920), 37, 40, 39; Hart, *Company K of Yesterday,* 50; White, *Panthers to Arrowheads,* 100–1.

[4] Chastaine, *Story of the Thirty-Sixth*, 36; *Wichita Daily Times*, August 21, 29, 1918; *Wise County Messenger*, August 23, September 20, October 18, 1918. In a humorous aside, another Wise County soldier, Bill Schulkey, who was not part of the 142nd Infantry, wrote home that when he marched off the boat onto French soil, he noticed a little girl standing nearby who burst out in a popular song of the day: "Hail, Hail, the gang's all here; so what the hell do we care!" *Wise County Messenger*, August 23, 1918; Chastaine, *Story of the Thirty-Sixth*, 39.

[5] White, *Panthers to Arrowheads*, 103; Chastaine, *Story of the Thirty-Sixth*, 41; RG 120, 36th Division records, box 3268, folder 4, G3 reports, table: 36th Division Arrival Strength in A.E.F. by unit and date; *Wise County Messenger*, October 18, 1918; William Hornaday Collection, Volume 4, page 237, Texas State Library and Archives, Austin, Texas.

[6] *Wise County Messenger*, September 13, 19, 20, 1918; *Clarendon News*, October 19, 1933; Hart, *Company K of Yesterday*, 53; Barnes, *History of the 142nd*, 27; Hornaday Collection, Volume 4, 238; Clark, *Aubyn's War*, 200.

[7] Hart, *Company K of Yesterday*, 54; Chastaine, *Story of the Thirty-Sixth*, 41, 45.

[8] RG120, 36th Division, 142nd Infantry Regiment, Box 14, Medical Report, 142nd Infantry, January 6, 1919; White, *Panthers to Arrowheads*, 104; Barnes, *History of the 142nd*, 27; Spence, "36th Division," 32.

[9] RG 391, 142nd Infantry, Correspondence, Supply Company, Memorandum to all brigade, regimental, and separate organization commanders, 2 October, 1918; *Wise County Messenger*, September 13, 1918; *Clarendon News*, September 19, 1918; Hart, *Company K of Yesterday*, 57; Clark, *Aubyn's War*, 201.

[10] *Clarendon News*, September 19, 1918.

[11] RG391, 142nd Infantry, Box 2400, Correspondence, Company K, Memorandum From: The Adjutant General, to: Commanding General 36th Division, subject: French Personnel, August 3, 1918; Spence, "36th Division," 35–37; *Wise County Messenger*, September 27, and October 25, 1918; Barnes, *History of the 142nd*, 27; White, *Panthers to Arrowheads*, 105; *Abilene Daily Reporter*, June 18, 1919; Mark Ethan Grotelueschen, *The AEF Way of War: The American Army and Combat in World War I* (New York: Cambridge, 2007), 40.

[12] *Wise County Messenger*, September 27, 1918.

[13] RG 391, 142nd Infantry, Box 2395, Correspondence, Supply Company, Memorandum from C.O. Co. A to Supply Officer, 142nd Infantry, subject: Rations, 14 September, 1918, and 2nd Indorsement, 16 September, 1918, D. M. Perkins, Captain 142nd Infantry, Supply Company; *Cleburne Enterprise*, October 24, 1918; *Wise County Messenger*, September 13, 27, October 25, 1918; *Clarendon News*, November 14, 1918; Clark, *Aubyn's War*, 202.

[14] *Clarendon News*, September 19, 1918; *Wichita Daily Times*, October 14, 1918.

[15] *Wise County Messenger*, October 18, 1918; *Wichita Daily Times*, August 21, 1918; *Cleburne Enterprise*, August 26, 1918.

[16] *Wise County Messenger*, September 13, 1918; *Wichita Daily Times*, October 14, 1918; *Clarendon News*, September 19, 1918.

[17] *Cleburne Enterprise*, October 24, 1918; *Wise County Messenger*, September 13, 1918.

[18] *Clarendon News*, November 14, 1918; *Wichita Daily Times*, October 14, 1918; *Wise County Messenger*, September 13, 27, 1918.

[19] *Wichita Daily Times*, October 14, August 29, and November 7, 1918; *Wise County Messenger*, September 13, 20, and October 4, 1918; *Clarendon News*, September 19, and November 14, 1918.

[20] *Cleburne Enterprise*, August 26, 1918; *Wichita Daily Times*, September 16, 1918. In this same letter, the soldier mentioned that the lieutenant who had been in command of their platoon had been transferred and their new lieutenant had been in France for a long time and had come up from the ranks as a private. *Clarendon News*, November 14, 1918; Clark, *Aubyn's War*, 201.

[21] *Cleburne Enterprise*, August 18, October 24, 1918; *Wichita Daily Times*, August 21, September 27, 1918; *Clarendon News*, September 19, 1918; *Wise County Messenger*, September 13, October 25, 1918; *Abilene Daily Reporter*, June 18, 1919; Clark, *Aubyn's War*, 201.

[22] *Clarendon News*, September 19, 1918; *Abilene Daily Reporter*, June 18, 1919; Clark, *Aubyn's War*, 201.

[23] RG 391, 142nd Infantry, Box 2395, Supply Company Correspondence, General Order No 14, 7 September, 1918; *Wichita Daily Times*, September 16, 1918.

[24] *Wise County Messenger*, September 14, 1918; *Wichita Daily Times*, October 14, 1918.

[25] *Wichita Daily Times*, August 22, 1918.

[26] *Wichita Daily Times*, August 22, 1918.

[27] RG 120, 36th Division, 142nd Regiment, Box 14, Medical Report, 142nd Infantry, January 6, 1919; Chastaine, *Story of the Thirty-Sixth*, 52.

[28] RG120, 36th Division, 142nd Regiment, Box 14, Medical Report, 142n Infantry, January 6, 1919.

[29] RG120, 36th Division 142nd Infantry Regiment, Box 14, medical report, 142nd Infantry, January 6, 1919; *Wichita Daily Times*, August 21, September 16, 1918.

[30] White, *Panthers to Arrowheads*, 107–108.

[31] RG391, Box 2395, Supply Company Correspondence, 36th Division, General Order No 10, 31 August, 1918; White, *Panthers to Arrowheads*, 108.

[32] Colonel Bloor, along with Colonel John Hoover of the 143rd Infantry, and Colonel Charles W. Nimon of the 111th, were appointed by General Smith as the division board charged with meeting from "time to time to examine into and report upon the capacity, qualifications, conduct, and efficiency of such commissioned officers of this command as may be ordered before it." The three men were to decide whether officers brought before the board should be retained or discharged, RG391, 142nd Infantry, Box 2395, Correspondence, Supply Company, 36th Division, General Orders No 4, 11 August, 1918.

[33] RG 391, 142nd Infantry, Supply Company Correspondence, 36th Division, General Order No 9, 31 August, 1918; Spence, "36th Division," 34–35; White, *Panthers to Arrowheads*, 107–9; Hart, *Company K of Yesterday*, 60; *Abilene Daily Reporter*, January 1, and June 18, 1919. According to the *Abilene Daily Reporter*, Captain Wagstaff was assigned to the School of the Line on September 28, and left for Langres on September 29. The paper stated that "the detail to this school was not solicited by Captain Wagstaff and was unknown to himself until orders were received at Bar-Sur-Aube." General Smith selected Wagstaff to attend the prestigious school. Although it was a worthwhile school, the timing of

Wagstaff's selection later caused him problems; see *Abilene Daily Reporter*, June 18, 1919.

[34] Roster of Officers from Barnes, *History of the 142nd*, 214–17, 245–47, 342–46.

[35] Barnes, *History of the 142nd*, 342–46.

[36] Barnes, *History of the 142nd*, 342–46.

[37] World War I Draft Registration Cards, National Archives Southwest Branch, Fort Worth, Texas.

[38] RG391, 142nd Infantry Regiment, Box 2400, Company K Correspondence, Letter, C.O. Company K, 142nd Infantry, to, C.O. Company I, 164th Infantry, 19 September, 1918; RG 391, Letter, Corporal Beasley to Captain S. G. Staniforth, September 6, 1918; *Wise County Messenger*, October 4, 25, 1918; Spence, "36th Division," 38; White, *Panthers to Arrowheads*, 109.

[39] RG 120, 36th Division, Box 2395, Supply Company, "Headquarters 36th Division, Memorandum No. 45," September 24, 1918; RG 120, 36th Division, 142nd Infantry Regiment, Box 14, Medical Report, 142nd Infantry, January 6, 1919; RG 391, 142nd Infantry, Box 2400, Correspondence, Company K, Memorandum, 18 September, 1918, Report on the Strength of the personnel of this company, Memorandum, 17 September, 1918, Report on the number of hours the personnel of this company has worn gas masks the past week, Memorandum, 9 September, 1918, Reference relative to unserviceable rifles, Memorandum, 6 September, 1918, Report on the religious census of this company, Memorandum, 10 September, 1918, Relative to Memo relative to gas masks; Spence, "36th Division," 40–41; *Wise County Messenger*, November 8, 1918; Grotelueschen, *AEF Way of War*, 265.

[40] Spence, "36th Division," 42, 46; Chastaine, *Story of the Thirty-Sixth*, 57; White, *Panthers to Arrowheads*, 116. AEF General Headquarters issued orders assigning the 2d and 36th Divisions to the French on September 23, 1918; see Historical Branch, War Department General Staff, Monograph No. 9, *Blanc Mont*, April 1920, 1, hereafter cited as *Blanc Mont*.

[41] RG 120, 36th Division, Box 8, Statement of Lt. Col. Hawley, Division Machine Gun Officer, no date, p. 2

[42] Spence, "36th Division," 44.

[43] RG 120, 36th Division, Box 8, Major General William R. Smith, Report on the Operations of the 36th Division with the French Armies, September 26, to October 29, 1918, 1–2; Spence, "36th Division," 37–38, 46–50; Trask, *The AEF and Coalition Warmaking*, 122; RG 120, 36th Division, Box 8, Statement of Lt Col Hawley, Division Machine Gun Officer, no date, p. 2–3; RG 120, 36th Division, Box 12, Report of 71st Brigade Operations, 5–11 October, p. 4; RG 391, 142d Infantry, Box 2400, Company K, Memorandum from C.O. Company K to Supply Officer 142d Infantry, "Report on Ordinance [*sic*] Equipment in the hands of this organization," September 21, 1918.

[44] RG 120, 36th Division, Report on the Operations of the 36th Division with the French Armies, September 26 to October 29, 1918, 1–2; *Fort Worth Star-Telegram*, October 23, 1918; Spence, "36th Division," 50; White, *Panthers to Arrowheads*, 118; Clark, *Aubyn's War*, 213.

[45] RG 120, 36th Division, Box 8, Smith, Report of Operations, 1; Spence, "36th Division," 53–54, 57; White, *Panthers to Arrowheads*, 123, 125–26; John A. Lejeune, *The Reminiscences of a Marine* (1930; repr., Quantico: Marine Corps Association, 1979), 360; Grotelueschen, *AEF Way of War*, 252–64.

[46] RG120, 36th Division, 142nd Infantry Regiment, Box 14, Personnel Experiences Folder, Thomas Barton, 1, Colonel Alfred W. Bloor, January 14, 1919, 1; RG 120, 36th Division, Box 12, Report of Operations, 71st Brigade, 5–11 Oct, p. 6; Spence, "36th Division," 55–60; Historical Branch, *Blanc Mont*, 8; Lejeune, *Reminiscences of a Marine*, 360; White, *Panthers to Arrowheads*, 127.

[47] RG 120, 36th Division, 142nd Infantry, Box 14, Personnel Experiences Folder, Irving Phillipson, 1; Alfred W. Bloor, 1–2; *Quanah Tribune Chief*, January 23, 1919; Spence, "36th Division," 61, 63–64; Historical Branch, War Plans Division, General Staff, *Blanc Mont (Meuse-Argonne-Champagne)*, Monograph No. 9, 1920, 26.

[48] RG 120, 36th Division, 142nd Infantry, Box 14, Personnel Experiences Folder, Irving Phillipson, 1; Alfred W. Bloor, 1–2; Spence, "36th Division," 64, 71–72.

[49] RG 120, 36th Division, 142nd Infantry, Box 14, Personnel Experiences Folder, Alfred W. Bloor, 2; Box 12, 36th Division, Report of Operations, 71st Brigade, 5–11 Oct, p. 5; Spence, "36th Division," 74–75.

NOTES TO CHAPTER 5

[1] John. W. Thomason, *Fix Bayonets!* (1925; repr., Charleston: Nautical and Aviation Publishing Company of America, 2007), 139; George B. Clark, *Devil Dogs: Fighting Marines of World War I* (Novato, CA: Presidio, 2000), 292.

[2] National Archives and Records Administration, RG 120, Records of the American Expeditionary Forces, 36th Division, 142nd Infantry Regiment, Box 14, Personnel Experiences Folder, Alfred W. Bloor, 3–4, hereafter cited as Personnel Experiences Folder; Spence, "36th Division," 73–78; *Congressional Medal of Honor, the Distinguished Service Cross, and the Distinguished Service Medal issued by the War Department*, Compiled by the Office of the Adjutant General of the Army (Washington: Government Printing Office, 1919), 871; *Blanc Mont*, 28.

[3] Personnel Experiences Folder, Barton, 1–2, Lillard, 1; *Clarendon News*, December 5, 1918; *Quanah Tribune Chief*, January 23, 1919; Spence, "36th Division," 76–77.

[4] Personnel Experiences Folder, Alfred W. Bloor, 4–5; Edwin B. Sayles, "From Somme-Py and Back," unpublished manuscript, Edwin B. Sayles Papers, 1892–1975 and undated, Military Activities Folder, 1892–1975, Literary Productions, 1918, Southwest Collection, Texas Tech University, Lubbock, Texas, hereafter cited as Sayles, Manuscript, 1; Spence, "36th Division," 79.

[5] Personnel Experiences Folder, D. M. Perkins, 3–5.

[6] Sayles, Manuscript, 1, 2, 4.

[7] Sayles, Manuscript, 7–10.

[8] Sayles, Manuscript, 11–12; Spence, "36th Division," 92–93.

[9] Personnel Experience Folder, Barton, 2, Phillipson, 3, Hawley, 5; Personnel Experience Folder, Intel Report. The lack of continuous trenches and shelter was also described in Historical Branch, War Department General Staff, Monograph No. 9, *Blanc Mont*, April, 1920, 8. See also Spence, "36th Division," 68, 81, 85; Hornaday Collection, Volume 12, 244.

[10] Sayles, Manuscript, 14, 25.

[11] Personnel Experiences Folder, Bloor, 5; Spence, "36th Division," 102; Lejeune, *Reminiscences of a Marine*, 361.

[12] Personnel Experiences Folder, Bloor, 5–6; Sayles, Manuscript, 25; *Abilene Daily Reporter*, June 18, 1919; Historical Branch, *Blanc Mont*, 10; Spence, "36th Division," 66, 93.

[13] Captain David R. Nelson took the place of Colonel Bloor's chauffeur, believing that he could drive

the regimental commander to the meeting more quickly. See RG 391, 142nd Infantry, Miscellaneous Correspondence File, Docs 150-700, Memorandum from Commanding Officer, 142nd Infantry, to Commanding General, 36th Division, subject: Distinguished Service Cross, 6 February, 1919; Personnel Experiences Folder, Bloor, 6; Spence, "36th Division," 97.

[14] Personnel Experiences Folder, Bloor, 6–7; Spence, "36th Division," 105.

[15] Personnel Experiences Folder, Bloor, 7–8; Historical Branch, *Blanc Mont*, Headquarters Second Division, Field Orders No. 40, October 7, 1918; Spence, 36th Division, 106.

[16] White, *Panthers to Arrowheads*, 133.

[17] Personnel Experiences Folder, Barton, 2.

[18] *Clarendon News*, December 5, 1918; *Quanah Tribune Chief*, January 23, 1919.

[19] Spence, "36th Division," 67, 85; White, *Panthers to Arrowheads*, 130–31; Barnes, *History of the 142nd*, 67.

[20] Spence, "36th Division," 81–82, 84; White, *Panthers to Arrowheads*, 131, 134.

[21] RG120, 36th Division, 142nd Infantry Regiment, Memorandum: to Captain Spence, December 21, 1918, outlines the assault arrangement of the 142nd Infantry; Personnel Experiences Folder, Elijah Horner, 1–2; Spence, "36th Division," 92; White, *Panthers to Arrowheads*, 136.

[22] *Foard County News*, June 7, 1918.

[23] Personnel Experiences Folder, Barton, 2–3, William Morrissey, 1; RG120, 36th Division, 142nd Infantry, Box 12, Special Report of tour in line of Seventy-First Brigade, 2; Spence, *36th Division*, 131–32; *Abilene Daily Reporter*, June 18, 1919.

[24] Personnel Experiences Folder, Horner, 3, Barton, 3; Barnes, *History of the 142nd*, 30.

[25] Personnel Experiences Folder, Gordon R. Porter, 1; Barnes, *History of the 142nd*, 124.

[26] Personnel Experiences Folder, Barton, 3; Spence, "36th Division," 133–34.

[27] *Clarendon News*, November 7, December 5, 1918; *Quanah Tribune Chief*, January 23, 1919; Adjutant General, *Medal of Honor*, 26.

[28] Barnes, *History of the 142nd*, 128–31, 134, 135–36; *Clarendon News*, December 5, 1918.

[29] Barnes, *History of the 142nd*, 143, 145, 158–62.

[30] William D. Hornaday, Volume 4, p. 238, William Deming Hornaday Transcripts of World War I letters and Personal Accounts, Archives and Information Serviced Division, Texas State Library and Archives Commission, Austin, Texas; Adjutant General, *Medal of Honor*, 26.

[31] Personnel Experiences Folder, Barton, 3.

[32] Personnel Experiences Folder, Steve Lillard, 1; Barnes, *History of the 142nd*, 146, 148, 151, 153; *Dallas Morning News*, November 10, 1918, and July 13, 1919. As Spence notes in the divisional history, the two Marine companies that were to move into Saint Etienne on the night of October 7, actually stopped about one kilometer south of the town and sent several patrols into the town. Accordingly, German soldiers filtered back into the town during the night and fired into the flanks of the 142nd Infantry on the morning of October 8. Spence, "36th Division," 112, 135–36.

33 Personnel Experiences Folder, Horner, 5, Lillard, 1.

34 Personnel Experiences Folder, Barton, 4, Lillard, 2; Spence, "36th Division," 138; Barnes, *History of the 142nd*, 152.

35 Personnel Experiences Folder, Lillard, 2, Barton, 4. Captain Greer and the men under his command eventually pulled back to the north slope of Blanc Mont Ridge on the night of the eighth. Spence, "36th Division," 153.

36 Personnel Experiences Folder, Lillard, 2, Barton, 4; Sayles, Manuscript, 29, 34; Hart, *Company K of Yesterday*, 73.

37 Barnes, *History of the 142nd*, 74–75; Spence, "36th Division," 151–52, 227.

38 Spence, "36th Division," 147, 230; Sayles, Manuscript, 40, 52–53; Personnel Experiences Folder, Perkins, 5, Barnes, 131; *Abilene Daily Reporter*, June 18, 1919. At one point in the fighting, the 142nd Infantry managed to bring water up to the ration dump by motorcycle. The driver took as many as fifty canteens and filled them at wells south of Blanc Mont. See Spence, "36th Division," 230.

39 Special Report Tour of the Line Seventy-First Brigade, 3; Personnel Experiences Folder, P. E. Barth, 2, Barton, 5; Barnes, *History of the 142nd*, 125, 139, 142, 157; *Abilene Daily Reporter*, June 18, 1919.

40 Sayles, Manuscript, 45, 50; Barnes, *History of the 142nd*, 69–70; Spence, "36th Division," 154–57.

41 RG 391, 142nd Infantry, Box 2389 Miscellaneous Correspondence Docs 150-700, Memorandum for Recommendation of Distinguished Service Cross to Major Robert Nelson, 6 February, 1919; Barnes, *History of the 142nd*, 69–70, 71; Personnel Experiences Folder, Phillipson, 6, Barton, 5; Spence, "36th Division," 154–57.

42 RG 120, 36th Division, Box 12, Report of Operations, 71st Brigade, 5–11 Oct, p. 9; Spence, "36th Division," 146, 158, 161, 192–93, 196–97; Barnes, *History of the 142nd*, 71, 156; Sayles, Manuscript, 54; Personnel Experiences Folder, Phillipson, 8, Barton, 5; Hart, *Company K of Yesterday*, 84; *Clarendon News*, December 5, 1918.

43 Spence, "36th Division," 193–95, 214, 217; Special Report tour in the line of Seventy-First Brigade, 3; Personnel Experiences Folder, Barton, 5; Historical Branch, *Blanc Mont*, 13; When General Naulin, XXI Army Corps commander, found out that both brigades were not to be put into the line abreast, he reportedly went to General Smith's command post and urged that they should be in the line together. When Smith explained the condition of the 71st Brigade, Naulin agreed that they should go into reserve. Spence, "36th Division," 205.

44 Spence, "36th Division," 204, 221; RG 120, 36th Division, 142nd Infantry, Box 14 G3 Memos, from Headquarters 142nd Infantry to Battalion Commanders, October 10, 1918; Barnes, *History of the 142nd*, 72; Sayles, Manuscript, 57–58. While in the town, the macabre sense of humor of soldiers in combat was evident when a sergeant approached Lieutenant Sayles and told him there was a "nice" room to rest in on the second floor of a nearby house. When Sayles went up to check it out, he found the room was full of dead French soldiers, some of whom had been there for a long time. Sayles, instead of being disgusted, wondered if they could remove the bodies and get rid of the odor. See Sayles, Manuscript, 59.

45 Spence, "36th Division," 118, 129, 140; Barnes, *History of the 142nd*, 69, 77–80; White, *Panthers to Arrowheads*, 139–40; *Wichita Daily Times*, November 6, 7, 1918; *Fort Worth Star-Telegram*, November 10, 1918; Personnel Experiences, Alvin Luebke, 2.

46 Spence, "36th Division," 115, 142–44; Barnes, *History of the 142nd*, 69, 73–76; Historical Branch, *Blanc Mont*, 11. Captain Ben Chastaine, who commanded Company A, observed soldiers walking upright

between the town and cemetery to get supplies, only taking cover for artillery, despite the "known presence of enemy snipers and machine gunners." Spence, *36th Division*, 115; Grotelueschen, *AEF Way of War*, 265; Hart, *Company K of Yesterday*, 108–9; *Official History of the Second Engineers in the World War, 1916–1919*, compiled by the Regimental Headquarters Second Engineers, circa 1922, 61.

47 *Blanc Mont*, 29–30.

48 Sayles, Manuscript, 61–62. A similar story about Perkins is repeated in Chastaine, *Story of the Thirty-Sixth*, 210; Spence, "36th Division," 256.

49 Sayles, Manuscript, 62.

50 White, *Panthers to Arrowheads*, 154–55, 159–60. The divisional command post in Dricourt was in a building that had once been a German recreation area, evident in part because soldiers found hundreds of empty beer bottles in the backyard of the place; see Spence, "36th Division," 257.

NOTES TO CHAPTER 6

1 Sayles, Manuscript, 66–68, 70, 71, 73.

2 Sayles, Manuscript, 72, 79; Hart, *Company K of Yesterday*, 138.

3 RG 120, 36th Division, 142nd Infantry, Box 14, Daily Operations Reports, October 16–18, 23–25, 1918; Spence, "36th Division," 273. See also Chastaine, *Story of the Thirty-Sixth*, 196, for a characterization of the regiment's time in front of Attigny.

4 Daily Operations Reports, October 16–27, 1918; Spence, "36th Division," 300. Spence wrote that the regimental gas officer decided to evacuate the town, which caused "friction" with Captain Lillard, who believed he would lose a significant number of support troops for the attack on Forest Farm; see Spence, "36th Division," 301.

5 Daily Operations Reports, October 17, 24, 26, 1918.

6 Daily Operations Reports, October 17–20, 1918; Sayles, Manuscript, 77.

7 RG 391, 142nd Infantry, Box 2389 Miscellaneous Correspondence Docs 150-700, Recommendation of Distinguished Service Cross for Sergeant Charles J. Lydell, 7 February, 1919.

8 RG 120, 36th Division, 142nd Infantry, Box 14, Patrol Reports, Memorandum from Private Lester Smith; Daily Operations Reports, October 19–22; RG 391, 142nd Infantry, Box 2389, Miscellaneous Correspondence Docs 150-700, Memorandum Recommending Major David Nelson for Distinguished Service Cross, 6 February, 1919.

9 RG 120, 36th Division, 142nd Infantry Regiment, Box 14, Field Messages, Memorandum from Intelligence OP with 142nd Infantry "No. 56 reports 18:00," signed Lt. Reid, no date; Daily Operations Reports, October 22, 25, 1918; Sayles, Manuscript, 76. A projector attack was a device resembling an "electric slingshot," that was used by both sides to fling gas shells. The British Livens Projector could launch a gas shell as far as 2,000 yards. See Michael S. Neiberg, *Fighting the Great War: A Global History* (Cambridge: Harvard University Press, 2005), 267.

10 Sayles, Manuscript, 83.

11 By this point, one of the active leaders of the regiment, Capt. Thomas Barton of Amarillo, who had been placed in command of 1st Battalion during the two weeks in front of Attigny, was summoned

to the division Chief of Staff. On the way, he believed he "had probably drawn a ticket to Blois"—the reclassification center. Instead, he found he had been placed in command of the 111th Military Police Battalion, and was no longer on the front. See RG 120 36th Division, 142nd Infantry, Box 14, Personnel Experiences, Thomas Barton, 5; White, *Panthers to Arrowheads*, 160.

[12] RG 120, 36th Division, 71st Brigade, Box 12, Combat Plans folder, Memorandum from CG, 71st Infantry Brigade to CG, 36th Infantry Division, subject: Preparation for Minor Operation, October 24, 1918; Spence, "36th Division," 308–11. Spence did note that several of Smith's objections were accepted, including having the brigade relief take place a day later than planned so they would have time to bury their dead and organize themselves. See Spence, "36th Division," 311.

[13] RG120, 36th Division, 142nd Infantry, Box 14, Memorandum from C.O. 142nd Infantry to Commanding General, 36th Division, subject: Transmitting Messages in Choctaw, January 23, 1919. Colonel Bloor wrote that some words had to be substituted for weapons, such as "big gun" for artillery, "little gun shoot fast" for machine guns, while the three battalions were identified as "one, two, or three grains of corn"; Spence, "36th Division," 319–20. General Smith briefed members of Congress on using the Choctaw code; see *Fort Worth Star-Telegram*, June 11, 1919.

[14] Personnel Experiences Folder, Lillard, 2–3; Spence, "36th Division," 320.

[15] Personnel Experiences Folder, Lillard, 3; Sayles, Manuscript, 88.

[16] Personnel Experiences Folder, Lillard, 3. On October 26, the Americans raised observation balloons to try to get a better look at the enemy positions. *Abilene Daily Reporter*, June 18, 1919; Spence, "36th Division," 313.

[17] RG 120, 36th Division, 142nd Infantry, Box 14 Forest Farm Engagement, Operations Report, October 27, 1918, 1–2; RG 120, 36th Division, Box 13, Operations Report—Forest Farm, 141st Infantry, 28 Oct 1918; RG 391, 142nd Infantry, Box 2400, Company I, Testimony of Sergeant Charlie Langford, and Testimony of Sergeant Ira Shockley, relative to the actions of Sergeant Albert Robinson while in action on October 27, 1918, March 25, 1919; Sayles, Manuscript, 89, 91; Spence, "36th Division," 314.

[18] Forest Farm Engagement, Operations Report, October 27, 1918, 2–3; RG 391, Testimony of Langford and Shockley, March 25, 1919; Sayles, Manuscript, 92; *Abilene Daily Reporter*, June 18, 1919; *Clarendon News*, November 7, December 5, 1918.

[19] Forest Farm Engagement, Operations Report, October 27, 1918, 3; RG 120, 36th Division, 142nd Infantry Regiment, Box 14, Memorandum from C.O. 142nd Infantry to Commanding General, 36th Division, subject: Machine Guns captured in Forest Farm engagement, November 6, 1918; Spence, "36th Division," 321–22, 324.

[20] Forest Farm Engagement, Operations Report, October 27, 1918, 3–4; Personnel Experiences Folder, Lillard, 3.

[21] Forest Farm Engagement, Operations Report, October 27, 1918, 3; Hart, *Company K of Yesterday*, 123–124; Barnes, *History of the 142nd*, 141, 143, 155. According to Corporal Hart, Lynch's shot did not kill the German soldier, whom they found with a terrible wound to his head. They pulled him out of his dugout and "laid him on the ground, within arm's reach of Cobb's lifeless body." When stretcher bearers took Cobb's body away, Hart asked them to come back and pick up the wounded German. Hart, *Company K of Yesterday*, 127.

[22] Forest Farm Engagement, Operations Report, October 27, 1918, 3; Personnel Experiences Folder, Rudolph E. Fried, 5–6; Hart, *Company K of Yesterday*, 144; Sayles, Manuscript, 95.

[23] Daily Operations Reports, October 28, 1918; Personnel Experiences Folder, Lillard, 3; Sayles, Manu-

script, 97–98.

[24] Daily Operations Reports, October 29–30, 1918; Sayles, Manuscript, 102, 104, 106, 107; Chastaine, *Story of the Thirty-Sixth*, 240; Spence, "36th Division," 329. Although most companies went into the line near full strength, Company K left the front lines with an effective strength of just three officers and sixty-four men. See RG 391, 142nd Infantry Regiment, Box 2400, Company K Correspondence, Form 30, "Condition of the Organization on the last day of October, 1918."

NOTES TO CHAPTER 7

[1] Spence, "36th Division," 332, 334–35; *Quanah Tribune Chief*, February 6, 1919, and January 17, 1919; Chastaine, *Story of the Thirty-Sixth*, 242–43, 246–47; Barnes, *History of the 142nd*, 41–42; William D. Hornaday, Volume 3, pp. 250–52, William Deming Hornaday Transcripts of World War I Letters and personal accounts, Archives and Information Services, Texas State Library and Archives Commission, Austin, Texas; *United States Army in the World War, 1917–1919, Military Operations of the American Expeditionary Forces, Volume 9* (1948; repr., Washington: Center of Military History, 1990), 480–81.

[2] Barnes, *History of the 142nd*, 142–43.

[3] Hornaday Collection, Volume 1, 298, Volume 5, 85–86, Volume 4, 241, Volume 2, 345, Volume 3, 250–52, Volume 4, 253–54, Volume 9, 258; *Wichita Daily Times*, 15 and 27 November, 1918.

[4] Chastaine, *Story of the Thirty-Sixth*, 248–49; Barnes, *History of the 142nd*, 46; Spence, "36th Division," 339.

[5] RG 391, 142nd Infantry Box 2389, Miscellaneous Correspondence Docs 150-700, Monthly Sanitary Report, 142nd Infantry, 2 March, 1919, and Memorandum from C.O. 142nd Infantry to C.O. 3th Division, Subject: Investigation of Pneumonia Cases, 17 February, 1919; Spence, "36th Division," 340–41; Barnes, *History of the 142nd*, 46–47; Hornaday Collection, Volume 5, 85–86; *Blum Bulletin*, January 9, 1919; Chastaine, *Story of the Thirty-Sixth*, 260.

[6] RG 120, 36th Division, 142nd Infantry Records, Box 14, "Field Order," 28 February, 1919, P.C. 142nd Infantry; Barnes, *History of the 142nd*, 47; Chastaine, *Story of the Thirty-Sixth*, 248; Hornaday Collection, Volume 2, 345, and Volume 9, 258.

[7] Spence, "36th Division," 348–349; *Abilene Reporter News*, September 27, 1942; *Amarillo Daily News*, November 30, 1919; *Quanah Tribune Chief*, January 23, 1919; Edwin Sayles Collection, Box 1, Officer's Record Book, Southwest Collection, Texas Tech University, Lubbock, Texas.

[8] RG 120, 36th Division, Box 14, Captain P. E. Barth, 142d Infantry, "Subject: Division History," 9 Jan 1919.

[9] Ibid.

[10] Ibid.

[11] Ibid.

[12] Ibid.

[13] RG120, 36th Division, Box 14, Captain P. E. Barth, 142d Infantry, "Subject: Division History," 9 Jan 1919; Keene, *Doughboys, the Great War, and the Remaking of America*, 105–118.

[14] RG 391, 142nd Infantry Regiment, Box 2400, Miscellaneous Correspondence, Testimony of Sergeant Elmer A. Blevins and Privates Frank Lynn and John H. Bynum with reference to wound of Corporal Lester E. Whatley, November 9, 1918, and Memorandum from C.O. Co. K, 142nd Infantry, to Sanitary Detachment, 142nd Infantry, Subject: Information with reference to wound of Corp. Lester E. Whatley, November 9, 1918.

[15] Hornaday Collection, Volume 1, 298, Volume 3, 250–52, Volume 5, 347, Volume 4, 253–55; *Abilene Reporter*, February 5, 1919.

[16] Spence, "36th Division," 344; Chastaine, *Story of the Thirty-Sixth*, 259–61.

[17] RG 120, 36th Division, 142nd Infantry Regiment, Box 14, Memorandum from: Entertainment Officer, Headquarters Company, 142nd Infantry, to: Regimental Entertainment Officer, 142nd Infantry, Subject: Entertainment report for the week ending March 21, 1919; Memorandum from: Entertainment Officer, 2nd Battalion, 142nd Infantry, to: Entertainment Officer, 142nd Infantry, subject: Report of Amusements for week ending March 22, 1919; Memorandum from: Entertainment Officer, 2nd Battalion, 142nd Infantry, to: Entertainment Officer, 142nd Infantry, subject: Report of amusements for week ending April 10, 1919; Memorandum from: Division Entertainment Officer, to: Lt. Chaplain F. W. Fann, 142nd Infantry, subject: Theatrical Contest; Hornaday Collection, Volume 8, 33.

[18] RG 391, 142nd Infantry, Box 2400, Memorandum from: Commanding Officer, Company I, 142nd Infantry, to Commanding Officer, 142nd Infantry, Subject: Officers and Men who desire to attend AEF University, March 2, 1919; RG 391, 142nd Infantry, Box 2400, Document 202, Memorandum from: Commanding Officer, Company I, 142nd Infantry, to Regimental School Officer, 142nd Infantry, Subject: Men who are qualified and desire to attend Division schools, February 27, 1919; Spence, "36th Division," 346; Chastaine, *Story of the Thirty-Sixth*, 262–63, 267. According to Spence, 348 officers and men of the division attended AEF programs at British and French universities; see Spence, "36th Division," 345.

[19] Samuel M. Sampler, Draft Registration Card, Jackson County, Oklahoma, National Archives and Records Administration, Atlanta, Georgia; *Fort Worth Star-Telegram*, June 16, 1919; Adjutant General, *Medal of Honor*, 26.

[20] Adjutant General, *Medal of Honor*, 702–4, 706, 708–10, 713–20; *Amarillo Daily News*, November 30, 1919; *Dallas Morning News*, July 13, 1919; *Cleburne Enterprise*, June 8, 1919; *Quanah Tribune Chief*, February 6, 1919; *Fort Worth Star-Telegram*, June 15, 1919; Spence, *36th Division*, 367.

[21] *Dallas Morning News*, August 14, 1919, July 2, 1919, April 26, 1919; *Gainesville Daily Register*, June 12 and 14, 1919; Spence, "36th Division," 367.

[22] *Abilene Reporter News*, September 27, 1942; *Amarillo Daily News*, November 30, 1919; *Gainesville Daily Register*, June 12, 14, and 18, 1919; *Clarendon News*, May 1, 1919; *Dallas Morning News*, August 14, 1919, July 2, 1919, April 26, 1919.

[23] Spence, "36th Division," 347.

[24] Hornaday Collection, Volume 1, 298, Volume 10, 65.

[25] *Wise County Messenger*, November 29, 1918; *Quanah Tribune Chief*, January 23, 1919, and January 2, 1919; Hornaday Collection, Volume 5, 321–323.

[26] *Quanah Tribune Chief*, February 6, 1919, and June 5, 1919; Hornaday Collection, Volume 3, 250–52.

[27] Hornaday Collection, Volume 3, 81, 217, 219, Volume 4, 241, Volume 4, 27–28; *Wichita Daily Times*, November 15, 1918.

[28] Hornaday Collection, Volume 2, 346, Volume 4, 28–29, Volume 7, 269.

[29] Hornaday Collection, Volume 4, 237; *Quanah Tribune Chief*, February 6, 1919, and January 23, 1919; Spence, "36th Division," 63.

[30] Hornaday Collection, Volume 5, 58–59, Volume 8, 229–30.

[31] Hornaday Collection, Volume 12, 321–22.

[32] Edwin B. Sayles Collection, Field Message Book Folder, 1918, Southwest Collection, Texas Tech University, Lubbock, Texas.

[33] Edwin B. Sayles Collection, Field Message Book Folder, 1918, Southwest Collection, Texas Tech University, Lubbock, Texas.

[34] *Quanah Tribune Chief*, January 23, 1919; Sayles Papers, Military Activities Folder, 1892–1975 and undated, undated newspaper clipping: "Sergt. Geo. W. Bolling Tells of Overseas Life."

[35] *Wise County Messenger*, June 27, 1919; Hornaday Collection, Volume 4, 58–59, Volume 6, 221–24.

[36] Hornaday Collection, Volume 4, 28–29.

[37] *Clarendon News*, December 5, 1918.

[38] *Clarendon News*, Dec 5, 1918; Clark, *Aubyn's War*, 52.

[39] *Clarendon News*, December 5, 1918; *Cleburne Enterprise*, June 22, 1919; Hornaday Collection, Volume 4, 237, Volume 8, 6; *Lubbock Avalanche*, January 2, 1919.

[40] Hornaday Collection, Volume 1, 298, Volume 5, 85–86, Volume 4, 241, Volume 2, 345, Volume 3, 250–252, Volume 4, 253–254, Volume 9, 258; *Wichita Daily Times*, 15 and 27 November, 1918.

[41] Hornaday Collection, Volume 2, 346, Volume 4, 27–28; *Cleburne Enterprise*, May 14, 1919; *Lubbock Avalanche*, January 2, 1919; Clark, *Aubyn's War*, 213.

[42] Hornaday Collection, Volume 4, 241–242, Volume 5, 58–59, Volume 11, 102.

[43] RG120, 36th Division, Box 2, Special Orders Number 67, 10 April, 1919; Chastaine, *Story of the Thirty-Sixth*, 271. Spence notes that there were rumors that the division would return home in March, as well as the unwelcome news that the division might end up in the Army of Occupation; Spence, "36th Division," 360.

NOTES TO CHAPTER 8

Chastaine, *Story of the Thirty-Sixth*, 277–78; Barnes, *History of the 142nd*, 43.

[2] White, *Panthers to Arrowheads*, 157–58; *New York Times*, October 20, 1918.

[3] *Wichita Daily Times*, October 20, 1918; *Wise County Messenger*, October 25, 1918; *Quanah Tribune Chief*, January 23, 1919.

[4] *Gainesville Daily Register*, June 9, 1919; *Fort Worth Star-Telegram*, November 7, 1918.

[5] *Fort Worth Star-Telegram*, November 6, 1918, June 15, 1919; *Gainesville Daily Register*, June 19, 1919;

White, *90th Division in World War I,* 194–95. As soon as the 36th Division arrived back in the United States, General Smith assumed command of Fort Totten, NY, and reverted to his original rank of colonel in the coast artillery; Spence, "36th Division," 363.

[6] *Clarendon News*, November 7, 1918; *Cleburne Enterprise*, June 20, 1919.

[7] *Clarendon News*, November 28, 1918.

[8] *Wise County Messenger*, November 22, 1918.

[9] *Abilene Reporter*, November 3, 1918.

[10] RG391, 142nd Infantry Regiment, Box 2400, Letter, Mrs. A. R. Childress to Chaplain George A. Nickles, February 5, 1919; Letter, 1st Lt. Joe A. Kell, 14nd Infantry, to Mrs. A. R. Childress, March 2, 1919.

[11] *Fort Worth Star-Telegram*, November 11, 1918; *Clarendon News*, November 14, 1918.

[12] *Clarendon News*, November 14, 1918; *Fort Worth Star-Telegram*, November 11, 1918. Another Tarrant County town, Keller, also buried the Kaiser with the assistance of 200 children from the public schools; *Fort Worth Star-Telegram*, November 11, 1918.

[13] *Wichita Daily Times*, November 11, 1918, May 12, 1957.

[14] *Abilene Reporter*, November 11, 1918; *Cleburne Enterprise*, November 11, 1918; Michael V. R. Thomason, "Mobile in World War I," in Olliff, *The Great War in the Heart of Dixie,* 121–40.

[15] Barnes, *History of the 142nd*, 48; Spence, "36th Division," 361.

[16] *Gainesville Daily Register*, June 9, 1919; Spence, "36th Division," 345; Chastaine, *Story of the Thirty-Sixth*, 271–72; RG120, 36th Division, Box 2395 Supply Company, "Headquarters 36th Division, General Orders, No. 15," September 19, 1918.

[17] Barnes, *History of the 142nd*, 49–50; *Cleburne Daily Enterprise*, June 24, 1919. Spence notes that the two men washed overboard were on the cruiser *Denver*; see Spence, "36th Division," 362.

[18] RG 391, 142nd Infantry Regiment, Box 2400, Doc number 262, Memo: Personnel Detachment, 142nd Infantry, From: R. E. Fried, Captain, April 12, 1919; Barnes, *History of the 142nd*, 53–54; White, *Panthers to Arrowheads*, 214; *Fort Worth Star-Telegram*, June 9, 1919.

[19] *Wichita Daily Times*, May 18, 1919; *Cleburne Enterprise*, June 2, 1919; *Lubbock Avalanche*, May 1, 1919. Spence notes that the 142nd Infantry disembarked at Boston, but that does not match newspaper reports of the time; Spence, "36th Division," 363.

[20] *Fort Worth Star-Telegram*, June 8, 1919; *Cleburne Enterprise*, June 16, 1919; *Gainesville Daily Register*, June 13, 14, 16, 1919.

[21] *Gainesville Daily Register*, June 14, 1919; *Fort Worth Star-Telegram*, June 11, 13, 14, 1919; White, *Panthers to Arrowheads*, 214–15. The *Fort Worth Star Telegram* reported that for the week ending May 31, 1919, Camp Bowie had already discharged 31,854 soldiers, *Star-Telegram*, June 8, 1919.

[22] Spence, "36th Division," 364; Barnes, *History of the 142nd*, 54; *Gainesville Daily Register*, June 13, 1919; *Fort Worth Star-Telegram*, June 12, 13, 1919.

[23] *Cleburne Enterprise*, June 8, 12, 1919; *Clarendon News*, April 10, 1919; *Quanah Tribune Chief*, July 10, 1919.

[24] *Abilene Reporter*, June 18, 1919; *Fort Worth Star-Telegram*, June 14, 1919.

[25] *Amarillo Daily News*, June 18, 19, 1919.

[26] *Gainesville Daily Register*, June 20–21, 1919.

[27] *Denton Record Chronicle*, June 17, 18, 1919.

[28] *Wise County Messenger*, June 20, 27, 1919.

[29] *Clarendon News*, June 19, 1919.

[30] *Clarendon News*, June 26, 1919.

[31] *Amarillo Daily News*, November 30, 1919.

[32] *Cleburne Enterprise*, June 8, 1919; *Lubbock Avalanche*, June 12, 1919.

[33] *Wise County Messenger*, November 22, 1918; *Abilene Reporter*, July 2, 1919.

[34] *Cleburne Enterprise*, June 9, 12, 1919; *Fort Worth Star-Telegram*, June 12, 1919.

[35] *Cleburne Daily Enterprise*, July 2, 6, 1919; *Dallas Morning News*, July 5, 1919.

[36] *Amarillo Daily News*, June 18, 28, 29, 1919; *Abilene Reporter*, July 2, 1919; *Foard County News*, June 20, 1919; *Gainesville Daily Register*, June 18, 30, 1919; *Lubbock Avalanche*, June 12, 19, 26, 1919; *Fort Worth Star-Telegram*, June 15, 1919.

[37] *Gainesville Daily Register*, July 2, 3, 1919; *Abilene Reporter*, January 22, 1919.

[38] *Amarillo Daily News*, July 4, 5, 1919; *Gainesville Daily Register*, June 24, and July 5, 1919; *Dallas Morning News*, July 3, 1918.

[39] *Abilene Reporter*, July 2, 3, 1919.

[40] *Abilene Reporter*, July 4, 6, 1919.

[41] *Clarendon News*, April 10, and July 3, 1919.

[42] Ruth Smith Truss, "Military Participation at Home and Abroad, 1917–1918," in Olliff, *Great War in the Heart of Dixie*, 24–40; Roberts, *American Foreign Legion*, 195, 199; Marshall, *Memories of World War I*, 164–65.

[43] *Clarendon News*, November 28, 1919.

[44] *Cleburne Enterprise*, January 5, 1919.

[45] *Wise County Messenger*, November 22, 1918; *Dallas Morning News*, March 30, 1919; *Gainesville Daily Register*, June 9, 1919.

[46] *Abilene Reporter*, July 6, 1919, and November 26, 1918; Hitt, Myers, Rich, and Statser, *Foard County and World War I*, 4–5.

[47] *Dallas Morning News*, November 6, 1920, and January 24, 1928; Roberts, *American Foreign Legion*, 201; Mark A. Snell, ed., *Unknown Soldiers: The American Expeditionary Forces in Memory and Remem-*

brance (Kent, OH: Kent State University Press, 2008), 18.

[48] Michael V. R. Thomason, "Mobile in World War I," 121–40, and Robert J. Jakeman, "Memorializing World War I in Alabama," in Olliff, *Great War in the Heart of Dixie,* 201–20; Roberts, *American Foreign Legion,* 199; Snell, *Unknown Soldiers*, 17.

[49] G. Kurt Piehler, "Remembering the War to End all Wars," in Snell, *Unknown Soldiers,* 28–59; *Fort Worth Star-Telegram*, October 28, 1918.

[50] *Cleburne Daily Enterprise*, November 9, 11, 1919.

[51] *Amarillo Daily News*, November 11, 12, 1928.

[52] *Dallas Morning News*, November 11, 1928; *Gainesville Daily Register*, November 12, 1928.

[53] *Dallas Morning News*, November 10, 11, 1938.

[54] *Abilene Reporter*, November 11, 1938.

[55] *Dallas Morning News*, November 11, 1948.

[56] *Dallas Morning News*, November 11, 1958.

[57] *Dallas Morning News*, November 10, 11, 1968; *Abilene Reporter*, November 11, 1968.

[58] *Dallas Morning News*, May 20, and September 10, 1921; Clark, *Aubyn's War*, 231–32.

[59] *Official National Guard Register for 1924*, Militia Bureau, Washington, D.C., May 1, 1924 (Washington: Government Printing Office, 1924), 764, 771–72, 774.

[60] *Official National Guard Register for 1930*, Militia Bureau, Washington, D.C., June 30, 1930 (Washington: Government Printing Office, 1930), 984; *Victoria Advocate*, March 8, 1995.

[61] *Dallas Morning News*, October 10, 1919.

[62] *Dallas Morning News*, September 11, 1922, October 9, 11, 1922, and October 8, 1930.

[63] *Dallas Morning News*, May 9, 1927, September 4, 1928, August 16, 1931, September 14, 1931, September 17, 1931, October 6, 1931, October 8, 1931, October 24, 1931. Governor Sterling, however, did not arrive, and sent Colonel Paul Wakefield, "of his personal staff," to represent him. The Lt. Governor, Edgar Witt, arrived for Sunday's ceremonies. See *Dallas Morning News*, October 25, 1931.

[64] *Dallas Morning News*, October 7, 1934, October 10, 17, 1938; Press Release, "36th Division Association—25th Annual Convention, Fort Worth, October 27–28, 1950," William Jary Collection, 89-4, Box 12, Special Collections, The University of Texas at Arlington Library.

[65] Roster, *Company G Association, 142nd Infantry, 36th Division, A.E.F.*, Amarillo, Texas, April 1, 1967, Homer Troy Merrill Papers, Folder: 1964 annotated, Southwest Collection, Texas Tech University, Lubbock, Texas.

[66] Historical Branch, War Department General Staff, Monograph No. 9, *Blanc Mont*, April, 1920; George C. Marshall, *Infantry in Battle*, 2nd ed. (Richmond: Garrett and Massie, 1939), iv, 164.

[67] *Amarillo Daily News*, July 22, 25, 1923; *Wise County Messenger*, November 1, 1918; *National Guard Register, 1924*, 763; *Texas Almanac*, Elections of Texas governors, 1845–2006, http://www.texasalmanac.

com/politics/gubernatorial.pdf (accessed 2 April, 2010).

[68] *Wise County Messenger*, February 11, 18, 1927.

[69] *Clarendon News*, June 26, 1919, and February 20, 1930; *The History of Donley County, Texas, 1879–1990, Presented by the Families of Donley County, Texas, both Past and Present* (Dallas: Curtis Media Corp, 1990), 385–386. For information on Everett Selden Simpson, see http://www.texasmilitaryforcesmuseum.org/articles/simpson.htm. (accessed April 1, 2010).

[70] Letter, A. W. Bloor to R. M. Wagstaff, July 11, 1920, Robert M. Wagstaff Papers, Box 4, Military Papers, Southwest Collection, Texas Tech University, Lubbock, Texas; *Handbook of Texas Online*, "Owsley, Alvin Mansfield, "http://www.tshaonline.org/handbook/online/articles/OO/fow2.html (accessed March 27, 2010); See also Marion S. Adams, *Alvin M. Owsley of Texas: Apostle of Americanism* (Waco: Texian Press, 1971); *Abilene Reporter-News*, March 15, and April 12, 1981; *Fort Worth Star-Telegram*, June 10, 1919.

[71] *Dallas Morning News*, December 18, 1920, April 3, 1925, May 6, 1927, February 11, 1933, April 9, 1933, October 21, 1933.

[72] *Dallas Morning News*, December 23, 1936, April 19, 1942, August 15, 1952.

[73] *Abilene News Reporter*, September 27, 1942; Hart, C*ompany K of Yesterday*; *Handbook of Texas Online*, "Texas Archaeological Society," http://www.tshaonline.org/handbook/online/articles/TT/bat1.html, (accessed April 3, 2010).

[74] Barnes, *History of the 142nd*, 57.

[75] *Cleburne Enterprise*, June 2, 1919; *Dallas Morning News*, March 29, 30, and August 27, 1919; *Journal of the Senate, State of Texas, Second Called Session Thirty-Sixth Legislature, convened June 23, 1919, adjourned July 22, 1919* (Austin: A. C. Baldwin, 1919), 91.

[76] Diploma, Major Alfred W. Bloor, School of the Line, June 21, 1921, Texas Military Forces Museum, Austin, Texas; Certificate, Major Alfred W. Bloor, General Staff School, June 30, 1922, Texas Military Forces Museum, Austin, Texas; Grade Sheet, General Service Schools, Major Alfred Bloor, June 23, 1922, Texas Military Forces Museum, Austin, Texas; James A Clark, with Weldon Hart, *The Tactful Texan: A Biography of Governor Will Hobby* (New York: Random House, 1958), 134.

[77] *Dallas Morning News*, February 27, 1930; *Austin American-Statesman*, July 4, 1952, and November 19, 1953; Certificate, Croix de Guerre, Major Alfred W. Bloor, July 28, 1924, Texas Military Forces Museum, Austin, Texas; Certificate, Domain of Neptunus Rex, Major Alfred W. Bloor, Texas Military Forces Museum, Austin, Texas; James E. Hewes, *From Root to McNamara: Army Organization and Administration* (Washington: Center of Military History, 1975), 383.

[78] *Abilene News Reporter*, September 27, 1942. For special designations see, http://www.history.army.mil/html/forcestruc/spdes-123-arng.html (accessed 9 Jan 11).

[79] Fifteenth Census of the United States, 1930, Population Schedule (Washington: Government Printing Office).

[80] Fifteenth Census of the United States, 1930, Population Schedule (Washington: Government Printing Office).

[81] Historical Branch, War Department General Staff, Monograph No. 9, *Blanc Mont*, April, 1920; Marshall, *Infantry in Battle*, iv, 164; *Wichita Daily Times*, October 20, 1918.

[82] RG 120, 36th Division, 142nd Infantry, Box 14 Forest Farm Engagement, Operations Report, October 27, 1918.

[83] National Archives and Records Administration, RG 120, Records of the American Expeditionary Forces, 36th Division, 142nd Infantry Regiment, Box 14, Personnel Experiences Folder, Lillard, 3

[84] Memorandum from C.O. 142nd Infantry to C.O. 36th Division, Subject: Transmitting Messages in Choctaw, 23 January, 1919, NARA, RG 120, 36th Division, 142nd Infantry, Box 14.

[85] Memorandum from C.O. 142nd Infantry to C.O. 36th Division, Subject: Transmitting Messages in Choctaw, 23 January, 1919, NARA, RG 120, 36th Division, 142nd Infantry, Box 14.

[86] Dawson, *The Texas Military Experience*, 84, 187; *Abilene Reporter News*, June 29, 1952. Robert Wagstaff's great-grandfather was Dr. Ducalion Aldrige Perry, who was assigned to "care for the women and children in the 'runaway scrape'" that eventually ended at San Jacinto.

[87] *Clarendon News*, June 19, 1919.

BIBLIOGRAPHY

Primary Sources: Unpublished

Armstrong, Hazen. Oral History #1214, Oral History Archives, University of North Texas, Denton Texas.

Blackmon, Daniel O. Collection. Southwest Collection, Texas Tech University, Lubbock, Texas.

Bloor, Alfred W., Papers. Texas Military Forces Museum, Camp Mabry, Austin, Texas.

Hornaday, William Deming. Transcripts of World War I Letters and Personal Accounts, Archives and Information Services Division, Texas State Library and Archives Commission, Austin, Texas.

Merrill, Homer Troy Papers, 1899–1964. Southwest Collection, Texas Tech University, Lubbock, Texas.

Record Group 120, Records of the American Expeditionary Forces, 36th Division, 71st Brigade, 142nd Infantry Regiment. National Archives and Records Administration, College Park, Maryland.

Record Group 391, Records of United States Regular Army Mobile Units, 142nd Infantry Regiment. National Archives and Records Administration, College Park, Maryland.

Sayles, Edwin B. Papers. Southwest Collection, Texas Tech University, Lubbock, Texas.

Texas National Guard Records, 1900–1964. Southwest Collection, Texas Tech University, Lubbock, Texas.

Thirty-Sixth Division Association Papers. Archives and Information Services Division, Texas State Library and Archives Commission, Austin, Texas.

Wagstaff, Robert M., Papers. Southwest Collection, Texas Tech University, Lubbock, Texas.

Government Documents

Congressional Record: Containing the Proceedings and Debates of the First Session of the Sixty-Fifth Congress of the United States of America, Volume 55, parts 1–8, and appendix. Washington, DC: Government Printing Office, 1917.

Crowder, Enoch H. *Second Report of the Provost Marshall General to the Secretary of War on the Operations of the Selective Service System to December 20, 1918.* Washington: Government Printing Office, 1919.

Journal of the House of Representatives of the Second Called Session of the Thirty-Fifth Legislature. Austin: Von Boeckmann-Jones Co., 1917.

Journal of the House of Representatives of the Regular Session of the Thirty-Sixth Legislature, convened January 14, 1919, and Adjourned March 19, 1919. Austin: Von Boeckman-Jones, 1919.

Journal of the Senate, State of Texas, Second Called Session Thirty-Sixth Legislature, convened June 23, 1919, adjourned July 22, 1919. Austin: A.C. Baldwin, 1919.

Militia Bureau. *Official National Guard Register for 1924*. Washington: Government Printing Office, 1924.

Militia Bureau. *Official National Guard Register for 1930*. Washington: Government Printing Office, 1930.

Report of the Acting Chief of the Militia Bureau, 1918. Washington, DC: Government Printing Office, 1918.

Report of the Chief of the Militia Bureau, 1917. Washington, DC: Government Printing Office, 1917.

Selective Service Registration Cards for World War I, M1509, Texas microfilm, National Archives and Records Administration Southwest Branch, Fort Worth, Texas.

Tenth Census of United States. Washington, DC: Government Printing Office, 1880.

Twelfth Census of the United States. Washington, DC: Government Printing Office, 1900.

Thirteenth Census of the United States. Washington, DC: Government Printing Office, 1910.

Newspapers

Abilene Reporter

Amarillo Daily News

Austin American Statesman

Blum Bulletin

Clarendon News

Cleburne Daily Enterprise

Dallas Morning News

Denton Record Chronicle

Foard County News

Fort Worth Record

Fort Worth Star-Telegram

Gainesville Daily Register

Houston Post

Lubbock News Avalanche

Quanah Tribune Chief

Victoria Advocate

Wichita Daily Times

Wise County Messenger

Published Primary Sources

Barnes, C. H. *History of the 142nd Infantry of the Thirty-Sixth Division, October 15, 1917 to June 17, 1919.* No City: Blackwell, 1920.

Brannen, Carl Andrew. *Over There: A Marine in the Great War.* College Station: Texas A&M University Press, 1997.

Chastaine, Ben H. *Story of the Thirty-Sixth: The Experiences of the Thirty-Sixth Division in the World War.* Oklahoma City: Harlow, 1920.

Ferrell, Robert S., ed. *A Youth in the Meuse-Argonne.* Columbia: University of Missouri Press, 2000.

Hallas, James H., ed. *Doughboy War: The American Experience in World War I.* 2000. Reprint, Mechanicsburg: Stackpole, 2009.

Hart, Archibald S. *Company K of Yesterday.* New York: Vantage, 1969.

History of Donley County, Texas, 1879–1990, Presented by the Families of Donley County, Texas Both Past and Present. Dallas: Curtis Media Corp, 1990.

Jackson, Warren R. and George B. Clark, ed.. *His Time in Hell: A Texas Marine in France.* Novato: Presidio Press, 2001.

Lejeune, John A. *The Reminiscences of a Marine.* 1930. Reprint, Quantico: Marine Corps Association, 1979.

Pershing, John J. *My Experiences in the First World War.* 1931. Reprint, New York: DaCapo, 1995.

Second Engineers, Headquarters Staff. *Official History of the Second Engineers in the World War, 1916–1919,* no date, circa 1922.

Texas Almanac and State Industrial Guide, 1914. Dallas: A.H. Belo & Company, 1914.

Thomason, John W. *Fix Bayonets!* 1925. Reprint, Charleston: Nautical and Aviation Publishing Company of America, 2007.

Secondary Sources

Books

Adams, Marion S. *Alvin M. Owsley of Texas: Apostle of Americanism.* Waco: Texian Press, 1971.

Adjutant General of the Army. *Congressional Medal of Honor, the Distinguished Service Cross, and the Distinguished Service Medal issued by the War Department.* Washington: Government Printing Office, 1919.

Allen, Hervey. *Toward the Flame: A Memoir of World War I.* 1926. Reprint, Lincoln: University of Nebraska Press, 2003.

American Battle Monuments Commission. *American Armies and Battlefields in Europe.* Washington: Government Printing Office, 1938.

Anderson, Fred. *A People's Army: Massachusetts Soldiers and Society in the Seven Years War.* Chapel Hill: University of North Carolina Press, 1996.

Barbeau, Arthur E. and Florette Henri. *The Unknown Soldiers: African American Troops in World War I.* 1974. Reprint, New York: DaCapo, 1996.

Blumenson, Martin. *Bloody River: The Real Tragedy of the Rapido River.* College Station: Texas A&M University Press, 1998.

Brager, Bruce. *The Texas 36th Division: A History.* Austin: Eakin Press, 2002.

Bricker, Richard W. *Wooden Ships from Texas: A World War I Saga.* College Station: Texas A&M University Press, 1998.

Britten, Paul Austin. *American Indians in World War I, at War and at Home.* Albuquerque: University of New Mexico Press, 1997.

Buenger, Walter E. *The Path to a Modern South: Northeast Texas between Reconstruction and the Great Depression.* Austin: University of Texas Press, 2001.

———. "World War I and Northeast Texas." *Locus* 8, no. 2 (Spring, 1996).

Campbell, Randolph B. *Gone to Texas: A History of the Lone Star State.* New York: Oxford, 2004.

Cantrell, Gregg. *Feeding the Wolf: John B. Rayner and the Politics of Race, 1850–1918.* Wheeling, IL: Harlan-Davidson, 2001.

Cappozzola, Christopher. *Uncle Sam Wants You: World War I and the Making of the Modern American Citizen.* New York: Oxford, 2008.

Chambers, John Whiteclay. *To Raise an Army: The Draft Comes to Modern America.* New York: Free Press, 1987.

Christian, Garna L. *Black Soldiers in Jim Crow Texas, 1899–1917*. College Station: Texas A&M University Press, 1995.

Clark, David G. *Aubyn's War and Tales from Mr. Billy's Family*. Colorado: Bingham Hill Press, 2009.

Clark, George B. *Devil Dogs: Fighting Marines of World War I*. Novato, CA: Presidio, 2000.

Clark, James A., with Weldon Hart. *The Tactful Texan: A Biography of Governor Will Hobby*. New York: Random House, 1958,

Clendenen, Clarence. *Blood on the Border: The United States Army and the Mexican Irregulars*. Toronto: Macmillan, 1969.

Coffman, Edward. *The War to End All Wars: The American Military Experience in World War I*. 1968. Reprint, Lexington: University Press of Kentucky, 1998.

Connally, Tom. *My Name is Tom Connally*. New York: Thomas Y. Crowell, 1954.

Cooke, James J. *Pershing and His Generals: Command and Staff in the AEF*. Westport: Praeger, 1997.

Cooke, James J. *The Rainbow Division in the Great War, 1917–1919*. Westport: Praeger, 1994.

Cooper, John Milton Jr. *Woodrow Wilson: A Biography*. New York: Alfred A. Knopf, 2009.

Cooper, Jerry. *The Rise of the National Guard: The Evolution of the American Militia, 1865–1920*. Lincoln: University of Nebraska Press, 1997.

Crager, Kelly. *Hell under the Rising Sun: Texas POWs and the Building of the Burma-Thailand Death Railway*. College Station: Texas A&M University Press, 2008.

Dawson, Joseph G., ed. *The Texas Military Experience: From the Texas Revolution through World War II*. College Station: Texas A&M University Press, 1995.

Dethloff, Henry C., and John A. Adams Jr. *Texas Aggies Go to War: In Service of Their Country*. College Station, Texas A&M University Press, 2004.

Eisenhower, John S. D. *Yanks: The Epic Story of the American Army in World War I*. New York: Free Press, 2001.

Faulkner, Richard S. "Disappearing Doughboys: The American Expeditionary Forces' Straggler Crisis in the Meuse-Argonne," *Army History* (Spring 2012): 7–25.

Ferrell, Robert H. *America's Deadliest Battle: Meuse-Argonne, 1918*. Lawrence: University of Kansas Press, 2007.

Ford, Nancy Gentile. *The Great War and America: Civil-Military Relations during World War I*. Westport: Praeger, 2008.

———. *Americans All! Foreign Born Soldiers in World War I.* College Station: Texas A&M University Press, 2008, paperback edition.

Glatthaar, Joseph T. *General Lee's Army: From Victory to Collapse.* New York: Free Press, 2008.

Gould, Lewis L. *Progressives and Prohibitionists: Texas Democrats in the Wilson Era.* Austin: Texas State Historical Association, 1992.

Grotelueschen, Mark E. *The AEF Way of War: The American Army and Combat in World War I.* New York: Cambridge University Press, 2007.

Hamilton, Richard F., and Holger H. Herwig. *Decisions for War, 1914–1917.* New York: Cambridge University Press, 2004.

Harris, Charles H., and Louis R. Sadler. *The Texas Rangers and the Mexican Revolution: The Bloodiest Decade, 1910–1920.* Albuquerque: University of New Mexico Press, 2004.

Harris, Stephen. *Harlem's Hell Fighters: the African-American 369th Infantry in World War I.* Dulles, VA: Potomac Books, 2003.

Harris, Stephen. *Duty, Honor, Privilege: New York's Silk Stocking Regiment and the Breaking of the Hindenburg Line.* Dulles, VA: Potomac Books, 2004.

Hegi, Benjamin Paul. "Old Time Good Germans: German-Americans in Cooke County, Texas, during World War I," *The Southwestern Historical Quarterly* 109 (Oct, 2005).

Hendrickson, Kenneth E., Jr. *The Chief Executives of Texas: From Stephen F. Austin to John B. Connally, Jr.* College Station: Texas A&M University Press, 1995.

Hewes, James E. *From Root to McNamara: Army Organization and Administration.* Washington: Center of Military History, 1975.

Historical Branch, War Department General Staff. Monograph No. 9. *Blanc Mont*, April 1920.

Hitt, Jo, Cynthia Myers, Jim Rich, and Faye Statser, *Foard County and World War I.* No publisher: 2007.

Johnson, Douglas V., and Rolfe L. Hillman, Jr. *Soissons, 1918.* College Station: Texas A&M University Press, 1999.

Katz, Friedrich. *Secret War in Mexico: Europe, the United States and the Mexican Revolution.* Chicago: University of Chicago Press, 1981.

Keene, Jennifer D. *Doughboys, the Great War, and the Remaking of America.* Baltimore: Johns Hopkins University Press, 2001.

Keith, Jeannette. *Rich Man's War, Poor Man's Fight: Race, Class, and Power in the Rural South during the First World War.* Chapel Hill: University of North Carolina Press, 2004.

Kennedy, David M. *Over Here: The First World War and American Society*. New York: Oxford, 1980.

Kennett, Lee. *The First Air War, 1914–1918*. New York: Free Press, 1991.

Lengel, Edward G. *To Conquer Hell: The Meuse-Argonne, 1918*. New York: Henry Holt, 2008.

Lowe, Richard. *Walker's Texas Division, C.S.A.: Greyhounds of the Trans-Mississippi*. Baton Rouge: Louisiana State University Press, 2004.

Marshall, George C. *Infantry in Battle*. 2d Ed. Richmond: Garrett and Massie, 1939.

Marshall III, R. Jackson. *Memories of World War I: North Carolina Doughboys on the Western Front*. Raleigh, NC: North Carolina Division of Archives and History, 1998.

Matthews, Matt M. *The US Army on the Mexican Border: A Historical Perspective*. Fort Leavenworth, KS: Combat Studies Institute Press, 2007.

Maxfield, Bernice Blanche Miller, and William E. Jary Jr. *Camp Bowie, Forth Worth, 1917–1918, An Illustrated History of the 36th Division in the First World War*. Fort Worth: B. B. Maxfield Foundation, 1975.

Mead, Gary. *The Doughboys: America and the First World War*. Woodstock: The Overlook Press, 2000.

Meinig, D. W. *Imperial Texas: An Interpretive Essay in Cultural Geography*. Austin: University of Texas Press, 1969.

Montejano, David. *Anglos and Mexicans in the Making of Texas, 1836–1986*. Austin: University of Texas Press, 1987.

Neiberg, Michael S. *Fighting the Great War: A Global History*. Cambridge: Harvard University Press, 2005.

Nenninger, Timothy K. "'Unsystematic as a Mode of Command': Commanders and the Process of Command in the American Expeditionary Forces, 1917–1918." *The Journal of Military History* 64 (July 2000): 739–68.

Olien, Roger M. *From Token to Triumph: The Texas Republicans since 1920*. Dallas: SMU Press, 1982.

Olliff, Martin T. ed. *The Great War in the Heart of Dixie: Alabama During World War I*. Tuscaloosa: University of Alabama Press, 2008.

Owen, Peter F. *To the Limit of Endurance: A Battalion of Marines in the Great War*. College Station: Texas A&M University Press, 2008.

Ramirez, Jose A. *To the Line of Fire! Mexican Texans and World War I*. College Station: Texas A&M University Press, 2009.

Roberts, Frank E. *The American Foreign Legion: Black Soldiers of the 93d in World War I*. Annapolis: Naval Institute Press, 2004.

Schaffer, Ronald. *America in the Great War: The Rise of the Welfare State*. New York: Oxford, 1991.

Selcer, Richard F. *Hell's Half Acre*. Fort Worth: TCU Press, 1991.

Shay, Michael. *The Yankee Division in the First World War*. College Station: Texas A&M University Press, 2008.

Schultz, Duane. *Crossing the Rapido: A Tragedy of World War II*. New York: Westholme, 2010.

Shenk, Gerald E. *"Work or Fight!" Race, Gender, and the Draft in World War I*. New York: Palgrave, 2005.

Skaggs, Jimmy M. "Lieutenant General Hulen," *Texas Military History* 18 (1970).

Slotkin, Richard. *Lost Battalions: The Great War and the Crisis of American Nationality*. New York: Henry Holt, 2005.

Snell, Mark, ed. *Unknown Soldiers: The American Expeditionary Forces in Memory and Remembrance*. Kent, OH: the Kent State University Press, 2008.

Spurlin, Charles. "The Victoria Sammies," *Texana* 7 (1969): 56–76.

Storey, James, and Mary E. Kelley. *Twentieth-Century Texas: A Social and Cultural History*. Denton: University of North Texas Press, 2008.

Trask, David F. *The AEF and Coalition Warmaking, 1917–1918*. Lawrence: University of Kansas Press, 1993.

Traxel, David. *Crusader Nation: The United States in Peace and the Great War*. New York: Knopf, 2006.

Twitchell, Heath. *Allen: The Biography of an Army Officer*. New Brunswick: Rutgers University Press, 1974.

United States Army in the World War, 1917–1919. *Military Operations of the American Expeditionary Forces, Volume 9*. 1948. Reprinted, Washington: Center of Military History, 1990.

Utley, Robert. *Lone Star Lawmen: The Second Century of the Texas Rangers*. New York: Berkeley, 2007.

Wagner, Robert L. *The Texas Army: A History of the 36th Division in the Italian Campaign*. Austin: State House Press, 1991.

Weaver, John D. *The Brownsville Raid*. New York: W. W. Norton, 1970.

White, Lonnie J. *The 90th Division in World War I: The Texas-Oklahoma Draft Division in the Great War*. Manhattan, KS: The Sunflower Press, 1996.

———. *Panthers to Arrowheads: The 36th (Texas-Oklahoma) Division in World War I*. Austin: Presidial Press, 1984.

———. "Chief of the Arrowheads: Major General William R. Smith and the 36th Division in France, 1918–1919." *Military History of Texas and the Southwest* 16 (1982).

———. "Major General Edwin St. John Greble." *Military History of Texas and the Southwest* 14 (1976).

Wilson, John B. *Maneuver and Firepower: The Evolution of Divisions and Separate Brigades*. Washington, DC: US Army Center of Military History, 1998.

Wooster, Ralph A. *Texas and Texans in the Great War*. Buffalo Gap: State House Press, 2009.

Wythe, Major George. *A History of the 90th Division*. New York: 90th Division Association, 1920.

Yockelson, Mitchell A. *Borrowed Soldiers: Americans under British Command, 1918*. Norman: University of Oklahoma Press, 2008.

Zieger, Robert H. *America's Great War: World War I and the American Experience*. Lanham: Rowman and Littlefield, 2000.

Electronic Sources

Handbook of Texas Online, "Owsley, Alvin Mansfield, "http://www.tshaonline.org/handbook/online/articles/OO/fow2.html (accessed March 27, 2010)

Handbook of Texas Online, "Texas Archaeological Society," http://www.tshaonline.org/handbook/online/articles/TT/bat1.html, (accessed April 3, 2010).

Texas Almanac, Elections of Texas governors, 1845-2006, http://www.texasalmanac.com/politics/gubernatorial.pdf (accessed 2 April, 2010).

Texas Military Forces Museum. "Everett Selden Simpson." http://www.texasmilitaryforcesmuseum.org/articles/simpson.htm. (accessed April 1, 2010).

University of Virginia. Historical Census Browser. "http://fisher.lib.virginia.edu/collections/stats/histcensus/php/state.php (accessed 30 November 2009).

A

B

C

D

F

G

H

L

M

N

O

P

Q

R

S

T

U

V

W

Z